ALSO BY THOMASINA MIERS

HOME COOK

Over 300 delicious, fuss-free recipes

THOMASINA MIERS

Photographs by Tara Fisher

First Published in 2017

by Guardian Books, Kings Place, 90 York Way, London N1 9GU

and Faber & Faber Ltd, Bloomsbury House, 74–77 Great Russell Street, London WC1B 3DA

Printed in China

A CIP record for this book is available from the British Library

ISBN 978-1-78335-096-4

Design Charlotte Heal Design
Photographer Tara Fisher
Home Economist & Food Stylist Rosie Ramsden

10 9 8 7 6 5 4 3 2 1

To Mark and my three girls:

Tati, Ottie and Isadora

CONTENTS

INTRODUCTION

When I sat down to write this book, I wanted to gather together the recipes that have meant the most to me over the years. They include family favourites, versions of dishes I grew up with and those I love cooking for my husband and children now. There are recipes that have been the biggest hits when feeding friends as well as exotic recipes that I've picked up on my travels. There are some I created on the hoof and others inspired by my much-loved, dog-eared cookbook collection.

I sit in my kitchen writing this, not as a chef or an entrepreneur, nor as a previous *MasterChef* winner or food writer, but as a busy, working woman with very little time but plenty of passion for cooking good food and eating well (and also for letting her hair down and having fun). My kitchen is the central part of our home and food connects our lives together with those of our friends and family. Over the years, I have spent thousands of happy hours – as a child, a student, a twenty-something-year-old singleton and now as a mother – in the company of those I love, sitting around a kitchen table breaking bread, being teased mercilessly and sharing stories. It is the way I communicate; it is how I nurture those closest to me.

The dishes in this book are achievable for any home cook. They will not only satisfy (and sometimes impress) the people you're feeding, but also fill your kitchen with great smells and a sense of adventure. I've designed *Home Cook* so that those short on time can weave good food into their lives and eat in a healthy, enjoyable way, any day of the week. These recipes are my kitchen essentials and they are delicious, fun and do-able. I've also made sure the book is full of tips and tricks to help you create a structure to your week's cooking: storing and reusing ingredients, making the best use of your freezer and store cupboard and using some of the time you do have to prep ingredients for those moments when you are madly busy. Whenever possible, I've included a 'why not try?' bonus dish that makes further use of an ingredient. Not only does this make financial sense, but it also creates a flow to your meals throughout the week, with one dish inspiring and providing ingredients for the next.

Home cooking is best when nothing is wasted, neither ingredients nor time, and when even if the rest of the day is manic, we make time to enjoy cooking and eating well with those closest to us.

A Modern Approach to Old-Fashioned Cooking

We have a tradition on this island of wasting nothing; it was an economical approach laid out in *Mrs Beeton's Book of Household Management* in 1861. When I was growing up, my parents didn't have much money but my mother always made the most sensational meals from left over ingredients. Making stocks or breadcrumbs was second nature to her, while the best part of Sunday lunch was soaking up the gravy with slices of buttered bread. To this day, if my father has jointed a whole chicken for a recipe he will chop up the leftover bones, stick them back in the oven covered in olive oil, salt and pepper, and we'll nibble on them as a snack before we sit down to eat.

One of my favourite ways of cooking is to open up the fridge or larder and see what I can make from what is in there. Just by rethinking the very word 'leftovers', a whole new world of flavours opens up. Every little bag of leaves, jar of paste or spice mix I've squirrelled away has the potential to transform a simple plate of pasta or bowl of soup. I think of them as cupboard gems that will help me whip up my next meal, plus there is something immensely pleasing about getting extra flavour without having lifted a finger or spent any more money.

What Healthy Eating Means to Me

I've mostly included recipes that have a healthy nutritional balance. There might be lots of butter in one dish but just a few drops of oil in the next. There are recipes with meat and fish but also an abundance of vegetables, in fact many dishes are what I think of as 'accidentally vegetarian'. During the week, when there is less time, vegetables are what I turn to for simplicity. At weekends we eat more meat and fish, because we have time to do them justice and share them with friends.

These days there are many books out there telling you how to eat better and eat 'clean'. I understand food and work with it every day, but even I find the mixed messages confusing: avoid carbs, avoid protein, only eat greens, eat fat, don't eat fat, eat grains, don't eat grains. I find all this conflicting advice unfathomable... and I know what I am doing in the kitchen. What about people who don't cook much but simply want to eat better? Which of the many conflicting food fads and eating plans should they follow?

After many years of trying any kind of diet that came my way, my simple answer now is to follow none but your own. Learn your own rhythms and metabolic pace and begin to understand what makes you feel good and your body feel happy. In my teens and throughout my twenties I developed an incredibly unhealthy attitude to food. I steadily put on weight and veered from bingeing to dieting, obsessing about all the 'bad' food I was desperate to eat, but feared would make me fatter still. When things felt particularly bleak I had the great fortune to meet Clarissa Dickson Wright, who sent me off to cookery school the moment she learnt how much I loved cooking. I began meeting incredibly inspiring chefs and cooks and noticed that most of them shared a common attitude to food: they took time to shop for ingredients, took time to prepare it, they always seemed to enjoy what they were eating and it never seemed to occur to them to say no to certain food types. Their attitude was wholly about embracing food for all its pleasure and enjoyment.

I realised that when I relaxed and spent half an hour in the kitchen chopping, sautéing, steaming and tasting food, part of that driving, raging hunger that held such power over me in my early twenties was already satiated by the time I sat down to eat. It was not real hunger that had had such control over me, but a hunger to feed an un-met emotion. I slowly stopped thinking that certain foods were the enemy. It dawned on me that I was at my happiest when I was feeding a room full of people, that playing with food or ingredients and making them taste good was one of the most satisfying things I did. Creating, eating and sharing food made me feel great.

The more I appreciated food, the more it appreciated me. I realised that denying myself certain things only made me crave them more, so gradually and unconsciously, I stopped the denial. As I started loving food again I found myself wanting the 'good' stuff as well as the 'bad'. I started becoming fascinated with fruits and vegetables and would visit greengrocers purely to discover new exotic ingredients that I hadn't cooked with before. I made salads in every which way, with glorious dressings of extra-virgin olive oils, walnut oils and different vinegars. I explored different cuisines around the world and learnt about spices. I travelled and learnt about different cooking techniques and styles and discovered new, exciting grains. Yes, I still sometimes went mad for puddings, but along the way I rediscovered my appetite's natural 'stop' button, that I lost in my teens.

After years of confusion and denial I have developed a food philosophy that is simple and easy to employ... and entirely guilt-free. I eat what I want, when I want and (almost) never give myself a hard time. I have learnt to listen to my body and be calm, even when I sometimes make the wrong choices.

The Power of Good Ingredients & Canny Shopping

My philosophy of food is deeply tied up with the environment: growing and transporting food is our most resource-intensive process. Generally speaking, the less meat we eat and the more locally we shop, the kinder our impact on the planet. Happily, this also equates to healthy eating. The closer you are to food at its source the better it is for you. Ready-made food has been variously sterilised, pasteurised and/or preserved and – at each of those processes – loses nutritional value. Ingredients are often living, breathing organisms and even time has an effect on their nutritional content and flavour. You only have to taste a recently picked broad bean or carrot and compare it to those in a supermarket that are grown thousands of miles away to realise this.

But we don't all live on a farm or grow our own veggies, so how do we get closer to natural food? Simple: shop intelligently and cook as much as possible from basic ingredients. The more you cook in this way, the more pleasure you get from eating and the more control you have over what you put into your body. What I do spend money on is certain key ingredients that I think give me vital nutrition for life, for example whole milk from grass-fed cows at my local market; it costs fractionally more than milk from the supermarket but I know that it is packed with more nutrients. Sourdough bread is expensive, but I use it to complete scores of meals. What is more it is intrinsically a whole food that is made with less intensively produced flours; while its slow-rise fermentation is also gentler on the digestive system. I buy organic meat when I can as I find the use of antibiotics in industrial animal-rearing – and its implications for the health of my family – terrifying, but normally I only buy it once a week, often choosing cheaper cuts. For the rest of the week we feed ourselves inexpensively on grains, vegetables and other delicious whole foods.

Prep Like a Master Chef

With *Home Cook*, I want to inspire you, not put pressure on you. Much of the food we see on television, on Instagram and in magazines is not about real life. When you make simple food, prepared with love, in a relaxed environment, people will always leave your home happy. The secret to that is simple organisation.

Mrs Beeton had it right: order in the kitchen is the key to good cooking. Naturally I am a spontaneous, fly-by-the-seat-of-my-pants person. In the early rounds of *Master-Chef*, John Torode would shake his head at my messy kitchen and chaotic approach. Com-peting in that show under the tutelage of John and Gregg soon taught me that getting organised saved me both time and stress. Now I lay out ingredients in the right weights before I start cooking (the *mise en place*) and have a bowl on my work surface for gubbins, which saves me untold numbers of trips to the bin. Even reading the recipe before I start cooking enables me to picture what I am trying to achieve at each stage and allows a calming rhythm to take pace, like completing the pieces of a jigsaw.

Time Well Spent

I love to cook but, like most of the people around me, I do not have enough spare time to devote to it. Living today is fast-paced and hectic with little chance to switch off. Sometimes, before I start cooking, the prospect of making dinner can feel like a total chore. Maybe I've got home from work late, or my daughters are in a bolshy mood, or I'm feeling rundown after a busy week (or a particularly fun weekend). I don't feel as though I have the time to make dinner, but I still want to fill my body with good food that tastes great.

Amazingly I am always glad when I do actually start cooking; it has become my form of daily mindfulness. I find it nearly impossible to make time for yoga and meditation, but cooking allows me the precious opportunity to disconnect from digital devices and live in the moment. It feeds my hunger for a more contemplative occasion in the day. It is the perfect pastime that gets the necessary done (feeding myself and my family and eating healthily) while fulfilling the need to chill out and switch off: a chance to take time out from the frenetic pace of life and breathe!

There is a skill in finding enough time to cook for yourself and still enjoy the process. Cooking and eating with friends and family have provided me with some of my favourite memories. Feeding people is the stuff of life, the magic that makes the world go round, the essence that binds people together and makes us human. Even in today's crazy world we can still find time for this fundamental pleasure in life. *Home Cook* will show you how.

Cook's Notes

— *All olive oil is a standard mild-tasting cooking olive oil, unless extra-virgin is stated, in which case I try to use the best one I can afford.*
— *All eggs are free-range or organic and are medium, unless otherwise stated. I keep mine out of the fridge; when cooking it's better if they are at room temperature.*
— *Onions and garlic are peeled, unless otherwise stated. Other than in summer, garlic contains an inner green shoot that tastes bitter. I always remove it before cooking.*
— *When zesting fruit, buy unwaxed or scrub clean.*
— *Although I spread salted butter on bread, I like to cook with unsalted butter. Unless otherwise stated, all butter in these recipes is unsalted, but feel free to use salted butter if you prefer; just adjust the seasoning accordingly.*
— *Salt is flaked sea salt and pepper is freshly ground black, unless otherwise stated. I use them in almost every recipe so they aren't listed in the ingredients lists.*
— *All parsley is flat-leaf, unless otherwise stated.*
— *Oven temperatures are non-fan assisted; please check your oven guide.*

Thomasina Miers
London 2017

Chapter ONE

GET GOING

GET GOING

My grandmother, my mother and two of my aunts all modelled at some stage in their lives and I grew up inheriting the idea that one could never be too glamorous or too thin. As a teenager I avoided breakfast like the plague and it was not until I had slowly sorted out my relationship with food that I started to embrace and enjoy breakfast. Now it is one of my favourite meals; delicious in its myriad forms (sweet, savoury, salty, healthy, fried, baked, poached) and having the advantage that the rest of the day stretches ahead, so you can eat a little too much and still go to bed feeling light and satisfied.

I try and treat this time of the day as an opportunity to have a sizeable dose of fairly healthy ingredients. It is probably something to do with having children and wanting them to start the day with something good inside them (having not much idea of what they will eat later on). I make giant vats of muesli every few months, which I pack with healthy nuts, seeds and exotic fruits.

In the summer we might have some overnight soaked oats, whether Bircher-style with apple or with blueberries. In the winter I might join the girls in their habitual bowl of porridge, which we lace with cinnamon and honey and a shake of 'magic sprinkles' (ground flaxseed). The girls' breakfast is never complete without a slice of hot, buttered toast topped with my mother's marmalade (see page 282); so ridiculously dark, rich and treacly that breakfast doesn't feel right without at least a spoonful. If I've started the day with something that is good for me, I feel I can handle whatever food the rest of the day holds (testing tacos at work, tasting ice cream samples, or judging a food award).

At weekends, breakfast – or more often than not, brunch – is a social affair. It is the easiest way to see other friends with children and it means we can all be fed and ready for an outing by 12 o'clock. This is when I get creative with eggs and I love getting the girls involved, whether cracking eggs, pouring batter or flipping pancakes. I might make a smoothie, bake some granola or even some cinnamon rolls … anything to celebrate the fact that we are not all having to whizz off to work and school.

Toasted Muesli with Almonds, Hazelnuts & Coconut

Commercial mueslis are often packed with sugar – and I find the healthier brands are crazily expensive – so I've started to make my own. I promise it takes very little time and is unbelievably easy. It also means you can pimp it as you like: try using dates, apricots or any other dried fruit you fancy. This recipe makes a large batch, but the quantities can easily be halved.

This version is full of low-gluten flakes such as rye, quinoa and oats, plus some bran for roughage. I like to toast the ingredients to bring out their flavour. Do play with the ratio of nuts to dried fruit to make your perfect blend. For a real treat the girls are allowed to grate over dark chocolate to make super-special chocolate muesli … it is amazing how far one tiny square goes with the help of a Microplane!

The muesli keeps for several months in an airtight container.

Preheat the oven to 180°C/gas 4.

Spread out half the flakes and oats between 2 baking sheets and gently toast in the oven for 15–20 minutes, stirring halfway through. Remove to a very large container and repeat with the second half. This way everything will be properly toasted. Now spread out the seeds on a baking sheet, the nuts on another and toast again, this time for about 10 minutes until the pumpkin seeds are puffed up and golden and the nuts are also pale golden. Keep an eye on them as they may take slightly different times. Allow to cool and then roughly chop the nuts in batches with a large chopping knife.

Lastly tip the coconut shavings onto a baking sheet and bake for 5–10 minutes, stirring halfway through so that the shavings are a deep golden and taste sweet and toasted. If you like a sweeter muesli try sprinkling them with a little caster sugar or agave syrup before you bake them, but take care as they will colour more quickly.

Toss all the toasted ingredients together with the wheat bran and dried fruits so that everything is thoroughly mixed. My grandmother would sprinkle this muesli with Demerara sugar and eat with milk *and* double cream. I sometimes add a dollop of Greek yogurt and some seasonal fruit purée.

Why not try Bircher muesli?

Mix together 200g rolled oats or muesli with 200ml apple juice, 250ml semi-skimmed milk, 1 coarsely grated apple, 100g raisins, 100g natural yogurt, 1 tbsp honey and 1 tsp mixed spice and leave to soak overnight. Play around with the ingredients, adding nuts and seeds, chia seeds or pear. Just make sure you have at least double the amount of liquid (juice, water, almond milk or whole milk) to oats. Serve topped with seasonal fruits and crunchy granola. Feeds 4.

500g barley flakes

500g rye flakes

1kg rolled oats

100g pumpkin seeds

100g sunflower seeds

150g almonds, skin on or off as you like

150g hazelnuts

200g unsweetened coconut shavings

200g wheat bran

200g raisins

100g goji berries

200g dried banana chips

How Do You
Like Your Eggs?

Eggs are small, versatile and perfectly formed. They are my fallback ingredient
for many fast and wonderful last-minute suppers, as well as the backbone to my
baking. I buy organic eggs from either the market or the local butcher because of
the now accepted wisdom that they contain higher levels of essential Omega fats,
vitamins and minerals than other eggs. Below are my much-tested and perfected
methods of cooking eggs in all their guises. I love mine fried best of all.

Poached Perfection

My husband makes a mean poached egg and this is his method. Place the egg in a
small cup. Bring a pan of water to the boil with 1 tbsp white wine vinegar (for flavour
more than anything else). Reduce the heat so the water is tremulous and lower in the
egg, slowly pouring it from the cup. Cook the egg for 2–3 minutes until the white is firm
and the yolk completely runny. Lift out with a slotted spoon, blot it on kitchen paper,
then serve. If poaching lots of eggs, don't be tempted to overload the pan. If cooking
ahead, place the eggs in ice-cold water after cooking, then reheat in simmering water
for 20 seconds when you are ready to serve. Note: if you like fancy kit, a sous vide
machine will make the most wonderful poached egg: just blanch in boiling water in the
shell, cook for 1 hour at 60°C then crack into 45°C water to finish cooking the white.

Rub a slice of toast gently with the cut side of a garlic clove and then more firmly
with a halved ripe tomato and serve your poached egg on top. Sprinkle with a pinch
each of crushed toasted cumin seeds and chilli flakes, drizzle over plenty of olive oil
and season. To go for broke, eat with blanched spinach, ham or smoked salmon and
my foolproof Hollandaise Sauce (see page 289).

Soft-Boiled Sustenance

Bring a pan of water to boiling point. Gently lower the egg into the water with a ladle
or spoon, reduce the heat a little to a gently rolling simmer and cook for 4–5 minutes,
depending on the size (the white will be just firm and the yolk runny). Remove with
the ladle or spoon and gently slide into an egg cup.

Hard-Boiled Heaven

Cook as for Soft-Boiled Sustenance (see left), but for 7 minutes for a perfect, squashy, cooked yolk with no grey in sight. Allow to cool for a minute, then peel.

Serve the peeled egg with blanched spears of trimmed asparagus wrapped in slices of Iberico ham. Or for dunking pleasure, put it in an egg cup and cut off the top. Marmite-buttered toast, cinnamon-and-sugar-dusted fried bread, green beans, cheese straws or fried celeriac chips all make excellent soldiers.

Or try a watercress pesto. Whizz a handful of chopped watercress, 4 tbsp olive oil, ½ garlic clove, a grating of lemon zest and 4 walnut halves in a food processor until smooth. Spread the pesto on 2 pieces of hot, buttered toast. Cut the peeled hard-boiled eggs into quarters, sprinkle with salt and squash them between the slices of toast.

My Favourite Fried Eggs

Pour 1cm olive oil (extra-virgin is best if you can spare some) into a sauté pan with 2 squashed garlic cloves and set over a medium-high heat. When shimmering slightly, slowly crack in an egg and fry for 30 seconds–1 minute, basting it in the olive oil throughout cooking, until the white is bubbling and golden. Remove with a slotted spoon and place on your serving plate.

OR

Heat a knob of butter in a frying pan and, when melted and bubbling, gently crack in an egg. Fry for 2 minutes until crisp and golden. Remove from the pan with a slotted spoon onto a serving plate (or slice of toast). Add 2 tsp good white wine vinegar to the butter and quickly reduce by half, then spoon over the egg to serve.

Serve with 250g girolles and ½ garlic clove, finely chopped, fried in 25g unsalted butter. Season the egg and the crisp and golden mushrooms with sea. Squeeze over lemon juice and grate on some lemon zest. Sprinkle with chopped parsley.

Hangover Tip:
Serve in a bap with Addictive Tomato-Bonnet Jam (see page 285) and crispy bacon.

Oat & Flaxseed Porridge

My father used to make a savoury porridge that swam in a pool of cold cream; I was not a fan. It was not until I had children that I became a convert. Now I mix oats with ground flaxseed, which we call 'magic sprinkles'. I use half milk (always whole) and half water so that the porridge isn't too rich. We all go off to work with a warm glow, fuelled for the day ahead. In the summer we have soaked oats that we leave in the fridge overnight and flavour with whatever berries we have; it somehow feels a little lighter when the weather is warm, but no less satisfying. If you are avoiding dairy use unsweetened almond or soya milk, and coconut yogurt instead of dairy yogurt.

Put the oats in a pan with the water and milk and place over a medium heat. The moment the liquid is hot, reduce the heat to low. Season with a pinch of salt and the cinnamon and – for sweetness – add the banana, currants or sugar.

Cook gently for 5–10 minutes until the oats are creamy and seem to have dissolved into the milk. Stir in the flaxseed. The porridge should fall off a wooden spoon like a creamy risotto. If it is too stiff, pour in another 50ml milk and warm through.

Serve the porridge in bowls topped with the yogurt, and fresh fruit if you like (we mostly prefer the pure, unadulterated version).

Why not try soaked oats?

Mix 150g jumbo rolled oats, 1 tsp chia seeds and ½ tsp vanilla extract in a glass jar or container. Pour over 250ml milk (cow's, goat's, almond or coconut), enough to cover the oats. Cover and leave in the fridge to soak overnight. Make a little compote by heating blueberries and raspberries with a drop of water in a pan until they soften and burst, then spoon them onto your soaked oats. Feeds 1–2.

50g rolled oats

130ml water

130ml whole milk

scant pinch of ground cinnamon

1 sliced banana, or 30g currants, or 1 tbsp brown sugar

25g ground flaxseed

2 tbsp Greek yogurt

Three Juices

Hugo's Juice

3 celery sticks, peeled and
    roughly chopped

3 sweet apples, peeled, cored
    and roughly chopped

juice of 1 orange

handful of mint leaves

small handful of parsley leaves

3 slices of pineapple, peeled and
    cored, or 2 ripe kiwis, peeled

Vampiro

2 apples, peeled, cored and
    roughly chopped

2 carrots, scrubbed clean, topped
    and roughly chopped

2 beetroots, scrubbed clean, topped
    and tailed and roughly chopped

juice of 2 limes

25g peeled and finely grated
    fresh ginger

Ginger Zing

2 carrots, roughly chopped

3 apples, peeled, cored and
    roughly chopped

25–35g peeled and finely grated
    fresh ginger, to taste

juice of 2 oranges

When I lived in Mexico, where breakfasts are done in proper style and the fruit is sweet and sun-drenched, I fell into the habit of drinking fresh juices most days. On every other street corner there are stands bedecked with kaleidoscopic tropical fruits. Mangoes, papayas, guavas, guanabanas and pineapples are combined with healthier ingredients such as celery, cactus, spinach, kale, cucumber, parsley, amaranth (a quinoa-like grain) or wheatgerm to make the most refreshing and revitalising juices. These are three of my favourites.

For each of these juices, place all the ingredients in a juicer or good blender and whizz until completely smooth. Pass through a sieve if you don't have a juicer and would rather not have the pulp. These are all best drunk as soon as they are made.

Hugo's Juice

This is inspired by the popular Mexican *jugo verde*, a green juice made from cucumber, parsley and fresh cactus (it is said its high-fibre content has the benefit of speeding up digestion), sweetened with fresh orange and pineapple. The girls have decided to call it Hugo, which is near enough to how it sounds in Spanish! It makes you feel fantastic.

Vampiro

After the late shifts in a bar I ran in Mexico City, I needed something uplifting, and this vibrant blood-red beetroot juice was just the thing. We now serve it at Wahaca; the colour is incredible.

Ginger Zing

My husband swears by this juice. When we first met I had terrible circulation and my fingers would turn white whenever there was a chill in the air. After a year of drinking this juice – and hot water with fresh ginger – I was cured (and am far less prone to catching colds).

Four Smoothies & Lassis

Berry & Oat Super Smoothie

1 large banana

300g mixed fresh (or frozen) berries,
    such as blueberries, raspberries,
    blackberries or strawberries

1 tbsp rolled oats

small handful of skin-on almonds

200ml natural yogurt

300ml coconut water or water

honey or maple syrup, to taste

Avocado Smoothie

2 avocados, flesh scooped out

200ml apple juice

juice of 1 large orange

juice of 1 lime

2 tbsp agave syrup or maple syrup

2 large handfuls of ice

100–120ml water, to thin to your
    desired consistency (add after
    blending the other ingredients)

Strawberry & Cardamom Lassi

200g natural yogurt

125g ripe British strawberries

seeds from 2 cardamom pods, ground

1 tbsp ground linseeds

50ml milk

1–2 tsp agave syrup (optional)

Date, Oat & Almond Smoothie

3 medjool dates, pitted
    (about 60g pitted weight)

200ml unsweetened almond milk

small handful of skin-on almonds

25g rolled oats

50ml water

Even freshly made fruit juices are fairly sugar-laden, but these smoothies and lassis retain the fibre you lose when you pass juices through a sieve. I load mine with gut-friendly probiotic yogurt, nuts, grains and seeds to give me energy and protein all morning.

For all five of these recipes, place all the ingredients in a blender and whizz until smooth. Pour over ice-filled glasses and serve with a straw.

Berry & Oat Super Smoothie

There are lots of oats in this, so it's halfway between a cold porridge and a smoothie, a bit like a Bircher muesli. If you want a real health kick add 1 tsp acai powder, spirulina or wheatgerm.

Avocado Smoothie

We used to make this when we opened the first Wahaca in Covent Garden and it set us up for the day. It was so popular that when we started serving breakfast in Oxford Circus we had to put it on the menu. It is sweet, smooth and wonderfully filling.

Strawberry & Cardamom Lassi

Brimming with fruit and wonderful live cultures from the yogurt, lassis are my new go-to breakfast drinks: smooth, sustaining and incredibly healthy.

Date, Oat & Almond Smoothie

This is as bewitchingly sweet as it is filling.

Olive Oil Granola with Oodles of Nuts & Seeds

I've always been a bit suspicious of granola because adding lots of oil and sugar to an otherwise healthy muesli doesn't seem a very sensible idea. Then I found a recipe that used extra-virgin olive oil, had less sugar than usual and was seasoned with sea salt, which counteracted the sweetness. I was intrigued, so I tried it and adapted it and – let me tell you – the smell of it baking in the oven is amazing. It is also great as a topping for ice cream, as a makeshift crumble topping (just add a touch of plain flour) or sprinkled on a baked apple (see page 262). It makes a fab present poured into a Kilner jar and wrapped up with a brightly coloured bow.

This makes a large batch that keeps for several months in an airtight container.

Preheat the oven to 140°C/gas 1.

Put all the ingredients into a large mixing bowl and stir well to mix them thoroughly. Spread the mix out across a few baking sheets in fairly thin layers.

Bake in the oven for about 1 hour, stirring the granola every 15 minutes, and circulating the trays to different levels of the oven and turning from back to front. The granola is cooked when it looks toasted and golden. Cool, stir well and season to taste with a little more salt if it needs it. Store in an airtight container.

Why not try my cheat's granola?

Dollop thick Greek yogurt between 2 bowls. Toast 1 tbsp quinoa in a dry frying pan over a medium heat until it starts to pop and transfer to a plate. Toast a handful of chopped nuts (walnuts, pistachios, skin-on almonds) in the same pan, shaking so as to toast them evenly. Roughly chop a handful of medjool dates and scatter over the yogurt with the nuts and quinoa. Season with grated lemon zest, a pinch of salt and a few tsp of your best extra-virgin olive oil and eat at once. Feeds 2.

500g rolled oats

125g almonds, roughly chopped

125g walnuts, roughly chopped

100g pumpkin seeds

100g sunflower seeds

100g linseeds

100ml apple juice

75g unsweetened coconut flakes

75g maple syrup

75ml extra-virgin olive oil

50g soft light brown sugar

1 tsp sea salt

½ tsp vanilla extract

Quinoa Porridge with Earl Grey Poached Prunes

FEEDS TWO—FOUR

This is virtuous (high in protein and low in gluten) and as comforting as rice pudding. You could also swap Earl Grey for smoky Lapsang Souchong, but do not over-brew the tea or the prunes will taste bitter. Mix it up by substituting dried apricots for the prunes and apple juice for the tea. My mother would make an unbeatable pudding with a similar mixture when we were little and I've included her recipe below.

First prepare the prunes. Brew the tea bags or leaves in 300ml just-boiled water for 4 minutes, then pour or strain over the prunes into a pan. Add the honey and lemon zest and juice. Bring to the boil and simmer for 8–10 minutes until the prunes are swollen and the liquid has reduced by half. Taste – you may want to add more honey. Leave to cool, preferably overnight. The prunes will last for several weeks in a sealed container. You can leave them whole or purée with a stick blender.

To make the porridge, place the quinoa in a pan and add the milk, vanilla pod and cardamom. Bring to the boil, then simmer over a low heat for 10 minutes until the quinoa is tender. Stir in the honey. Serve with the prunes and, if you like, a dollop of natural yogurt or toasted flaked coconut. It is also delicious with slices of ripe mango in the summer.

Why not try my mother's prune & Armagnac pud?
This is particularly popular with the men in my life; they do seem to love nostalgia puddings. Prepare the prunes as above and then purée in a blender with 2 tbsp Armagnac or good brandy. Add icing sugar to taste, perhaps 1 tsp. Fry 150g stale breadcrumbs (see page 277) in 60g butter with several pinches of salt and 30g soft brown sugar until crisp and golden. Whisk 300ml double cream to soft peaks and stir in 300g strained Greek yogurt and 2 tsp sifted icing sugar. Layer half the puréed prunes in a large glass bowl or individual glasses followed by a layer of the breadcrumbs and a grating of dark chocolate (if you are using a Microplane or fine grater you will only need about 10g to get a lovely carpet). Top with the cream and more shavings of dark chocolate. Repeat the layers to get a double stack. Chill. This is also delicious with an apricot purée made as above and lightened with Muscat.

For the Porridge
150g quinoa, rinsed and drained

350g whole milk or unsweetened almond milk

1 vanilla pod, split lengthways

1 cardamom pod, crushed

1 tbsp honey

yogurt or toasted flaked coconut, to serve (optional)

For the Prunes
2 good-quality Earl Grey tea bags (the best you can find) or 2–3 tsp Earl Grey tea leaves

200g soft pitted prunes

1 tbsp honey, or to taste

finely grated zest and juice of ½ lemon

Waffles with Sweet-Roasted Grapes

Turn on the music, put on the coffee and whip up a batch of these bad boys. I love waffles, all springy and fluffy, with those dimples that are perfect for collecting little wells of melted butter and maple syrup. I discovered roast grapes thanks to the chef Anna Hansen. They add wonderful bursts of sweetness and I find we get through far less maple syrup now! Sensational.

Preheat the oven to 160°C/gas 3.

Put the grapes in a roasting tin just large enough to hold them. Drizzle with the pomegranate molasses or maple syrup, then sprinkle over the sugar and lemon zest and roast for 15–20 minutes. The grapes should just be beginning to break down. Remove from the oven and leave to cool in their juices.

Meanwhile sift the flour, baking powder, cinnamon and salt into a large mixing bowl. Whisk the egg yolks in a separate bowl with a fork until light and fluffy. Beat in the yogurt and one-third of the milk until fully incorporated into the egg mixture. Beat in the rest of the milk to get a smooth batter.

Make a well in the centre of the dry ingredients and slowly beat in the yogurt mixture. Whisk 5 tablespoons of the melted butter into the batter, keeping the rest for brushing onto the toasted waffles. Beat the egg whites with an electric hand whisk until they have formed stiff peaks. Gently fold a little of the batter into the whites with a large metal spoon to loosen them and then fold this mixture back into the whites, trying to keep as much air in the mixture as possible.

Fry or grill the streaky bacon and keep somewhere warm, reserving the fat for the waffle iron or frying pan. Heat the waffle iron or frying pan until smoking hot and brush with a little bacon fat or butter. Pour in a ladleful of batter and cook until golden brown (if making pancakes, cook until bubbles appear, then flip to cook the other side; if your mixture is a little wet, sift in a little extra flour).

Dish up the waffles as they are cooked so that they are eaten while hot. Brush them with the extra melted butter and top with the grapes, bacon, a dash of maple syrup and a bowl of yogurt to dollop on the side, giving a cool creaminess to the hot toasted waffles.

Kitchen Note:
I have an old-fashioned waffle iron left to me by my American grandmother, but most sandwich-maker machines have a waffle fitting. You could also make fat American-style pancakes in a hot frying pan.

For the Waffles
250g white spelt flour
1 tbsp baking powder
pinch of ground cinnamon
½ tsp salt
2 large eggs, separated
3 tbsp natural or Greek yogurt
350ml whole milk
100g butter, melted

For the Grapes
250g red seedless grapes
1 tbsp pomegranate molasses
   or maple syrup
2 tbsp Demerara sugar
finely grated zest of 1 lemon

To Serve
streaky bacon
maple syrup
thick Greek-style natural yogurt

Huevos Rancheros

Mexicans breakfast like kings and – out of their extraordinarily large repertoire of recipes – very little beats the light and spicy *huevos* (pronounced 'wayvoss') *rancheros*. The dish is wonderfully quick. Have all the vegetables chopped and the salsa blitzed, coffee on the go, any fresh juice already squeezed and tortillas toasted and kept warm in a tea towel. Then get everyone sitting down ready to eat. These are essentially scrambled eggs with the brilliantly vibrant and healthy additions of tomatoes, chillies and onion; they do not like sitting around.

Dry-roast the tomatoes, onion and garlic for the salsa in a dry frying pan for 10–15 minutes until blackened all over. Blitz with the rest of the salsa ingredients, apart from the chilli, in an upright blender. Taste and stir in as much chilli as you like, seasoning with salt, pepper and lime juice to taste.

Heat the oil in a large, heavy non-stick frying pan. When hot add the onion and cook over a medium heat for 5 minutes until it turns translucent. Add the garlic and chilli, season with salt and pepper and cook for another couple of minutes before adding the tomatoes and cooking for a further few minutes.

About 10 minutes before you want to sit down, beat the eggs and milk together briefly and add to the onion mix. Cook slowly over a gentle heat, stirring continuously with a wooden spoon. If they look like they are cooking too fast, take them off the heat for a few seconds before putting back on. When they start to thicken, take them off the heat and keep stirring, remembering that they will keep cooking for several more minutes away from the heat.

Toast the tortillas for 10–15 seconds each side over a gas flame, or heat in the oven or microwave, wrapped in cling film, and keep warm stacked in a tea towel.

Serve the eggs at the table on warm plates with a bowl of the salsa and a basket of tortillas for everyone to help themselves.

Kitchen Note:

For a more substantial brunch serve the eggs with strips of skirt steak, seasoned with salt and pepper and flash-fried in a dash of olive oil, or some slices of grilled chorizo, or maybe just some good British bacon.

For the Eggs

1–2 tbsp olive oil

1 onion, finely chopped

2 garlic cloves, finely chopped (optional)

½–1 jalapeño chilli, finely chopped (or ½ dried chilli, deseeded)

3–4 tomatoes, deseeded and finely chopped

10 free-range eggs

40ml semi-skimmed milk

8–12 tortillas

For the Salsa

3 large, ripe plum tomatoes, cored and deseeded

½ onion, peeled and cut into wedges

1 garlic clove, unpeeled

2 tsp olive oil

handful of fresh coriander leaves

pinch of brown sugar

juice of 1 lime, plus extra to taste

1 jalapeño chilli, finely chopped

Moreish Muffins

These muffins are sticky, sweet treats for breakfast and very simple to make. And they are good for you! I've used spelt as my flour here. These days most flours are made from intensively grown strains of wheat that are hard for us to digest, and they are milled so thoroughly that they are stripped of most of their essential nutrients. By using less intensively produced flours, such as spelt or kamut, in both their white and wholewheat forms, we can start getting nutrition back into our baking and eat a more easily digestible grain.

Marmalade & Poppy Seed Muffins

Preheat the oven to 180°C/gas 4 and line a deep 12-hole muffin tin with paper cases.

In a large mixing bowl, whisk together the marmalade and melted butter, then whisk in each egg in turn before slowly whisking in the orange juice and milk.

In a separate bowl, sift together the flour, baking powder and salt and stir in the poppy seeds and sugar. Stir the dry ingredients into the wet and stir until well combined. Spoon into the cases so that they are two-thirds full and bake on the middle shelf of the oven for 25–30 minutes until golden and an inserted skewer comes out clean.

While the muffins are in the oven, melt 4 tbsp of marmalade for the glaze. As soon as they come out of the oven, transfer to a wire rack to cool and liberally paint the top of the warm muffins with the extra marmalade. Leave to cool before eating; these are best eaten within a couple of days and are delicious reheated.

Seed, Oat & Fruit Breakfast Muffins

Preheat the oven to 190°C/gas 5 and line a deep 12-hole muffin tin with paper cases. Whisk the eggs (or use chia seeds for a dairy-free alternative) into the olive oil, then whisk in the yogurt followed by the fruits and vegetables.

Sift the flour, baking powder and salt into a bowl, then stir in the oats, sugar, maple syrup, spices, raisins, seeds and walnuts. Fold this into the wet ingredients, then spoon into the cases so that they are two-thirds full and scatter over some extra seeds to decorate. Bake on the middle shelf of the oven for 25–30 minutes until golden and an inserted skewer comes out clean. Leave to cool before eating.

Marmalade & Poppy Seed Muffins

200g thick-cut marmalade
(for home-made, see page
282), plus extra to glaze
120g butter, melted
2 eggs
2 tbsp orange juice
250ml whole milk
300g wholemeal spelt flour, sifted
3 tsp baking powder
½ tsp salt
50g poppy seeds
100g soft light brown sugar

Seed, Oat & Fruit Breakfast Muffins

3 eggs (or 3 tbsp chia seeds
soaked in 3 tbsp water)
200ml olive oil
200g natural yogurt or coconut yogurt
2 ripe bananas, peeled and mashed
1 red apple, grated
1 carrot or parsnip, grated
250g wholemeal spelt flour
1 tbsp baking powder
½ tsp salt
50g quick-cook porridge oats
75g soft light brown sugar
50g maple syrup
½ tsp grated nutmeg
½ tsp ground cinnamon
100g raisins or sultanas
50g mixed pumpkin and sunflower
seeds, plus extra to sprinkle
50g walnuts

Scandi-Style Breakfast

FEEDS FOUR

Thanks to a local diner, Snaps and Rye, I am, at last, getting sucked into the Scandinavian food craze. Here is a dish that typifies its fresh and fiery flavours. You will need a box grater, a mandoline (if you have one) and a sharp knife.

To make the rösti, coarsely grate the celeriac and potatoes and mix in the onion. Add half the salt and set in a colander over a bowl to drain off any excess liquid.

For the rémoulade, fill a bowl with cold water and add half the lemon juice to stop the celeriac from discolouring. Use a mandoline or large sharp knife to cut the celeriac into thin slices, about 2–3mm thick. Cut each slice into matchsticks and add to the water.

Whisk together the crème fraîche, remaining lemon juice, mustard and olive oil in a large bowl and season generously with salt and pepper. Add the horseradish and dill. Peel and coarsely grate the apple, and stir into the horseradish dressing. Drain the celeriac matchsticks, tip onto a tea towel and dry thoroughly. Add to the dressing and mix well. Check the seasoning, cover and leave to chill in the fridge.

Squeeze out any excess liquid from the grated potatoes and celeriac. Whisk the egg with the flour and remaining ½ tsp of salt and mix into the vegetables. Form little patties in the palm of your hands; you should get about 8 röstis. Generously cover the base of a large frying pan with oil and warm over a medium to medium-high heat. Fry the röstis in batches, ensuring that they do not touch each other. Cook for about 5 minutes each side until crisp and golden, then remove and drain on kitchen paper. Keep warm in a low oven while you cook the remaining batches.

Serve the röstis with a dollop of crème fraîche, a few slices of smoked salmon, a sprinkling of extra dill, a wedge of lemon and the delicious, fiery rémoulade on the side.

Why not try my perfect Bloody Mary?
Mix 1.5 litres tomato juice in a jug with the juice of 1 lemon, ½ glass of red wine, 1 tbsp Worcestershire sauce, 1 tsp Tabasco, several good grindings of pepper, ½ tsp celery salt, 1 tsp flaky sea salt, 1 tbsp freshly grated horseradish and 50ml sherry. Stir well. Taste and adjust the balance of spicy, savoury and sour with Tabasco, salt and lemon juice, as you like. Fill highball glasses to the brim with ice, add 40ml vodka to each and top with the mix. Serve with a celery stick and a good grinding of black pepper.

For the Rösti
½ celeriac (about 350g), peeled
300g floury potatoes
    (such as Maris Piper), peeled
½ onion, finely chopped
1 tsp salt
1 egg
2 heaped tbsp plain flour
vegetable oil, to fry

For the Rémoulade
juice of 1 lemon
½ celeriac (about 350g), peeled
4 tbsp crème fraîche
1½ tbsp Dijon mustard
1 tbsp olive oil
2 tbsp grated horseradish (fresh is
    best, avoid the horseradish creams)
small handful of dill fronds, finely
    chopped, plus extra to serve
2 green apples

To Serve
crème fraîche
200g smoked salmon
1 lemon, quartered

Eggs in Pots

There is something extremely comforting about dipping your spoon into the molten collection of ingredients below, especially if you have a hunk of fresh crusty bread at your side.

You can play around with the contents of your fridge and cupboard to make your own variations, but I have included some ideas as a launch pad.

Cover the porcini in boiling water and leave to soak for 10–15 minutes, then squeeze out the excess water in your hands and finely chop.

Preheat the oven to 180°C/gas 4. Warm the butter and the splash of oil in a frying pan over a medium-low heat and add the shallots and a pinch of salt. Cook for 5 minutes until soft, then increase the heat to medium-high and add the garlic, chestnut mushrooms, porcini, thyme and chilli, if using. Cook, stirring, until the mushrooms begin to soften, then take off the heat, add a squeeze of lemon juice and season to taste. Stir in the crème fraîche and parsley and divide between 4 ramekins. Make a small indentation in the centre of each, break in an egg and season.

Boil a kettle. Place the ramekins in a baking tin, then place on the oven shelf and pour in enough boiling water to come halfway up the sides of the ramekins. Bake for 12–15 minutes until the whites are cooked and the yolks still runny; keep half an eye on them as they can suddenly turn from under- to over-cooked. Serve immediately.

Why not try it with smoked salmon, chives & crème fraîche?
Mix 70g torn smoked salmon, 200ml crème fraîche, freshly chopped chives, a squeeze of lemon juice and lots of black pepper and spoon into 2 buttered ramekins. Add an egg to each and bake as above. Squeeze a little lemon juice on top to serve. Feeds 2.

Or Parma ham, Gruyère & cream?
Curl up 2 slices of Parma ham in a buttered ramekin and drizzle over 35ml double cream and 15g grated Gruyère. Crack an egg on top, grate over a little more Gruyère and sprinkle with chilli flakes. Bake as above. Feeds 1.

Or Moroccan tomatoes?
Mix 1 chopped beef tomato, a pinch of thyme leaves, ½ tsp sweet smoked paprika and 2 tbsp natural yogurt. Spoon into a buttered ramekin. Add an egg then bake as above. Feeds 1.

15g dried porcini (optional)

30g butter

splash of olive oil

2 small banana shallots, finely chopped

2 garlic cloves, finely chopped

6 chestnut mushrooms, roughly chopped

3 sprigs of thyme, leaves picked

pinch of chilli flakes (optional)

squeeze of lemon juice

4 tbsp crème fraîche or double cream

small handful of parsley leaves, finely chopped

4 eggs

Cornbread with Goat's Cheese & Honey Butter

FEEDS FOUR

A trip to California got me into cornbread. The corn was quite unlike English corn, so juicy and sweet. The Californians seemed to eat variations of this bread with everything from rich meat braises to light salads and eggs for breakfast.

This recipe is always a total hit when we put it on the Wahaca menu, and was developed from a recipe in an old Chez Panisse cookbook. We serve it with a chipotle honey butter, using the smokiness and heat from the chillies to balance the sweetness of the honey.

For the Cornbread

100ml whole milk

240ml buttermilk

3 eggs

165g sweetcorn kernels,
    frozen or cut from a fresh cob

100g plain flour

180g fine polenta

30g soft brown sugar

1 tsp fine salt

1 tbsp baking powder

80g butter

3 spring onions, halved lengthways
    and very finely sliced

For the Goat's Cheese

250g soft goat's cheese

75ml whole milk

25ml olive oil

For the Chipotle Honey Butter

125g butter

35g chipotle in adobo,
    very finely chopped

50g honey

generous squeeze of lime juice

To Serve

butter, to fry

4 eggs

large handful of rocket, dressed
    with olive oil and lime juice

To make the cornbread, preheat the oven to 180°C/gas 4 and butter a 900g loaf tin.

Blend together the milk, buttermilk, eggs and 100g of the sweetcorn. Put the flour, polenta, sugar, salt and baking powder into a large bowl and whisk well to combine. Melt the butter in a pan and add to the dry ingredients, along with the egg mixture, spring onions and remaining sweetcorn. Mix briefly to bring everything together.

Pour the mixture into the prepared tin and bake for about 45 minutes or until an inserted skewer comes out clean. Allow to cool in the tin for 30 minutes before turning out onto a wire rack to cool.

While the cornbread is baking, blitz the goat's cheese, milk and olive oil in a food processor or blender, seasoning with salt and pepper. It should be light and fluffy and easy to spoon onto a plate.

For the chipotle honey butter, melt the butter in a pan, add the chipotle and honey and whisk until everything is incorporated. Season with the lime juice and salt, to taste.

Cut the bread into slices the thickness of two £1 coins and fry in a little butter to warm through. Crack the eggs into a hot frying pan (see the second method on page 19, omitting the vinegar) and fry until crisp. Serve the bread with 1–2 heaped tbsp of the goats' cheese, a handful of dressed rocket, a fried egg and a generous drizzle of smoky-sweet chipotle honey butter.

Why not try corn & double cheese muffins?

Add 50g grated Cheddar, 50g crumbled feta, 4 sprigs of thyme (leaves picked) and a pinch of cayenne to the cornbread mix. Bake in muffin trays lined with paper cases for 25–30 minutes. A top-notch breakfast with or without a few rashers of bacon.

No-Fuss Cinnamon, Maple & Hazelnut Buns

MAKES TWELVE

I've been hooked on cinnamon buns since my gap year in Mexico, where I'd eat them fresh from the oven. Here I have adapted a recipe from my friend Claire Ptak's wonderful book, *The Violet Bakery Cookbook*. The buns don't need long proving, so you can make them first thing in the morning ready for a mouth-watering breakfast.

Preheat the oven to 200°C/gas 6 and butter a 12-hole muffin tin.

Prepare the filling by melting the butter. In a separate bowl, mix together the sugar, cinnamon and chopped and ground nuts (save the maple syrup for later).

Mix together the flour, baking powder, salt and cardamom with the chilled butter in a food processor until you have something that resembles fine breadcrumbs. Slowly pour in the milk and pulse until you have a wettish ball of dough. Turn the dough out onto a lightly floured surface and leave to rest for 5 minutes.

Fold the dough over itself once or twice, then rest again for 10 minutes. Dust the surface again with flour and then roll out the dough to a 5mm-thick rectangle. Brush the surface with half the melted butter and then evenly sprinkle over the sugar, cinnamon and nut mix.

Starting from a longer side, roll up the dough into a sausage, as tightly as possible, then squeeze it along its length so that you have an even spiral. With a knife, score a light mark at quarter stages along the sausage, and then mark each quarter into three. This will make slicing the roll into 12 even pieces a cinch. Once you have 12 rolls, pull the loose end of each roll over one side of the spiral to cover and hold in the filling (don't fret if the dough tears, they'll still be great). Put the spirals in the holes of the muffin tin, covered sides down, squashing them down a little with the palm of your hand. Sprinkle with any excess cinnamon sugar, mix the maple syrup into the remaining butter and drizzle evenly over each bun.

Bake the buns for 25 minutes. Using an oven glove, immediately remove the buns from the tin, swirl facing upwards, onto a wire rack. Eat while still warm.

For the Filling
100g butter, plus extra for the tin
175g soft light brown sugar
2 tsp ground cinnamon
50g hazelnuts, half finely chopped,
    half ground to a coarse powder
2 tbsp maple syrup

For the Cinnamon Buns
560g plain flour, plus extra to dust
2 tbsp baking powder
2 tsp fine salt
seeds from 10 cardamom pods, ground
240g chilled butter, diced
300ml chilled milk

Kitchen Note:

These do not keep well so, if you are not eating them straight away, reheat in a preheated 200°C/gas 6 oven, brushed with butter and a sprinkling of sugar. Serve with vanilla ice cream for an indulgent pudding.

Chapter
TWO

A COMFORTING BOWL

A COMFORTING BOWL

A bowl of hot food is always comforting. If it only uses one pan or pot in the making, better still!

I particularly love how soups can be a last-minute invention, a simple matter of a few sweated vegetables, spices or herbs and some stock. The Beetroot & Fennel Seed Soup with Ginger Crème Fraîche and the Carrot Soup with Spiced Brown Butter in this chapter were created when I needed to cook something fast using what I had at home; they have since become firm family favourites. Do play with what you have in the fridge; you can transform a simple bowl of broth with a jazzy garnish, a seasoned dollop of yogurt, some fried chorizo or toasted nuts. Even a drizzle of cream, or of truffle or olive oil, can be all you need to lift flavours and make them sing.

Stock is key to this type of cooking, not only adding enormous flavour to whatever you are making but also vital goodness. Happily it is absolutely painless to make and having stock in your freezer is a great asset when making food at a moment's notice.

One last word on this: soups and stews should always be served either very hot or very cold. The act of cooking down firm, robust ingredients into comfortingly soft purées and serving them lukewarm makes them dangerously similar to baby food. Heat is a defining feature that brings alive the clarity of flavours. With this in mind, always heat up bowls before you serve soup, or chill them in the freezer if you are making a cooling vichyssoise or gazpacho; I know it sounds prescriptive but it really does make all the difference.

A Summer Bowl

FEEDS FOUR—SIX

50ml olive oil

knob of butter

1 red onion, finely sliced

200g Jersey Royals or other waxy
    new potatoes such as Pink Fir
    Apple, cut into chunks

2 fat garlic cloves, finely sliced

¼ tsp fennel seeds

¼ tsp chilli flakes

1 fennel bulb, cut into 4cm slices

1 large yellow courgette
    (about 300g), halved lengthways
    and cut into thick diagonal slices

500ml good-quality vegetable
    or chicken stock

175g runner beans, trimmed, de-stringed
    if needed, and cut into 4cm pieces

150g fine green beans, halved

100g podded broad beans

1 tbsp oregano leaves, roughly chopped

handful of basil leaves, torn

50g Parmesan, grated

finely grated zest of ½ lemon

mascarpone or your best extra-virgin
    olive oil, to serve (optional)

Calling this recipe a soup or a stew fails to capture the light, summery collection of textures, shapes and flavours that sit together in the bowl. Beautiful summer beans, courgettes, new potatoes and summer garlic cook in a soupy broth until just tender, brought together by a few summer herbs and gentle seasonings. Finish off with a dollop of creamy mascarpone or a slick of your best extra-virgin olive oil and bring it all together with a generous grating of Parmesan and you are in for a real treat.

Melt the oil and butter together in a large pan or wok and fry the onion, potatoes, garlic, fennel seeds, and chilli flakes with a pinch of salt until the onion has softened.

Add the fennel and courgette and fry for 5 minutes, then pour in the stock. Bring to the boil and simmer gently for 8–10 minutes, then add the runner and green beans. Simmer for 5 minutes until the beans are tender, then add the broad beans and cook for a further 3 minutes. You want the vegetables to be tender but not overcooked and mushy.

Season to taste then stir in the herbs, Parmesan and lemon zest. Immediately ladle into deep warmed bowls and, if you like, drop in a dollop of mascarpone or drizzle with extra-virgin olive oil.

Kitchen Note:

I love this soup with a few chunks of potatoes in it but you could equally add some freshly soaked and cooked borlotti beans, or leave both out and keep the soup lighter, mopping it up with hunks of fresh bread or garlic-rubbed toast (see page 277). For extra richness, spoon in a herb pesto or oil. Do experiment with what you can find; if you are making this in early summer, you might try asparagus, fresh peas, ripe tomatoes, fennel, spinach or sorrel or any combination of the above.

Making Stock

Forget any cheffy connotations, making stock is easy and a fine example of getting something for almost nothing. Re-use the bones from your roast, cover them with water and let them do all the work. If you don't have the energy to deal with making stock straight after a filling roast dinner, then you can leave it until the next day to strain, cool and store it. I use clean plastic milk cartons to store my stock in the fridge or freezer.

Bear in mind the source of your stock; high-quality meat from farms or good butchers means strong bones that give beautifully jellied, highly nutritious stock. Here are some simple recipes for every stock occasion.

Chicken Stock

Probably the most useful of all the different kinds, a chicken stock will add flavour to sauces, risottos, stews and soups and can transform store cupboard noodles into exotic bowls of Asian pho. The most obvious way to make a chicken stock is by using the bones and leftovers from a roast, but if you are making a stock from a fresh, raw chicken, begin by cooking the chicken in a hot oven for 20 minutes to get some caramelisation and depth of flavour. If you are using a leftover carcass, adding the raw neck, or gizzard, and some giblets will improve the taste; they usually come free with the bird from a butcher or farmer's market.

Put all the ingredients into a pan just large enough to fit them and cover with water. Bring to the boil, then reduce the heat and simmer gently for 2–3 hours. Top up the stock with hot water as it evaporates so that the ingredients are always covered, but never boil vigorously or the stock will taste bitter. Strain and cool, then chill in the fridge. When cold, spoon off any fat that has collected on the surface.

1 chicken carcass with all the
    leftover gunk (skin, fat, jelly etc.)
1 large onion, cut into chunks
2 carrots, cut into chunks
2 celery sticks, cut into chunks
1 tsp whole peppercorns
few sprigs of parsley or thyme
2 bay leaves, preferably
    (but not necessarily) fresh
2 unpeeled garlic cloves (optional)

To freeze the stock, pour into clean plastic water bottles or milk containers and mark the contents and date on them with a freezer pen (it keeps happily for 6 months). Alternatively reduce the stock right down after you have strained it to produce a highly concentrated essence. You can then freeze this in ice-cube trays; perfect if a recipe calls for only a small amount of stock.

Kitchen Note:
Never add salt to stock in case you need to reduce it later; the salt levels can become too concentrated the more it is reduced.

Vegetable Stock

Heat 2 tbsp olive oil in a large pan and sweat 2 roughly chopped onions for a few minutes. Add 4 chopped carrots, 3 chopped celery sticks and 1 sliced fennel bulb and sweat for a further few minutes. Add 4 chopped cabbage leaves, 3 halved garlic cloves, 2 washed and chopped leeks, 1 bouquet garni, a few sprigs of chervil, the pared zest of 1 lemon, 2 bay leaves and 8 peppercorns and cover with 2 litres of water. Bring to the boil, then reduce the heat and simmer for 1 hour, topping up with water if needed to ensure that the ingredients are always covered. Strain, cool and use.

Beef Stock

Preheat the oven to 200°C/gas 6. Wash 2.5kg beef bones thoroughly, place in a roasting tray and roast for 30 minutes with 2 quartered onions until well browned. Heat 1 tbsp vegetable oil in a stock pot and fry 2 chopped carrots and 2 washed and chopped leeks until taking on a bit of colour, then add the bones and onion. Cover with water and add 1 bouquet garni, 2 bay leaves and 10 black peppercorns. Simmer gently for 3–5 hours, skimming off any scum as it emerges, and topping up with hot water as needed. Strain well, the second time through a chinois or fine-mesh sieve, and cool. Chill and skim off the fat. If you want to freeze the stock, return to a clean pan and simmer until reduced, intensifying the flavour. Pour into ice-cube trays and freeze.

Fish Stock

Heat 2 tbsp olive oil in a large pan and add ½ sliced fennel bulb, 1 quartered onion, 1 chopped carrot and 1 washed and chopped leek. Slowly cook until softened but not coloured. Add 700g white fish bones, the zest of 1 lemon, 1 bouquet garni and 250ml white wine and bring to the boil. Reduce the heat and simmer for 5 minutes. Cover with water and simmer for 20 minutes (no longer), skimming off any scum that rises to the surface. Strain through a fine-mesh sieve, cool and use within a day, or freeze for up to 3 months.

Fast, Unbeatable Shellfish Stock

Heat 2 tbsp olive oil in a large pan with 4 unpeeled garlic cloves, smashed once. Add 500g prawn shells and heads (use the bodies to make a delicious prawn cocktail, see page 76 for a modern, smoky take on the classic Marie-Rose dressing) and cook over a medium heat for 2–3 minutes until the shells are pink and aromatic. Add 1 tbsp tomato purée and cook for another 30 seconds before pouring in 2.5 litres fish stock (see above) and a few sprigs of parsley. Bring to the boil and simmer gently for 20 minutes, then strain and chill.

Celeriac, Crème Fraîche & Chive Soup

When I first entered *MasterChef* I remember John Torode telling us to read, read, read; this was when I first discovered two of the great female British food writers, Elizabeth David and Jane Grigson. I particularly fell in love with Grigson's take on traditional English food; her celeriac and apple soup was one of the first recipes I tried on one of my days off during the competition.

For my version of this soup I've added potato, which softens the intense flavour of the celeriac and makes the texture silkier. I like to garnish it simply with a few snipped chives but, if I were serving this for a smart dinner, I might sprinkle it with some fried croutons, or roast celeriac cubes, or caramelised apple slices with a slick of truffle oil.

Melt the butter and oil in a deep pan over a medium-low heat and add the onion, celery, apple and a good pinch of salt. Sweat them without colour for 10–12 minutes until soft and sweet. Stir in the celeriac, potato and thyme leaves and cook for a further couple of minutes to give the celeriac a little colour, then pour over the stock and season well. Bring to the boil, then reduce the heat and leave to simmer for 20–25 minutes until the celeriac is just soft.

Meanwhile, toast the hazelnuts in a dry pan over a medium heat, shaking continuously until they begun to turn golden, about 3 minutes. Remove from the heat and finely chop, or place in a clean tea towel and bash with a rolling pin.

Take the soup off the heat and use a stick blender to blitz until smooth. Stir in the crème fraîche, add a squeeze of lemon juice to taste and adjust the seasoning if needed. Transfer to warmed bowls and add a big dollop of crème fraîche, a sprinkling of toasted hazelnuts and a scattering of chives before serving.

Why not try burnt butter celeriac dip with broccoli?

Fry a peeled and diced head of celeriac with 6 whole garlic cloves and 2 sprigs of thyme in 3 tbsp olive oil over a high heat for 5 minutes, then over a low heat for 10 minutes until soft. Brown 30g butter (see page 52), then add to the celeriac with 100g yogurt. Whizz to a purée in a food processor or blender. Serve with blanched Tenderstem or purple sprouting broccoli and a sprinkle of Dukkah (see page 294).

40g butter

splash of olive oil

1 large onion, finely chopped

2 celery sticks, finely chopped

1 apple, cored and chopped

1 celeriac, peeled and roughly chopped

1 medium potato, peeled and roughly chopped

4 sprigs of thyme, leaves picked

1.5 litres hot chicken or vegetable stock (for home-made, see pages 46–7)

4 tbsp peeled hazelnuts

150ml crème fraîche, plus extra to serve

squeeze of lemon juice

a few chives, finely chopped

Smoky Udon Mackerel Soup

FEEDS TWO

Junya Yamasaki, once head chef at London restaurant Koya, kneaded the dough for his thick, firm, yielding noodles with his feet. One of my favourite of his dishes was a smoky noodle broth with mackerel and miso. Sadly he returned to Japan, so I had to come up with my own version. This is easy, speedy, and mouth-wateringly good.

Miso paste comes in three types with increasing pungency: white, brown or red. I use white for a cleaner flavour, or sometimes brown for more depth.

In a pan, gently heat the vegetable oil over a medium heat and add the ginger and garlic. After a minute of sizzling take off the heat and add the soy, mirin, honey and sesame oil. Return to the heat for just a second to make sure it's hot, but don't let it boil. Add the mackerel in large chunks, tossing it gently in the sauce, trying not to break it up too much, until it is completely coated, then put to one side.

To cook the egg, bring a pan of water to the boil and carefully lower in the egg. Reduce the heat to a simmer and leave to cook for 6 minutes (for a medium egg), then remove and peel under cold running water. Place the peeled egg in the pan with the warm mackerel and smother it in the sauce; the longer you can leave it in there the better.

Bring a pan of water to the boil and cook the noodles according to the packet instructions. Meanwhile, in a separate pan, bring 750ml water to the boil and stir in the miso paste until it disappears. Drop in the cabbage and the spring onions, leaving until they just wilt. Drain the noodles and stir them into the pan with the cabbage. Transfer to 2 bowls then spoon the mackerel and its sauce over the top. Halve the egg, sit a half on each bowl, and serve with a little soy for people to add themselves.

Why not try smoked mackerel rillettes?

Take 4 smoked mackerel fillets and mash them with a fork with 150ml crème fraîche, 30ml best extra-virgin olive oil and 1 tbsp finely chopped chives. Season with salt and pepper and the juice of ½ lemon. Serve with sourdough toast and a beautiful side salad of castelfranco, pink chicory or radicchio leaves (see page 96–7 for a photo of these). Or you could have it with a green bean, caper and shallot salad for a snazzy starter.

2 tsp vegetable oil

1 tsp peeled and finely grated fresh ginger

1 garlic clove, finely grated

5 tbsp soy sauce, plus extra to serve

4 tbsp mirin

2 tbsp honey

2 tsp sesame oil

2 smoked mackerel fillets, skinned

1 egg

150g udon, or other noodles

4–5 tbsp miso paste, to taste

6 Savoy cabbage leaves, very finely shredded

4 spring onions, finely sliced on the diagonal

Carrot Soup with Spiced Brown Butter

FEEDS FOUR

The spices in this delicious soup bring out all the flavour of the sweet carrots; it is made more warming and exotic by the nutty brown butter seasoned with a touch of Turkish chilli. I always try to buy my carrots at the market; for me it is the one vegetable where you really notice the difference in taste between those that have come straight from the ground and those that have spent time on the shelves.

If you want to make this soup a little more substantial, crumble some feta on top with the chopped dill and serve with flatbreads.

Heat a large, wide pan over a medium heat and gently warm the spices until smelling fragrant. Tip into in a spice grinder or pestle and mortar and grind to a powder. Melt the butter in the same pan, seasoning generously with salt and pepper, and fry the onion and celery, again over a medium heat, for about 10 minutes until soft. Add the ground spices and carrots, stir to coat well, then cover with a circle of baking parchment and a lid. This will allow the carrots to gently 'steam' in their own juices. Cook for about 15 minutes, stirring every 5 minutes to make sure the carrots are not sticking to the bottom, and adding a splash of water if you find that they are.

Pour in the stock, bring to the boil and simmer for 10 minutes until the carrots are completely soft. Using a stick blender or a food processor, whizz until completely smooth. Check and adjust the seasoning.

For the spiced butter, place the butter in a small pan over a medium heat and cook until it turns deep brown and smells nutty. Add the chilli flakes and lemon juice (take care as the fat may spit a little when the lemon juice is added) and remove from the heat. Serve the soup in warmed bowls with dollops of yogurt, a scattering of chopped dill and spoonfuls of the nutty butter.

Kitchen Note:
The chilli butter above is also delicious on lamb chops. Serve them with a bulgar wheat salad with masses of parsley, mint and coriander leaves flecked throughout; adding pomegranate seeds, feta or diced cucumber if you like.

For the Soup

2 tsp coriander seeds

½ tsp cumin seeds

50g butter

1 onion, chopped

2 celery sticks, chopped

600g carrots, preferably organic for flavour, roughly chopped

1.2 litres chicken or vegetable stock (for home-made see pages 46–7), or water

For the Spiced Butter

50g butter

1 tsp Turkish chilli flakes or smoked paprika

juice of ½ lemon

4 tbsp Greek yogurt, to serve

handful of dill, to serve

Beetroot & Fennel Seed Soup with Ginger Crème Fraîche

I'll never forget a dinner we had for a huge gaggle of our Wahaca staff at Hartwood, a smart beachside restaurant in Tulum, Mexico. They served giant whole beets they'd roasted in their wood-fired oven, sitting on beautifully seasoned labneh (this region of Mexico, the Yucatan, is heavily influenced by Lebanese cuisine); our team couldn't believe how good they were. This soup is my take on borscht, with fennel seeds and chilli adding wonderful accents of flavour.

Top and tail the beetroot, rinse the top stalks and any leaves in cold water, roughly chop and set aside. Scrub the beets and potatoes clean with a coarse scourer and roughly dice the beets (I always use rubber gloves for this to avoid pink-stained fingers). Peel the potatoes and dice into the same size as the beets (the actual size doesn't matter, although the smaller they are the faster they will cook).

Heat 3 tablespoons of the oil in a large casserole over a medium heat and add the onions, fennel seeds and chilli. Sweat for about 8 minutes until the onion is soft and translucent, then add the garlic and vegetables. Cook the vegetables in the oil for about 5 minutes, stirring them to coat in the spices. Season generously with salt and pepper, pour in the stock to cover and simmer gently for 30 minutes, by which time the vegetables should be completely soft. Blitz with a stick blender and adjust the thickness by adding more water, or simmering to reduce and thicken.

Meanwhile grate the ginger into the crème fraîche. Add the lime zest and juice and season with a pinch of salt.

Just before serving, heat the remaining oil in a frying pan and sauté the beet tops for a few minutes until soft and hot. Season with a pinch of salt. Serve the soup in warmed bowls with a dollop of the crème fraîche and a sprinkling of the tops. It is delicious right away but improves substantially if you can rest it overnight; mostly I am too impatient.

For the Soup

6 medium beetroots

3–4 floury potatoes (about 500g)

4 tbsp olive oil

2 small onions, finely chopped

1 tsp fennel seeds

a few pinches of chilli flakes (optional)

2 fat garlic cloves, finely chopped

1.5 litres chicken, beef or
  vegetable stock (for home-made,
  see pages 46–7)

For the Crème Fraîche

large thumb-sized piece
  of fresh ginger, peeled

250ml crème fraîche

finely grated zest of 1 lime
  and juice of ½ lime

Why not try salmon ceviche with roast beetroot, pumpkin seeds & tarragon?
Cut 800g peeled, trimmed beetroot into slender wedges and toss in 2 tbsp olive oil, salt and pepper. Roast in a preheated 180°C/gas 4 oven for 1 hour until tender. Meanwhile, toast 40g pumpkin seeds. When the beetroot is cooked toss in 1 tbsp cider vinegar, a big handful of chopped tarragon leaves and the pumpkin seeds. Slice 2 organic salmon fillets into wafer-thin slices and dress with lemon juice, finely chopped green chilli and a slick of pumpkin seed oil. Serve with the beets on the side. Feeds 4.

A Comforting Bowl

Sprout & Squash Laska

FEEDS FOUR

I am helping to create an open-air classroom and garden for my local school. I held a dinner to introduce some of the main players to each other. It felt stressful as I didn't know anyone terribly well and three of my guests were either vegetarian or vegan. I opted for Thai, knowing that my local supermarket stocked galangal, lime leaves, lemon grass and dairy-free coconut milk.

I was working that day so, true to form, I was flying by the seat of my pants. Three of my guests ended up slicing Brussels sprouts and chopping coriander but, despite my lack of planning, we all had great fun and the laksa was a hit. If you think you hate Brussels sprouts you could use green beans instead, but I urge you to try this recipe as written before you do … you might be amazed!

1½ tbsp groundnut oil

1 red onion, half finely chopped,
    half finely sliced

2 garlic cloves, finely chopped

1–2 bird's eye chillies, finely chopped

2 tsp peeled and finely grated
    fresh ginger

1 lemon grass stick, chopped

large bunch of coriander, stalks
    finely chopped, leaves picked

1 x 400ml can coconut milk

400ml vegetable or chicken stock
    (for home-made see pages 46–7),
    plus extra if needed

2 tbsp fish sauce

10 fresh or frozen lime leaves

500g butternut squash,
    peeled and chopped

300g Brussels sprouts,
    trimmed and quartered

juice of 1 lime

200g cooked black rice noodles, to serve

In a wok or large pan, heat 1 tbsp of the oil over a medium heat. Add the chopped onion, garlic, chillies, ginger, lemon grass and coriander stalks and fry for 2 minutes.

Add the coconut milk, stock, fish sauce, lime leaves and squash, season well and bring to the boil briefly. Reduce to a low simmer and cook for 25 minutes or until the squash is tender. Add a little more stock if the liquid has reduced too much. Season again, to taste.

Meanwhile, heat the remaining ½ tbsp of oil in a pan and fry the sprouts and sliced onion for 4 minutes, so the sprouts take on just a little colour but are still a little raw and crunchy. Season and squeeze over the lime juice.

Spoon the laksa over cooked black rice noodles in large warmed bowls and sprinkle with the sprouts.

Why not try pan-fried sprouts with sweet soy glaze, toasted almonds & feta?

Mix 30g soft brown sugar, 60ml soy sauce, 30ml fresh lime juice and 50ml water. Trim and halve 250g sprouts. Heat 20g butter in a large frying pan or wok and throw in the sprouts. Fry for a few minutes over a high heat, before pouring in the soy glaze. Continue to fry for a few minutes until the sprouts are caramelised and tender, adding a splash of extra water if needed. Serve on their own, or on a bed of noodles scattered with a small handful of toasted, slivered almonds, 40g crumbled feta (optional) and sweet soy sauce (kecap manis). Feeds 1–2.

Simple Moroccan Fish Stew

FEEDS FOUR

I spent the third year of my Spanish degree in Santiago, where I befriended a mad bunch of Chileans. One weekend we went to the coast to go fishing and met a Moroccan fisherman who, that night, made a fish stew for all of us with our catch in a huge oil drum over a fire. He kept adding layer upon layer of garlic, onion, spices, herbs, potatoes, fish and shellfish. The stew was extraordinary – fresher than anything I had ever tasted – still alive with the sea.

All coastal cultures have a version of this stew: France has bouillabaisse with tomato, fennel and anise; Kerala has red fish curry, with coconut milk and tamarind; Mexico's fish stew is made with crab and smoky, rich red chillies. Prepare your base early, then put in the seafood at the last minute, as guests arrive.

Warm the oil in your widest pan (or a large frying pan with a lid) over a medium heat and add the onions, garlic, coriander, chilli and oregano along with a good pinch of salt. Cook gently for 8–10 minutes until everything is completely soft.

Increase the heat to medium-high and add the soaked saffron followed by the preserved lemon, tomatoes, potatoes and wine. Simmer for 12 minutes, stirring occasionally to prevent sticking, until the sauce has thickened slightly, then season to taste. Reduce the heat to low.

Lightly season the fish, then very gently fold into the stew. Scatter the mussels on top and cover with a lid. Allow to cook over a low heat for 4–5 minutes, then check to see if the mussels have opened. If not, replace the lid for another few minutes until they have all opened (discard any that remain closed).

Carefully spoon the fish stew into bowls and scatter over the herbs. Serve at the table with the yogurt, harissa oil and crostini or fresh crusty bread.

For the Stew

3 tbsp olive oil

2 onions, finely sliced

3 garlic cloves, finely sliced

1 tbsp coriander seeds

1–2 pinches of chilli flakes

1 tsp dried oregano

½ tsp saffron threads,
   soaked in boiling water

1 preserved lemon, pulp scraped
   away, rind finely chopped

2 x 400g cans plum tomatoes,
   drained, rinsed and chopped

600g floury potatoes, peeled and
   cut into walnut-sized chunks

250ml white wine

600g cod loin, skinned,
   cut into 3cm chunks (or
   use red mullet or gurnard)

500g mussels, scrubbed
   and de-bearded

To Serve

small handful of either
   dill or coriander leaves
   (or both), finely chopped

Greek yogurt

2 tbsp extra-virgin olive oil mixed
   with 2 tbsp rose harissa (shop-bought
   or for home-made see page 296)

Crostini (optional, see page 277)

Why not try a garlicky sopa de ajo?

Fry the finely chopped cloves from 1 whole head of garlic in 100ml olive oil and 1 tsp sweet smoked paprika until soft and pale golden. Season and add to a pan with 1.5 litres hot fresh chicken stock and a small pinch of saffron threads. Now fry 400g stale bread pieces in the garlicky oil with another pinch of saffron until the bread is golden. Just before serving, bring the stock to the boil, reduce to a simmer and drop in 4 eggs from a cup, one at a time. Cook for 2–3 minutes until the whites have just set, then ladle into warmed bowls with the bread in the bottom. Drizzle with the saffron oil left in the pan and add a dusting of smoked paprika and chopped parsley to serve. Feeds 4.

Chestnut, Spelt & Chorizo Soup

FEEDS FOUR

When I began learning Spanish as a teenager I spent my summers working in Spain and fell in love with the people, the country and its gutsy food. I found a job in a little village in the Pyrenees, with a family who owned the local bar. I remember making endless plates of *pan con tomate* (see page 277), but the thing I most loved was an incredible chestnut and chorizo soup that the family would make in cooler weather. The garlicky, spiced oil from the chorizo seeped through the grainy, sweet nutty body of the soup. This version is inspired by that recipe and a soup from *Moro: The Cookbook*, one of my all-time favourite cookery books. It is a rich, comforting, deeply satisfying bowl of soup.

Buying whole fresh chestnuts in the supermarket and cooking them yourself is a lot cheaper than buying them cooked and vacuum-packed, and the texture tends to be much smoother, but if you are time-poor, buy them ready to go.

100g pearled spelt,
   pearl barley or buckwheat
1.6 litres water or chicken stock
   (for home-made see pages 46–7)
4 tbsp olive oil
1 large Spanish onion, finely chopped
1 carrot, finely diced
1 celery stick, finely sliced
120g sweet cooking chorizo,
   cut into 1cm cubes
2 garlic cloves, finely sliced
1 tsp ground cumin
1½ tsp finely chopped
   fresh thyme leaves
2 small dried red chillies, crushed
2 tomatoes, fresh or
   canned, roughly chopped
250g cooked peeled chestnuts
   (fresh or vacuum-packed),
   roughly chopped
20 saffron threads, infused
   in 3–4 tbsp boiling water

Rinse the grains you are using under cold, running water then place in a pan, cover with the water or stock and bring to the boil. Simmer for 30 minutes while you make the rest of the soup.

In a large pan, heat the oil over a medium heat. Add the onion, carrot, celery, chorizo and a pinch of salt and fry for about 20 minutes, stirring occasionally, until everything caramelises and turns quite a dark brown. This will give the soup a wonderfully rich, deep flavour.

Add the garlic, cumin, thyme and chillies and cook for 1 more minute, then follow with the tomatoes and, after about 2 minutes, the chestnuts, grains and their cooking water. Give everything a good stir, season generously with salt and pepper, then add the saffron-infused liquid and simmer for 10–15 minutes, by which time the chestnuts will be disintegrating into the soup. Remove from the heat, check the seasoning and serve in warmed bowls. The soup will be chunky and delicious.

Why not try chestnut purée meringues?

Blitz 500g cooked chestnuts with 250ml double cream, 3 tbsp dark rum, 1 tsp vanilla extract, 90g unrefined caster sugar and 100ml water. Use to sandwich meringues together and drizzle with Chocolate Sauce (see page 249), or use to fill a tart case (see page 302) and serve with chocolate ice cream.

Tomato Gazpacho with Summer Strawberries

FEEDS SIX—EIGHT

For the Soup

60g blanched almonds

2 fat garlic cloves

1 tsp salt

small bunch of basil
(save some for the garnish)

1 red chilli, stem removed,
plus extra if needed

1 Lebanese cucumber
(or ½ a large one)

300g strawberries, hulled

6 tbsp extra-virgin olive oil

2 tbsp sherry vinegar,
plus extra if needed

1.2kg very ripe tomatoes

To Serve

2 small Hass avocados

few strawberries

juice of 1 lime

extra-virgin olive oil

This soup is the essence of summer, using tomatoes when they are heavy and fragrant, and balancing their acidity with sweet strawberries. The chilli and bitter notes of the olive oil give it a more grown-up, savoury edge, while the almonds provide a lovely background nuttiness. It should be served very cold. It makes a refreshing starter, managing to be both light and filling. If you are allergic to nuts, replace the almonds with a slice of stale country-style or sourdough bread.

Put a frying pan over a medium heat. Toast the almonds, shaking the pan occasionally, until they are pale golden and smelling deliciously nutty. Blitz them in a food processor with the garlic, salt, basil and chilli until the almonds have been ground to dust. Top and tail the cucumber and add to the food processor along with the strawberries, olive oil and sherry vinegar and blitz again until you have a smooth purée. Finally add the tomatoes and plenty of black pepper. If you find you have too much in the food processor, remove half and blitz in 2 batches.

Now taste; chilling food dulls the flavours so make sure that you can taste all the ingredients, seasoning with more salt, pepper and vinegar if needed. You may want to whizz in another chilli, but finely chop it first so it can be fully incorporated.

Chill the gazpacho for a few hours in the fridge. When you are ready to eat, roll the remaining basil leaves into a cigar and finely shred. Finely dice the avocados and strawberries and season with salt and pepper, the juice of the lime and a few tbsp of olive oil. It should taste delicious. Serve in small chilled bowls (it is very filling) with spoonfuls of the avocado relish and a scattering of basil.

Green Coriander & Pearl Barley 'Risotto'

The renewed interest in long-forgotten grains has been one of the most exciting food trends in the last five years. These grains were staples in my grandmother's cooking as well as in the dishes still found in so many food cultures, from Mexico to India to the Middle East. Grains are full of nutrition, largely gluten-free and reduce or eliminate the need for meat, making them an inexpensive but healthy option for recipes. Here I've taken a very British grain and given it a Mexican makeover, using an Italian cooking style. The result is a really wonderful risotto, green, herby and alive with flavour.

Place the pearl barley in a pan with plenty of salted water, bring to the boil and cook for 35–40 minutes until tender. Drain and set aside.

Put the butter in a pan over a medium heat and, once melted, add the sweetcorn, garlic, onion and a big pinch of salt and sweat for 5–7 minutes until tender. Stir in the cream and milk and cook for a further 5 minutes until the mixture has reduced slightly. Transfer to a blender or food processor and whizz until smooth. Return to the pan, stir in the drained pearl barley and keep warm.

Place the coriander, spinach, green chilli and garlic in a food processor and blitz until coarsely chopped, then add the lime juice and blitz again. With the motor running, slowly pour in the oil until you have a glossy green purée. Season to taste, then stir into the sweetcorn and barley. Gently warm up, then transfer to plates. Grate over the ricotta before serving with a few sweetcorn kernels scattered over, if you like.

Why not try roast squash with labneh & coriander oil?

Halve, peel and deseed a butternut squash and cut into thick slices. Rub the slices with 2 tbsp olive oil, a sprinkling of Turkish chilli flakes, a pinch of dried oregano and a pinch of sumac. Roast in a preheated oven at 200°C/gas 6 for 30 minutes. Top with dollops of labneh, sprinkle over 2 tbsp toasted sunflower seeds and drizzle with 2 tbsp coriander purée (see above). Serve with warm flatbreads. Feeds 3.

For the Risotto

120g pearl barley, rinsed

40g butter

200g fresh sweetcorn kernels
(cut from 2 sweetcorn cobs),
plus extra to serve (optional)

2 garlic cloves, finely chopped

½ white onion, finely chopped

120ml single cream

120ml whole milk

For the Coriander Purée

bunch of coriander, leaves and stalks

3 handfuls of spinach leaves

1 green chilli, seeds left in
and roughly chopped

½ garlic clove, roughly chopped

juice of 1 lime

60ml olive oil

75g salted ricotta, to serve

Black Rice with Smoked Oysters & Smacked Cucumber

FEEDS THREE—FOUR

My mother always had a tin of smoked oysters in the cupboard to use with some other everyday ingredient, transforming them into something quasi-exotic for a fast weekday dinner. Whether she used them to add a smoky deliciousness to a tomato sauce, or to add some oomph to her mouth-watering fish pies, she had a knack of getting the maximum flavour from affordable ingredients. I like to think her imaginative use of the humblest of ingredients has informed all my cooking since.

This dish is a doddle to make. I love the combination of the warming, inky black rice and oysters and the way you are transported to the Far East by the punchy, fiery smacked cucumber relish. Simple, tasty and a feast to look at.

For the Black Rice

200g black rice

500ml chicken or vegetable stock
(for home-made see pages 46–7)

olive oil, for frying

80g pancetta, finely chopped

3 banana shallots, finely chopped

3 fat garlic cloves, finely chopped

large thumb-sized piece of fresh
ginger, peeled and finely grated

1 x 400g can plum tomatoes

4 tbsp Shaoxing wine or
Manzanilla sherry

2 x 85g cans smoked oysters

For the Cucumber

1 cucumber

½ tsp salt

2 tsp finely grated garlic

2 tsp soy sauce

2 tsp brown rice vinegar

¼ tsp chilli flakes

2 tbsp olive oil (or chilli oil if
you have it in your store cupboard,
for home-made see page 295)

Soak the rice for 10 minutes, then drain under running water. Empty into a pan, cover with the stock and bring to the boil. Season well with salt and pepper, reduce the heat and simmer gently for 50 minutes or until rice is just cooked. It should be tender but still slightly chewy in the middle. You may need to add a little boiling water towards the end of cooking, if the pan seems to be getting dry.

Meanwhile, fry the pancetta in a little olive oil over a medium heat for 5 minutes before adding the shallots and cooking for a further 5 minutes. Add the garlic and ginger and fry for a few more minutes before adding the tomatoes and Shaoxing wine or sherry. Simmer gently while the rice cooks.

Make the smacked cucumber. Put the cucumber on a wooden board and smack it several times with the flat blade of a large chopping knife or a rolling pin. This will help the cucumber to absorb the flavours. Quarter lengthways and then cut each length diagonally into 1cm chunks. Toss these in the salt and leave to drain for 10 minutes in a colander over a sink. Rinse away the salt and drain thoroughly, then transfer to a small serving bowl. Toss through the remaining ingredients and set aside.

When the rice is cooked, stir through the tomato sauce, add the smoked oysters and stir to heat through, being careful not to break up the oysters. Season to taste, then serve with the cucumber salad.

Kitchen Note:

Smoked oysters are also rather good with pasta. Use them instead of pancetta in a classic carbonara sauce for a rich and warming, comforting bowl of food. Shaoxing wine is now available online from larger retailers and from Asian stockists, but Manzanilla sherry is a great alternative. It adds a wonderful savoury, rich flavour to noodle dishes.

Lamb Harira

FEEDS SIX—EIGHT

I love lamb, perhaps more than any other meat. The nuances of flavour that you get from a slightly older animal, either hogget or mutton, is exceptional and very popular in countries such as Mexico, Morocco and India. Try ordering some from your local butcher; it is sometimes more expensive than regular lamb but you need very little. Have this harira on its own on a weekday, or serve it with a steaming mound of saffron-spiced couscous flecked with herbs, nuts and dried fruit for a sumptuous weekend feast. If you can, make it a few days ahead so that the spices and meat have a chance to relax into one another.

Warm the oil in a large, deep pan over a medium heat and add the onion, carrots, garlic and coriander stalks, along with a big pinch of salt. Cook for 8 minutes until softened slightly.

Season the lamb, increase the heat a little and add it to the pan. Fry for a few minutes until the lamb begins to take on colour, then stir in all the ground spices (except the saffron) along with plenty of black pepper. Cook for a further minute until the spices begin to smell fragrant.

Stir in the bay leaves, tomatoes and saffron, then pour in enough hot water to cover everything by 5cm. Bring to a simmer and cook for 1½ hours until the meat is completely soft, adding the parsnips, chickpeas and lentils after 1 hour. The pulses will thicken the soup, so keep adding water as it needs it.

Meanwhile melt the butter in a small pan and, once melted, season generously with salt and pepper and increase the heat a little. Simmer until the solids are turning a golden brown and the butter starts smelling nutty. Turn off the heat the moment the butter has turned hazelnut in colour and stir in the yogurt to stop it any further. Season with a squeeze of lemon juice.

Stir the harissa into the soup and taste, checking for heat levels and adding a little more if you like. Check and adjust the seasoning and stir in the coriander leaves. Serve with the lemon quarters, offering the burnt yogurt in a bowl to hand round.

Why not try a classic Irish stew?

Add an extra onion, swap the coriander for parsley, skip the spices and add a few sprigs of thyme instead. Instead of the pulses, add 4 medium cubed potatoes and allow to simmer for a further 45 minutes until the potatoes are tender. Serve with redcurrant jelly and mint sauce.

3 tbsp olive oil

1 large onion, roughly chopped

2 carrots, roughly chopped

3 garlic cloves, finely chopped

½ bunch of coriander, stalks and leaves separated, both finely chopped

300g lamb, hogget or mutton neck fillet, cut into 1–2cm cubes

1 tsp ground cinnamon

1 tsp ground turmeric

2 tsp ground cumin

1 tsp sweet paprika

½ tsp ground ginger

2 bay leaves

1 x 400g can chopped plum tomatoes

pinch of saffron threads, soaked in boiling water

2 parsnips, peeled & roughly chopped

1 x 400g can chickpeas, rinsed and drained

1 x 400g can lentils, rinsed and drained

75g butter

200g Greek yogurt

squeeze of lemon juice

2 tbsp harissa, plus extra to taste

lemon wedges, to serve

Simple Spiced Dhal with Spinach & Yogurt

Lentils and dried peas used to have a reputation for tasting a bit dull, but once you've tasted the richly spiced dhals of India you realise that lentils can be the base for some magnificent main meals, varied and heady with aromatics.

This recipe uses the classic Indian technique of tempering spices: heating seeds, leaves or chilli flakes in hot fat to release their flavours, ready to scatter over the dhal just before serving.

Put the split peas in a sieve and run under cold water until the water runs clear. Place in a pan with the whole garlic cloves, bay leaves and whole chilli and pour in enough water to cover everything by 5cm. Bring to the boil and cook for 40–45 minutes until tender and falling apart, skimming the water occasionally. Discard the bay and chilli and use a stick blender or potato masher to create a smooth-ish texture. Season to taste.

Heat the oil for the temper in a frying pan over a medium heat. When hot, add the onion and fry for 5 minutes or until it turns translucent. Increase the heat a fraction, add the mustard seeds and, as soon as they pop, add the curry leaves, frying for a moment until they turn translucent. Add the sliced garlic and crumbled red chilli, fry for a couple of minutes until the garlic is beginning to colour, then stir in the garam masala, coriander and turmeric. Cook for a further 30 seconds until the spices begin to smell fragrant, then add the tomatoes and allow to sizzle in the hot oil for a minute.

Warm up the split peas, adding a ladle of water or vegetable stock if you need to loosen them. Stir in the tempered spices with the spinach and season to taste. Add a squeeze of lemon juice and serve with chapattis and yogurt. It's also good topped with a fried egg or as an accompaniment to other curries.

For the Dhal

400g yellow split peas

4 garlic cloves, 2 left
   whole, 2 finely sliced

a few bay leaves (fresh if
   you can get them)

2 Kashmiri, arbol, or other dried red
   chillies, 1 left whole, 1 crumbled

a little vegetable stock,
   if needed (optional)

200g spinach leaves, washed

squeeze of lemon juice, to taste

chapattis & natural yogurt, to serve

For the Temper

6 tbsp vegetable oil

1 large onion, finely chopped

2 tsp black mustard seeds

small handful of fresh curry leaves

1 tsp garam masala

½ tsp ground coriander

½ tsp ground turmeric

2 ripe tomatoes, or drained and rinsed
   canned plum tomatoes, chopped

Why not try using Indian flavours with mussels?

Fry 1 chopped onion and 1 crushed garlic clove in 2 tbsp oil until softened. Add 2 cans chopped tomatoes, 1 tsp brown sugar, a pinch of chilli flakes and 1 tbsp tomato purée and season with salt and pepper. Meanwhile heat 4 tbsp oil over your highest heat and fry the temper spices as above for a minute to release the aromatics. Add 2kg scrubbed, de-bearded mussels, cover and cook for a minute before pouring in 200ml boiling water or fish stock and covering again. Take out the mussels with a slotted spoon as they open and add to the sauce, discarding non-openers. Strain the cooking liquid from the mussels through a muslin into the sauce and stir in 3 tbsp crème fraîche. Serve with hot crusty bread and plenty of coriander leaves. Feeds 4.

Sichuan Aubergines

I find Sichuan food intoxicating: the vibrant combination of fried garlic, ginger, dried chilli and Sichuan pepper does it for me. Sichuan food has become so popular that is now easy to find its ingredients online or in larger supermarkets. Invest in a few dried chillies, a small packet of Sichuan pepper and a bottle of Shaoxing rice wine.

Aubergines are the perfect sponge for these gutsy flavours. Rather than deep-frying them as is customary, I prefer roasting, which uses less oil and makes less mess. The result is a soft, silky heap of aubergines doused in a deeply fragrant sauce. And, if you like, try scattering over 150g crispy wok-fried minced pork.

Cut the aubergines into rounds about 1–2cm thick and then cut the rounds in half. Sprinkle them with a little fine sea salt and leave to drain in a colander in the sink or on the draining board for at least 30 minutes, to draw out any excess water.

Preheat the oven to 220°C/gas 7. When the aubergines are drained, tip into a roasting tin, toss them well in the vegetable oil and roast in the oven for 40–50 minutes until they are completely soft and temptingly golden on the outside.

Meanwhile get the sauce ready. Mix the cornflour with 2 tbsp of water. Heat the oil in a large wok and, when hot, add the chilli bean sauce. As soon as it starts sizzling, add the chillies, ginger and garlic and stir-fry for a minute or so, taking care not to burn the chillies and garlic. If necessary take the wok off the heat for a few minutes.

Pour in the stock and cornflour paste and cook for a few minutes to allow the sauce to thicken, then add the sherry, sugar and vinegar and simmer together for a few minutes to allow the flavours to meld.

Meanwhile, cook the udon noodles according to the packet instructions. Serve with the aubergines in warmed shallow bowls with the sauce poured over and scattered with the spring onions and coriander.

Why not try blackened aubergine purée?

Char the skin of 2 aubergines, either on a barbecue or using tongs over a gas hob, until they have blistered and blackened (you can place them under a very hot grill too but this will take longer). Then roast them in a preheated 200°C/gas 6 oven for 15 minutes until the flesh has softened. Blitz in a food processor, skin and all, with 2 tbsp tahini, 2 garlic cloves, 100ml olive oil, 50ml extra-virgin olive oil, ½ tsp hot smoked paprika, 1 tsp salt, juice of ½ lemon and a handful of torn mint leaves. Serve warm or cold as a dip or as a topping for bruschetta.

For the Aubergines

4 large aubergines (about 1.2kg),
    topped and tailed
100ml vegetable oil
400g fat udon noodles
4 spring onions, finely sliced
small bunch of coriander,
    roughly chopped

For the Sauce

3 tsp cornflour
3 tbsp vegetable oil
2 tbsp Sichuan chilli bean paste
2 large red dried chillies, crumbled
    (you can use Sichuan, Mexican
    chile de arbol, Italian pepperoncino
    or even chilli flakes)
2cm piece of fresh ginger, peeled
    and finely chopped
3 garlic cloves, finely chopped
250ml chicken or vegetable stock
    (for home-made see pages 46–7)
2 tbsp Shaoxing wine or
    Manzanilla sherry
1–2 tbsp soft light brown sugar
1 tbsp brown rice vinegar

SMALL BITES & SALADS

SMALL BITES & SALADS

When I'm planning a dinner or lunch I always have the most fun dreaming up the starter. Although it is easiest to balance everything around the main course, it is often the first morsels of food that people try, when their hunger is acute, that give the most pleasure. When I'm reading the menu at a restaurant it is always the starters to which I am drawn: small, beautifully prepared plates of food that both whet the appetite and create a visual feast. And there's no need to over-complicate things; a simple well-dressed salad (see page 79), a home-made pâté, or a plate of beautifully cooked seafood are all hard acts to follow.

For me, the start of a meal often includes bread (see 'A Few Thoughts on Bread', page 276). I always have a loaf of sourdough in my freezer ready to transform into a starter, whether it be garlicky fried crumbs, roasted croutons or simply a chargrilled slice of toast rubbed with garlic and oil to accompany a home-made dip. I could never forgo the pleasures of good bread.

The recipes in this chapter are designed to be versatile: they could be starters, salads, party nibbles or simple meals when you are after something light and colourful.

Grilled Asparagus with Romesco

Romesco is a Catalan classic. The sweet, charred roast tomatoes, peppers, garlic and nuts with the flavour and body of dried red chillies and sweet paprika make it without doubt one of my favourite salsas. It'll go with absolutely anything, but here I pair it with the grassy greenness of chargrilled asparagus.

Heat an old frying pan over a medium heat, then toast the ancho chilli pieces, if using, for a minute or so until puffed up a little and fragrant. Tip into a bowl, cover with boiling water, leave to soak for 15 minutes until soft, then drain.

Roast the peppers over a direct flame on a gas hob until blackened all over, then put them in a bowl, cover with cling film and leave for 10 minutes. Now peel the peppers, discarding the skin, core and seeds. Dry-roast the tomatoes, fresh chillies and garlic in the pan you used for the ancho until the tomatoes and chillies are blackened all over and the garlic is soft, about 15–20 minutes, and transfer to a third bowl; the garlic cloves will be ready 5–10 minutes before the tomatoes and chillies, so transfer to the bowl once softened. Gently toast the hazelnuts until pale golden all over.

Heat 2 tablespoons of the olive oil in the same pan, and gently fry the bread until golden on both sides. Using a large pestle and mortar or food processor, grind the hazelnuts, garlic, fresh and ancho chillies, paprika, bread and salt until you have a smooth paste. Pummel in the tomatoes and peppers until incorporated, then work in the vinegar and remaining olive oil. Taste for seasoning, adding more salt if needed (if the tomatoes are a little unripe you may also need a pinch of brown sugar). If you feel the sauce is too thick, thin it with oil or water.

Trim the ends off the asparagus. Drop into a pan of boiling water for 2 minutes until vibrant green. Drain, refresh under cold water, then brush with oil and season. Heat a griddle pan, then chargrill the asparagus for 3 minutes each side, to get good char marks. Serve the asparagus drizzled with the romesco sauce.

For the Asparagus
400g asparagus spears
olive oil, to brush

For the Romesco
1 ancho chilli, stem removed, deseeded,
    flesh torn into small pieces (optional)
2 red peppers
2 large ripe tomatoes
2 fresh red chillies
6 unpeeled garlic cloves
60g hazelnuts
140ml extra-virgin olive oil
1 small slice of sourdough or
    other peasant-style bread
2 tsp sweet smoked paprika
½ tsp salt
2 tbsp red wine vinegar
pinch of brown sugar (optional)

Why not try sautéed asparagus with anchovy crumbs & a fried egg?
Blanch 200g asparagus spears, refresh under cold water and set aside. Now fry 50g sourdough breadcrumbs (made with week-old bread) in 2 tbsp oil, 1 crushed garlic clove, 1 tbsp chopped parsley and 4 chopped anchovy fillets until golden and crisp; this will be more than you need but the result is an amazing topping for lots of dishes. Remove to a plate. Add a little more oil to the pan and fry the asparagus for a few minutes until nicely coloured, seasoning well. Top with fried eggs. Feeds 2.

A Few Things on Toast

Get the hard work done early so you can have fun with your friends as they arrive for dinner. Outsource the toast-making to said friends while you artfully and casually put the finishing touches to the delicious accompaniment. Experiment with the bread you buy, whether sourdough, raisin and walnut, rye or granary. You could make toast, or chargrill the bread for more texture. Drizzle with your best olive oil, rub with garlic, or leave plain. Here are a few recipes so you can start your evening with a swing. Serve chopped up on a board with drinks, or beautifully plated up at the table.

Delicious Chicken Liver Pâté

It is hard to beat home-made chicken liver pâté and livers are packed with iron and other good minerals. I love to serve it with a crisp salad dressed with good olive oil and sherry vinegar.

Cut away any white membranes from the livers and cut the bacon into 3cm pieces.

Heat a knob of the butter in a frying pan until sizzling hot, season the livers generously with salt and pepper and fry in 2–3 batches for a minute each side so that the outsides are nicely coloured but the insides are still pink. Transfer the livers to a food processor as they are cooked. Make sure the frying pan gets smoking hot between batches and add a little more butter as needed.

Now add another knob of butter to the pan, fry the bacon until caramelised and lightly crisp and transfer to the food processor. Finally add another knob of butter to the pan and sauté the shallots gently over a medium heat until softening. Season generously with salt and pepper, add the garlic and herbs and fry for another 5 minutes until the onions are translucent. Add 1 tbsp of brandy, increase the heat and bring to a simmer.

Transfer the shallots and herbs to the food processor with all but 50g of the remaining butter, the remaining brandy, port and jelly. Blitz everything until completely smooth and check for seasoning before transferring to a bowl. Melt the reserved butter and allow to cool slightly before pouring over the top of the pâté (it will make it last longer). Chill in the fridge until set, before serving with toasts and a green salad, or freeze for up to 3 months.

500g chicken livers

8 rashers of streaky bacon

500g softened butter

8 shallots, finely chopped

3 garlic cloves, finely chopped

handful of thyme sprigs,
    leaves picked

2 fresh bay leaves

2 tbsp brandy

2 tbsp port

1 tbsp quince or redcurrant jelly

Smoked Cod's Roe with Olive Oil & Crème Fraîche

Smoked cod's roe is inexpensive and really good. Blitzed with olive oil and crème fraîche it makes the most delicious of starters.

65g stale sourdough or other
   coarse-textured bread
200g smoked cod's roe
2 garlic cloves, roughly chopped
75ml extra-virgin olive oil
75ml vegetable oil
60ml freshly squeezed lemon
   juice (from about 1 lemon)
2 heaped tbsp crème fraîche (optional)
lemon wedges, to serve

Soak the bread in 100ml water for 5–10 minutes. Meanwhile pierce the membrane that encases the roe with a sharp knife and carefully peel it away, scraping the cod's roe into the bowl of a food processor.

Squeeze any excess water from the bread, add it to the bowl with the garlic and blitz for a few seconds, then slowly add the olive and vegetable oils in a thin, steady stream until thoroughly combined. Add the lemon juice and plenty of black pepper and check to see if needs any salt; it probably won't. I like to add crème fraiche here which smooths down the smoky flavour, but you can leave out. Chill in the fridge and serve with toast and lemon wedges. It will keep happily in the fridge for up to 10 days.

Roast Aubergine with Mint, Ricotta & Addictive Tomato-Bonnet Jam

The tomato-chilli jam I use here is an absolute essential in our household; we eat it with sausages, toasted cheese sandwiches and everything in between.

For the Aubergines

4 medium aubergines,
   topped and tailed
2½ tsp sea salt
4 fat garlic cloves
3 tbsp pomegranate molasses
120ml olive oil

To Serve

100g rocket leaves
handful of mint leaves
handful of basil leaves
150g ricotta
3 tbsp extra-virgin olive oil
finely grated zest of 1 lemon
   and juice of ½ lemon
75g Addictive Tomato-Bonnet Jam
   (see page 285)
80g soft black olives, pitted

Cut the aubergines in half lengthways and cut each half into long slender wedges (about 4–5 wedges per half). Toss them in 2 tsp of the salt and leave to sit for 30 minutes to coax out the bitter juices. Preheat the oven to 220°C/gas 7.

Meanwhile crush the garlic cloves and molasses to a paste in a pestle and mortar with the remaining ½ tsp salt. Rinse the aubergines in cold water and pat dry between clean tea towels. Tip into a roasting tin, toss in the olive oil and garlic-molasses paste and roast for 25 minutes. Pour off any excess oil (you can keep this for roasting other vegetables), then roast for another 10 minutes until the aubergine is golden, soft and slightly crispy at the edges.

Wash the leaves and herbs and spin dry. Beat the ricotta with the olive oil, lemon zest and most of the juice and season generously with salt and pepper. Swirl in the tomato-chilli jam. Spread this ricotta jam on your toast, top with a heap of the leaves and finally with wedges of the aubergine. Scatter over the olives, squeeze with a final few drops of lemon juice and serve, or freeze for up to 3 months.

Mexican Crab Mayonnaise

FEEDS FOUR

When I was very little we would sometimes go to stay with my grandparents on our own; when we were good they would take us out for lunch in a restaurant. There was almost always prawn cocktail on the menu and that was absolutely my favourite thing in the world (it was pink, I had a thing for pink). I created this recipe in remembrance of those exciting prawn cocktail moments, using crab instead of prawns. Both kitsch and modern, this starter is a winner in the height of summer when crab is at its sweetest.

Snip the chillies open, discarding the stalk and seeds. Place a dry pan over a medium heat and, when hot, add the chillies, gently toasting each side for a couple of minutes until they begin to smell fragrant; take care not to burn them. Cover in boiling water and simmer for 15 minutes to soften. Meanwhile prepare the apple and fennel for the salad and place in a bowl of iced water with a squeeze of lemon juice (to get ahead you can do this an hour or so before you eat).

Drain the chillies, setting aside the water, and transfer to a food processor. Whizz until puréed, adding a dash of the chilli water to loosen if necessary, then add the egg yolks, mustard and a pinch of salt. With the motor running, very slowly start to drip the oil through the funnel of the processor until the mayonnaise starts to thicken and emulsify, then pour in the remaining oil in a thin stream. Stir in the lime juice, ketchup and Worcestershire sauce and season to taste.

Stir together equal quantities of the mayonnaise and the crab (the remaining mayo will keep in the fridge for at least a week). Add more lime, ketchup or Worcestershire sauce to taste; it should be smoky and tangy but with the crab flavour shining through.

Drain the apple and fennel and pat dry. Add to a bowl with the watercress, a few squeezes of lime juice and some olive oil and season with salt and pepper. Toss and transfer to plates. Halve, pit and peel the avocados, then place half an avocado on each plate. Spoon the crab mayonnaise over the avocados and serve.

For the Crab

2 chipotle chillies

2 egg yolks

1 tsp Dijon mustard

400ml mild olive oil

juice of 1 lime, plus extra to taste

1½ tbsp tomato ketchup,
    plus extra to taste

½ tbsp Worcestershire sauce,
    plus extra to taste

250g fresh white crab meat

For the Salad

1 apple, finely sliced

1 fennel bulb, outer layer
    removed, finely sliced

squeeze of lemon juice

55g watercress

juice of 1 lime

extra-virgin olive oil

2 avocados

Kitchen Note:

Try this mayonnaise with the fried squid on page 83, or try it spread on barbecued corn with lime juice, feta and chilli powder.

Beautifully Quick Baked Prawns with Cherry Tomatoes, Garlic & Chilli

My friend Saritha makes these prawns when she throws a big party. They are quite the most wonderful, garlicky, olive oil-doused jewels. Guests greedily mop up the juices with fresh, crusty bread and fights over the last prawn are not uncommon.

I try to always ask my fishmonger where the prawns have come from and look for Marine Stewardship Council (MSC)-certified prawns in supermarkets, which have been sustainably caught.

Preheat the oven to 190°C/gas 5.

Toss the tomatoes, garlic, olive oil, chilli flakes, thyme and a generous few pinches of salt and grindings of pepper together in an ovenproof dish. Cook for 10 minutes until the tomatoes have released their juices, the oil is bubbling gently and the garlic is lightly golden.

Add the prawns and cook for about 3 minutes until the prawns have just turned pink. Serve hot, straight from the dish, scooping up the juices with hunks of crusty bread.

300g cherry tomatoes
  on the vine, halved
4 garlic cloves, thickly sliced
100ml extra-virgin olive oil
1 heaped tsp chilli flakes, or to taste
1 sprig of thyme, leaves picked
250g raw king prawns, preferably
  MSC-certified, peeled and deveined
crusty bread, to serve

Why not try melon & tomato panzanella?

Crush 1 tsp chilli flakes with 1 tsp salt, the zest of 1 lime and ¼ tsp sugar and set aside. Mix 500g quartered, mixed tomatoes with 2 very finely sliced baby shallots, 1 tsp brown sugar, 2 tbsp extra-virgin olive oil and salt and pepper. Leave to macerate at room temperature for 1 hour, covered. Preheat a grill, mix 250g stale bread, torn into chunks, in 2 tbsp rapeseed oil and grill for 3–4 minutes, tossing occasionally, until crisp and golden. Add to the tomatoes with 600g honeydew melon in bite-sized chunks or balls. Tear in a small handful each of basil and mint leaves, add a squeeze of lime juice and sprinkle with the chilli salt. Serve within 4 hours. Fantastic with grilled fish. Feeds 4.

My Perfect Salad

Salads are a passion of mine; not only are they a brilliantly easy meal in themselves, they are also make a sprightly, healthy beginning to a big dinner. There is little I like more than the textures of seasoned crisp leaves, juicy fruits and crunchy toasted nuts. You can make salads wholesome and filling by adding grains, noodles or poached eggs, or you can keep them light with slivers of carrot, apple, tomato or fennel. The variety of salad leaves – kales, mustard leaves, rocket, spinach, sorrel – can add intricate flavours to the base of your salad. We grow herbs such as thyme and borage in our small garden, as well as edible flowers such as nasturtiums, chive blossoms and rocket flowers; picking a handful of these vitamin- and mineral-rich ingredients to pepper and colour a salad gives me enormous pleasure. Even if you have only a small window box, you can experiment with growing your own herbs and scatter them freshly picked into the bowl.

A good dressing (never stingily applied) is vital. I go by the ratio of 1 part vinegar to 2½ parts oil, as a rule of thumb. Vinegars, oils, mustards or miso, sugar or garlic, plus salt and pepper, transform a salad and many of those are packed with nutrients. The cheapest way to buy oils is online; I buy 5-litre tins of good-quality extra-virgin olive oil from small Italian, Greek or Spanish suppliers, then decant into wine bottles. Nut oils are an expensive luxury I sometimes use for special occasions, but they go rancid all too quickly so I keep them in the fridge, extending their shelf life by several months. Sesame oil is good for Asian salads, while rapeseed, vegetable and coconut oils are best reserved for frying. Mainly though, I just love a great olive oil.

I am hooked on vinegars too. In Mexico, where they are used extensively to lift and sharpen the flavours of earthy chillies and slow-cooked braises, many housewives will make their own from apples, pineapple and other fruit. They do wonders for the digestive system – like any fermented foods they encourage the growth of good gut bacteria – and when you notice how much you can spend on a good-quality vinegar, making your own suddenly becomes appealing. I now save leftover red wine in an old ceramic crock to ferment and then use later when I am making a dressing. Balsamic has been all the rage for over a decade, but it is only the really expensive balsamic that is delicious. Try experimenting with sherry vinegar for a subtlety and lovely roundness of flavour, or red wine vinegar for body. Raspberry vinegar adds delicate sweetness to leaves, cider vinegar gives a clarity and purity of flavour that works brilliantly in marinades, while rice wine vinegar is soft and sweet. Try different vinegars and find your own favourites.

I find that if I make My Classic Vinaigrette (see page 290) in a large batch, so it lasts over a few weeks, I am more likely to choose to eat salad. It means you are only ever minutes away from a good lunch. I am convinced that this is why my children love salads so much: they are used to trying them whenever we have lunch together as I pull them out as a quick fix … and who can resist pretty slivers of fruit and vegetables when glistening with a wonderful dressing?

Cold Udon Salad with Crisp Prawns & Sesame Dressing

FEEDS FOUR

For the Salad

400g udon noodles

½ cucumber

150g beansprouts

¼ red cabbage, finely shredded

3 spring onions, finely sliced

big handful each of coriander and
mint leaves, roughly chopped

For the Prawns

vegetable oil, to fry

300g raw prawns, preferably
MSC-certified (see page 78),
peeled and deveined

2 tbsp plain flour

1–2 red chillies, finely chopped, to serve

handful of coriander leaves, to serve

1 lime, quartered, to serve

For the Dressing

½ garlic clove,
crushed with a little salt

3 tbsp sesame oil

1 tbsp rice wine vinegar

1½ tbsp soy sauce

juice of 1 lime

1 tsp sugar

2 tbsp toasted sesame seeds

This is a gutsy little salad. Almost everything can be made ahead: prep and store the salad ingredients and garnishes in containers in the fridge (cover them with damp kitchen paper and they will stay perfect for half a day) and get the dressing ready in an old jam jar and you can feel calm and relaxed. Then all you have to do is wait for your guests to arrive, fry the prawns and conjure it up in front of their eyes, Singaporean street food style.

Bring a pan of salted boiling water to the boil and cook the udon noodles according to the packet instructions, then drain and rinse them under cold water until cool. Peel the cucumber of its skin and then peel long, thin strips of it, working all round until you reach the seeds in the centre. Put the strips into a big salad bowl with the drained noodles and other salad ingredients.

Put the dressing ingredients into a small bowl or jam jar and whisk or shake to combine. Taste and adjust the seasoning. Pour over the salad, toss well and divide between plates or bowls. Set aside while you cook the prawns.

Pour enough oil into a deep frying pan so that it comes 5mm up the sides. Place over a medium-high heat. Season the prawns, then toss them in the flour. When the oil is hot, add the prawns (you may have to do this in batches), turning them as they crisp up and become orange. Once cooked through and crisp, drain on kitchen paper while you cook the rest, then sit on top of the salads. Sprinkle over the chillies and coriander and serve with lime wedges.

Kitchen Note:

For a wonderful vegetarian salad, replace the prawns with fried tofu. Soak diced firm tofu in salted hot water for 10 minutes, then pat dry and fry as above. Or top the salad with stir-fried chicken strips and a handful of toasted peanuts: simply double the amount of soy sauce in the dressing and whisk in 3 tbsp crunchy peanut butter.

Mango & Coconut Rice Salad

One of the signs that summer is around the corner is the sight of boxes of Alphonso mangoes stacked up outside my local Lebanese grocer. They are so sweet and juicy that it is impossible to eat them without getting into a sticky mess.

When we have this salad during the week we have it as is, but at the weekend I serve it with barbecued or grilled chicken; it also makes an amazing salad with some grilled prawns tossed in. Be sparing with the chillies if you are feeding children.

Put the rice in a pan, pour in the coconut milk and 200ml of water and season with the fish sauce and a generous grinding of black pepper. Bring to a simmer, then put a lid on and cook over a gentle heat for 10 minutes before turning off the heat. Taste it for seasoning, adding a little salt if you think it needs it, and cover again, leaving for another 10 minutes for the grains to absorb the rest of the liquid; they should be swollen and tender. Leave covered, somewhere warm.

Toast the quinoa in a dry pan for a minute, cover with salted boiling water and simmer for about 20 minutes until the grains are tender and just uncurling. Drain and set aside.

Meanwhile, peel and chop the mangoes into 1cm dice, squeezing out any excess juice into a bowl to add to the dressing and putting the flesh into a large salad bowl. Combine the mango juices with the rest of the dressing ingredients, whisk well to combine and set aside.

Toast the peanuts, if using, in a preheated (150°C/gas 2) oven or dry frying pan over a gentle heat until they are pale golden, then roughly chop them and add to the mangoes.

Add the rest of the salad ingredients to the salad bowl, along with the coconut rice and quinoa, and toss with the dressing.

Why not try chilled mango salad with cinnamon & star anise?

To make a syrup, simmer 150g sugar, 50ml water, 2 star anise, 1 cinnamon stick, 1 tsp coriander seeds and 1 finely chopped red chilli together, stirring until the sugar has dissolved. Increase the heat and, without stirring, simmer briskly until the syrup starts to darken in colour. Once it turns a deep nutty brown, turn off the heat and pour in 100ml water and the zest and juice of 2 limes. Return the heat to low and stir gently until any crystallised sugar has dissolved. Once cool, pour the syrup over 4 diced mangoes or a sliced pineapple and marinate for 1 hour in the fridge. Serve with scoops of vanilla ice cream and torn mint leaves. Sweet and refreshing, a great way to round off a meal. Feeds 4–6.

For the Salad

200g white rice

1 x 400ml can coconut milk

2 tbsp fish sauce

120g red quinoa

3 small or 2 large ripe mangoes

50g unsalted peanuts (optional)

½ red onion, finely chopped

large handful each of mint,
    coriander and basil leaves
    (Thai if you can get it)

3 celery sticks, finely chopped

½ cucumber, deseeded and chopped

For the Dressing

1 tsp brown sugar

finely grated zest and juice of 2 limes

2 tbsp rice vinegar

1 tbsp sesame oil

small thumb-sized piece of fresh
    ginger, peeled and finely grated

1 tbsp fish sauce

2 bird's eye chillies, finely chopped

Squid, Lemon & Broad Bean Salad

This salad is fresh, citrusy and very quick to make, with no need for any dressing; you just throw all the ingredients together in a salad bowl. Do not be tempted to fry the squid for too long or it will toughen up. For tender squid the rule is to cook slow and low or, as here, hot and fast.

Bring a large pan of well-salted water to a rolling boil and cook the orzo until al dente, or according to the packet instructions. Drain and toss in 2 tbsp of the olive oil. Simmer the beans in the same water until tender, about 3–4 minutes, then drain and refresh under cold water. Add to the orzo.

If cleaning the squid yourself, rinse them, scoop out the soft gunk inside with your fingers and pull off the thin film from the outside. Shake them dry, pull away the fins from the body and cut them in half. Cut open the bodies like a book and scrape out any residue. Finely slice the bodies and blot dry with kitchen paper. Cut the tentacles into thirds or quarters, cutting away and discarding the eyes and beak, if present.

Slice the preserved lemon in half and scoop out and discard the pulp. Finely slice the rind (or very finely chop if you prefer).

Meanwhile place a wok or large, heavy-based frying pan over a high heat and add the remaining olive oil. Throw in the squid, season generously with salt and pepper and stir-fry for a few minutes until it is curling up, beginning to brown and is tender.

Toss the squid through the cooked orzo and beans in a serving dish, along with the preserved lemon, lemon zest and juice and the herbs. Using your fingers, squash the olives over the top of everything to remove the stones, so their juices run into the orzo. Scatter over the sumac, chilli flakes and almonds. Lastly, run a vegetable peeler up and down the cucumber over the dish in quick motions so you get lovely thin shavings. Give the top of the salad a final loose toss, then serve.

Why not try deep-fried hot & spicy squid with aioli?

Toss 1kg baby or sliced squid (cleaned and trimmed) in 100g seasoned gram flour, 1 tsp cayenne pepper or ground Sichuan pepper and ½ tsp ground cumin. Fill a pan two-thirds full with sunflower oil and heat until it reaches 180°C on a kitchen thermometer, or until a piece of bread dropped in the oil turns golden in 40 seconds. Fry the squid in batches for 2 minutes until crisp and golden, then remove with a slotted spoon and drain on kitchen paper. Season and serve with aioli (see page 288), lemon wedges and chopped parsley leaves. Feeds 4–6.

300g orzo pasta

6 tbsp extra-virgin olive oil

200g podded young broad beans

700g squid, ideally ready-cleaned
    (ask your fishmonger),
    with tentacles if possible

1 preserved lemon

finely grated zest and juice of 1 lemon

small handful of marjoram
    or oregano leaves, finely chopped

handful of mint leaves, finely chopped

handful of dill or fennel fronds, chopped

65g whole black Kalamata olives

1 tbsp sumac

½ tsp chilli flakes

50g flaked almonds, toasted

½ cucumber

Smoked Squash Salad with Hazelnuts, Chicory & Blue Cheese

FEEDS FOUR AS A MAIN OR
EIGHT AS A STARTER

This exotic salad was inspired by Yotam Ottolenghi's recipe, where he smokes beetroot for a salad. I felt the same simple technique could be applied to other root vegetables and this is the wonderful result.

Preheat the oven to 240°C/gas 8.

Cut the squash in half, deseed and cut each half into rough slices, about 6 per half.

Line a large frying pan or wok with 2 large sheets of foil with plenty of overhang (for the smoking to work you will need to seal in the squash completely). Pour the rice into the pan with the pared lemon rind (I use a vegetable peeler) and thyme. Sprinkle over 2 tbsp of water. Pop the squash on top of the rice, put a lid over the pan and wrap the foil tightly around the lid. Place over your highest heat; after 4–5 minutes you should see a little whiff of smoke threading out. If in doubt have a sniff, you should be able to tell that the rice is smoking. Smoke for exactly 8 minutes, then remove from the heat.

Transfer the squash to a roasting tray and throw away the remaining contents of the parcel. Roast in the oven for 35 minutes until a knife can pierce it easily. Set aside to cool, then toss in the olive oil and season well with salt and pepper.

Reduce the oven temperature to 160°C/gas 3 and roast the hazelnuts on a baking sheet for 10–12 minutes until a pale golden.

Put the sugar and 2 tbsp of water into a small pan and stir to melt the sugar over a gentle heat. Once the sugar has melted stop stirring, increase the heat a little and cook until the sugar has turned into a nut-brown caramel, swirling the pan around to evenly disperse the darker patches of brown. Immediately remove from heat, add the nuts, stir to coat and pour the lot onto a tray lined with baking paper. Allow to cool, then roughly chop.

Meanwhile, blitz the dressing ingredients with a stick blender and season generously with salt and pepper.

To assemble the salad, separate the chicory into leaves, cut in half and wash and dry well. Wash and dry the mint and roughly chop. Toss the chicory, nuts, shallot and mint in the salad dressing and check the seasoning. Scatter over the roasted squash at the last minute. Check the seasoning again and serve.

For the Salad

1 large butternut squash

250g long-grain rice

pared rind of 1 lemon

small bunch of thyme

1 tbsp olive oil

70g hazelnuts

50g caster sugar

3 heads of chicory

handful of mint leaves

½ large banana shallot, finely sliced

For the Dressing

70g blue cheese (something peppery such as Stilton or Roquefort)

½ garlic clove, finely grated

4 tsp sherry vinegar

80ml extra-virgin olive oil

handful of chives, finely chopped

Small Bites & Salads   84/85

Kale Caesar!

FEEDS FOUR

For the Salad

finely grated zest
    and juice of 1 lemon
6 anchovies (from a jar or can)
1–2 garlic cloves
1 egg yolk
100ml olive oil, plus extra
    to massage the kale
400g red or green kale, coarse stalks
    removed, well washed and dried
100g Parmesan, shaved
    with a vegetable peeler

For the Croutons

150g stale sourdough bread,
    torn into chunks
60g pumpkin seeds
35g caraway seeds
50ml olive oil

The kale is used as a leaf here and kept raw. If you'd prefer a milder, warm salad, quickly blanch the kale in boiling water and drain well; you'll need double the amount of kale this way as it will wilt during cooking. The garlic is raw, so use less if you know you are sensitive to it!

Preheat the oven to 200°C/gas 6.

Use a large pestle and mortar to grind the lemon zest, anchovies and garlic together until you have a rough paste. Stir in the egg yolk and a little lemon juice, then very slowly and evenly drizzle in a thin stream of the olive oil, grinding or whisking as you go to incorporate it. You can add the oil faster once the dressing starts to emulsify. Stir in a little more lemon juice and 1 tsp of water every now and then. Taste and season, cover in cling film and set aside.

To make the croutons, place the torn sourdough on a baking sheet and sprinkle with the pumpkin seeds, caraway seeds and olive oil. Season with salt and pepper and toast in the oven for about 10 minutes until golden and crisp.

Rub the kale between your hands in 1–2 tbsp olive oil until the leaves have softened and broken down a little. Mix the warm croutons with the kale and Parmesan in a large serving bowl and drizzle over the dressing.

Why not try smoked salmon salad with warm anchovy cream dressing?
Fry 6 roughly chopped anchovies from a jar in 25g unsalted butter with 2 crushed pink peppercorns, squashing the anchovies lightly with the back of a wooden spoon. When the anchovies have dissolved, pour in 125ml double cream. Briefly simmer to thicken, then squeeze in a little lime juice, stir and season to taste. Serve warm over a salad of smoked salmon and chicory leaves. Feeds 4.

Three Bean Salad with Carrot & Ginger Dressing

FEEDS FOUR—SIX

This vivid carrot and ginger dressing adds bright Asian flavours and beautiful colour to a salad of green summer beans; the toasted seeds add a wonderful, nutty crunch and earthy flavour.

I love to use the runner beans that we grow in the garden every year (they are deliciously sweet and remind me of my grandmother), plus sugar snaps and broad beans, but experiment with whatever beans you can find in the shops or use grilled Tenderstem broccoli in the winter. You can make it more substantial with black quinoa or have this as is with steamed fish or lamb chops.

To make the dressing, whizz together all the ingredients except the vegetable oil in a powerful upright blender, then slowly pour in the oil until fully incorporated. Loosen with water; I find about 4 tbsp gives the right consistency.

Top and tail the runner beans, cut away the stringy sides and then cut the beans into 5cm pieces. Bring a pan of water to the boil and blanch the beans for a few minutes until tender. Scoop out, run under cold water and set aside. Using the same water, blanch the sugar snaps for 1–2 minutes until tender, scoop out and refresh under cold running water. Repeat with the broad beans, cooking them for a few minutes.

Meanwhile, toast the sesame seeds in a dry frying pan over a medium heat until golden all over. Set aside in a small bowl. Repeat with the buckwheat, transferring to the same bowl when golden and crisp. Do the same with the sunflower seeds.

Spread all the beans out onto a large, wide serving plate and drizzle with the dressing. Scatter with the buckwheat, seeds, sprouted seeds and coriander. Dust over a little chilli and, if you like, the feta, although the salad is delicious without. For more body, toss in 100g black quinoa which you have simmered until tender, about 20 minutes.

Why not try wok-fried green beans?

Whizz together a peeled thumb-sized piece of fresh ginger, 3 garlic cloves, 5 sun-dried tomatoes, 1 lemon grass stick, 1 tsp sugar, 1 tbsp sesame oil, 1 tbsp soy sauce and 1 tbsp sesame oil until you have a paste. Fry for 1 minute in another 1 tbsp sesame oil, then toss in 400g green beans. Add a splash of fish sauce and stir-fry, adding splashes of water until the beans are softened and beginning to wrinkle. Check for seasoning and serve sprinkled with nigella seeds. Feeds 4 as a side.

For the Salad

250g runner beans, trimmed, de-stringed if necessary

150g sugar snaps, halved at an angle

250g baby broad beans

1 tbsp each black and white sesame seeds

50g buckwheat

25g sunflower seeds

100g sprouted seeds, well washed and shaken dry

small handful of coriander leaves, roughly chopped

few pinches of Aleppo pepper, or other chilli flakes

100g feta, crumbled (optional)

100g black quinoa (optional)

For the Dressing

2 carrots, roughly chopped

2 round shallots, roughly chopped

50g fresh ginger, peeled and roughly chopped

1 tbsp white miso paste

60ml rice wine vinegar

1 tbsp honey

2 tbsp toasted sesame oil

small handful of thyme leaves

120ml vegetable oil

Pretty & Pink Pickled Egg, Beetroot & Tarragon Salad

FEEDS FOUR

This is the prettiest of salads. The eggs turn a beautifully deep neon pink and taste great with the crisp leaves in the rich, thick Dijon dressing. I love the way it turns an old English chip shop staple into something so contemporary and delicious.

Bring a pan of salted water to the boil and add the beetroots. Boil for 30–40 minutes (depending on size), or until you can pierce them easily with a sharp knife. Drain, reserving a cup of the cooking liquid, and return the liquid to the pan to make the pickling liquor. Add the vinegar, sugar, peppercorns and allspice berries and return to the heat. Cook for a minute or so until the sugar dissolves. Pour into a large, sterilised jar that will comfortably fit the eggs and beetroot and drop in the tarragon sprigs.

Fill a medium pan with water and bring to simmering point. Lower in the eggs so that they are covered, bring to the boil and simmer gently for 7 minutes.

Wearing gloves to avoid staining your hands a deep beetroot colour, rub away the skin from the beetroots and slice into quarters. Once the eggs are cooked, cool under cold running water, then peel and add to the jar along with the beetroots and sliced shallots. Seal tightly, then very gently tip up to mix everything together and place somewhere dark and cool for at least a week.

To assemble the salad, toss all the dressing ingredients together in a clean jar with a tight-fitting lid and shake thoroughly to combine. Serve the watercress and tarragon leaves with wedges of the beetroot and pickled egg, drizzled with the creamy dressing.

Why not try a Middle Eastern beetroot borani?

Quarter 600g beetroots, place in a foil parcel and toss with 1 tbsp oil, a pinch of ground cumin, salt and pepper. Roast in a preheated 200°C/gas 6 oven for 45 minutes until tender. Peel, then place in a food processor with 1 crushed garlic clove, 45g toasted walnuts, 3 tbsp cider vinegar, 6 tbsp Greek yogurt and 100ml olive oil. Blitz, leaving a little texture. Sprinkle with extra chopped walnuts, feta and mint leaves. An amazing dip to have with pitta crisps, crudités and quail's eggs.

For the Salad

4 small red beetroots, scrubbed

6 eggs

2 banana shallots, finely sliced

2 large handfuls of watercress

small bunch of tarragon,
   leaves picked

For the Pickling Liquor

400ml red wine vinegar

4 tbsp caster sugar

1 tbsp black peppercorns

1 tsp allspice berries

4–5 sprigs of tarragon

For the Creamy Dijon Dressing

3 tbsp red wine vinegar

1 tbsp honey

1 tbsp Dijon mustard

1 small garlic clove,
   very finely chopped

75ml extra-virgin olive oil

75ml sunflower oil

Grilled Halloumi & Peach Salad

FEEDS FOUR—SIX

6 small courgettes

4 peaches, cut into thick wedges

big handful of mint leaves,
    roughly chopped

juice of 1 large lemon,
    plus extra to taste

4 tbsp extra-virgin olive oil,
    plus extra to taste

20g butter

50g skin-on almonds,
    roughly chopped

¼ tsp smoked paprika

500g halloumi, cut into 1cm slices

Halloumi is a wonder ingredient, best when it sees a flame. Here I toss juicy peaches with wafer-thin courgette ribbons, nutty almonds fried in butter and slices of halloumi whipped straight from the barbecue to the plate (halloumi doesn't do sitting around). Ideal for sunshine and the outdoors.

Light a barbecue an hour before you want to eat, or use a griddle pan.

Using a vegetable peeler, peel the courgettes into long strips, rotating them around as you do and stopping when you get to the seedy centre (you can keep the middles for stewing in olive oil for a soup or side dish). Put the ribbons in a salad bowl with the peaches, mint leaves, lemon juice and 3 tbsp of the oil. Toss well and set aside.

Put a small frying pan over a medium heat, add the butter and season generously with salt and pepper. Melt the butter and cook it, swirling continuously, for 2–3 minutes until it starts darkening. Add the chopped almonds and paprika and cook for another minute or so until the butter is a dark, biscuit colour and the almonds are golden. Scatter the almonds and butter over the salad.

Rub the halloumi slices in the remaining 1 tbsp of oil, then place on the hottest part of the barbecue. Grill for 30–60 seconds on each side until char marks appear and they soften. Cut the halloumi pieces in half, toss into the salad and taste. You may want a scrunch more of black pepper, a squeeze more lemon juice or a touch more olive oil. Season appropriately and serve immediately.

Why not try grilled peaches with ice cream?
Preheat the grill to high. Halve and pit 3 ripe peaches and place in an ovenproof pan. Sprinkle over the finely grated zest of ½ lemon, 1 tbsp coconut sugar (or use Demerara), 1 tsp chilli flakes and top each half with ½ tsp unsalted butter. Grill for 5–7 minutes until almost blackened and caramelised on top. Remove, allow to cool slightly, then serve in bowls with any pan juices and scoops of ice cream. Feeds 2.

Cauliflower Salad with Carrot, Orange, Za'atar & Toasted Buckwheat

FEEDS FOUR AS A STARTER OR
TWO AS A LIGHT LUNCH

This salad was born from rooting around in my fridge and using up what I could find in the crisper one lunchtime. Apart from the herbs, it contains little that you would not have lying around in your fridge or cupboard, yet it's a stunning example of how a few simple ingredients thrown together can be transformed into a seriously good plate of food.

Toast the buckwheat in a dry frying pan until crunchy but not burnt, then set aside. In the same pan, toast the cumin seeds for the dressing and then grind in a spice grinder or by hand with a pestle and mortar. Set aside.

Fry the raisins in the olive oil over a medium-high heat for 2–3 minutes until plumped up and round.

Thinly slice across the cauliflower and then chop the slices into small pieces. Put the cauliflower into a salad bowl with the remaining salad ingredients, including the toasted buckwheat and fried raisins.

Mix the dressing ingredients together, season generously with salt and pepper and pour into the salad. Toss together and serve.

Why not try crab & buckwheat salad?

Toast 150g buckwheat in a pan over a medium heat for 5 minutes. Bring 1 litre salted water to the boil and add the buckwheat. Simmer for 10 minutes until the grains are almost tender and have absorbed most of the water, then drain and drizzle with olive oil. Cool then toss through ½ chopped cucumber, a small bunch of chopped dill, 2 thinly sliced spring onions, 1 segmented grapefruit and 200g white crab meat. Season well. Whisk 1 tbsp cider vinegar with the juice of 1 lime and 4 tbsp rapeseed oil and drizzle over the salad. Feeds 4.

For the Salad

40g buckwheat

60g raisins

½ tbsp olive oil

1 medium cauliflower, including
   tender inner leaves

80g black olives, preferably
   Kalamata, pitted and chopped

1 large orange, peeled and segmented

2 carrots, coarsely grated

large handful each of dill, parsley
   and mint leaves, finely chopped

3 tsp za'atar

For the Dressing

1½ tsp cumin seeds

1½ tsp soft light brown sugar

3 tbsp red wine vinegar

120ml olive oil

Chapter FOUR

WEEKEND

WEEKEND

My weekends are all about spending time with my children, family and friends, relaxing and having fun; for me this is inextricably bound up with cooking and eating. Without the time pressure of the week days, there is space to experiment with new ingredients and to play with food ideas and combinations that have been gently bubbling in my mind.

It is also the time I go to the farmer's market near where we live in Queen's Park. There I buy almost everything I need for Sunday lunch and the week ahead. My husband is lured by the promise of good coffee and a sausage sandwich and the children know they'll bump into local friends. I take my granny-chic shopping trolley so that I am limited in what I can carry and just buy what we need. From here I can stock the freezer with milk from grass-fed cows, with sourdough bread, with organic meat and with extremely fresh fish caught by day boats off the Norfolk coast the night before. Buying directly from the farmers keeps down the cost of this marvellous quality food, especially the meat and fish. Shopping at the market keeps me in touch with the seasons and gives me the chance to buy locally grown ingredients picked at their best.

The food we eat at the weekend can be divided into two distinct categories. Firstly there is the food that you will find in this chapter, more relaxed in feel and generally what I would cook for just a few friends or family; recipes that are pretty easy to put together quite swiftly. The recipes in the next chapter, 'Feeding the Troops', feel a bit more extravagant and – as the title suggests – are for big group meals.

In both chapters there are opportunities to add some useful store cupboard ingredients and mouth-watering leftovers to the fridge and freezer, so both are well stocked for the week ahead. Always consider making extra; it is such a relief when you come home midweek to find you've already done most of the work towards a meal. Perhaps on Saturday you made some extra Charred Tomato Dressing to go with the corn on the cob recipe here, which on Wednesday you can combine with lentils and feta to make a satisfying little salad. If I am making lamb meatballs, or bread dough, or pastry, I almost always double up the quantities so that I have leftovers for midweek or for the freezer. This is the nuts and bolts of my column in the *Weekend* magazine of *The Guardian*.

Gruyère and Bacon Quiche

FEEDS SIX—EIGHT

My extremely glamorous grandmother was a great cook and made a mean leek quiche with the crumbliest, flakiest shortcrust pastry ... I have been a quiche nut ever since. This version was inspired by the quiche Lorraine at the famous Clarke's delicatessen in London. Sally Clarke uses sweet Gruyère and salty, streaky bacon. I can still remember the day I first tried it and the intense pleasure of the first bite.

The key to avoiding a rubbery, overly eggy quiche is to use plenty of cream and not overcook it. Take it out when still slightly quivering in the middle and let it cool until just warm. There is little as unappetising as a cold quiche so, if you have made it in advance, always let it come to room temperature, or warm it gently in the oven. For a vegetarian version, leave out the bacon and add more spring onion and herbs, or some chard, mushrooms, leeks or spinach. Serve with a crisp green salad.

Roll out the pastry and lay it across a 23cm flan tin, pressing the dough into the corners. Chill in the freezer for 15 minutes while you preheat the oven to 180°C/gas 4.

Cover the pastry with baking paper and a layer of baking beans and bake in the oven for 15 minutes. Remove the paper and beans and return to the oven for a further 5 minutes, or until pale golden. Transfer the flan tin to a baking sheet.

Meanwhile, melt the butter in a frying pan over a medium heat. When bubbling, add the bacon and fry until crisp and golden on both sides. Remove and drain on kitchen paper. Add the spring onions and thyme to the pan and cook for a few minutes until the onions are softened. Leave to cool.

Whip the cream until slightly thickened, then whisk in the eggs and Gruyère. Season with a little salt (be sparing as the cheese and bacon are both quite salty) and pepper, then grate in plenty of the nutmeg, about 7–8 good gratings.

Ingredients

320g all-butter shortcrust pastry, either bought or home-made (see page 303)
15g butter
6 very thin rashers of smoked streaky bacon
6 spring onions, finely sliced
few sprigs of thyme, leaves picked
250ml double cream
4 eggs
75g grated Gruyère
freshly grated nutmeg
30g Parmesan, finely grated

Break the bacon pieces into halves or thirds and put them over the base of the tart with the spring onions. Pour in the egg mix so that it comes right up to the edge and then sprinkle over the Parmesan. Carefully transfer the baking sheet to the middle of the oven and bake for 25–30 minutes until golden on top and set, with just a slight wobble in the middle. Leave to cool and firm up a little before serving.

Why not try fiery cheese straws?
Preheat the oven to 200°C/gas 6. Roll a 320g sheet of shortcrust pastry onto a large baking sheet and brush evenly with 1 tbsp English mustard. Sprinkle with ½–1 tsp cayenne pepper and 40g grated Gruyère. Season generously. Slice into 12 long strips and carefully twist each to create a spring shape. Brush with beaten egg, then bake on the baking sheet for 10 minutes until golden and crisp. Serve immediately, dusting with finely grated Parmesan. Makes 12.

Avocado Four Ways

Avocados originate in Mexico and it is said that they are packed with so much nutrition that you could live off them. In the ancient Aztec language Nahuatl the word for avocado is *ahuacatl*, which translates as 'testicle'; Aztec warriors would eat them to make them more virile, either before going into battle or leaping into other physical activities! I prefer this reason for the avocado's appeal over the contemporary one of 'eating clean'.

Avocados in their unadulterated form are blank canvases, needing citrus juices, vinegars or other zingy flavours to make them come alive. Here are some of my favourite ways to serve them.

Diced Avocado with Mango, Black Beans & Pickled Jalapeño

150g mango, diced

½ small red onion, finely chopped

juice of 1 lime

small handful of coriander,
  roughly chopped

75g cooked black beans

1–2 tbsp chopped pickled jalapeños

2 medium Hass avocados

pinch of cumin seeds

½ small garlic clove, crushed

2 tbsp extra-virgin olive oil

bread or pitta, to serve

This spicy, mouth-tingling salad is wonderfully fruity and satisfyingly filling. You can use black beans from a can or a carton.

Mix the mango with the red onion, lime juice, coriander, beans and jalapeños. Remove the flesh from the avocados, chop roughly and stir into the mango salad.

Grind the cumin seeds with the garlic and a little salt in a pestle and mortar and stir in the olive oil. Use this to dress the mango salad; check for seasoning.

Toast 2 slices of sourdough or granary bread or some pitta and serve with the salad. This is delicious with My Favourite Fried Eggs on the side (see page 19). *Feeds 2.*

Watermelon, Feta & Avocado Salad With Grilled Flatbreads

2 large flatbreads
  (for home-made, see page 125)

4 tbsp extra-virgin olive oil

2 medium Hass avocados

2 tbsp lemon juice

80g watermelon, chopped

small handful of mint leaves,
  finely chopped

40g feta cheese, crumbled

large handful of sprouted seeds (optional)

½ tsp za'atar

These chorizo and avocado toasts are earthy, garlicky and splendidly delicious.

Preheat the grill to medium-high and cut open the flatbreads. Brush the insides of the breads with half the olive oil and season with salt and pepper. Grill for a few minutes until gently toasted. Set aside.

Remove the flesh from the avocados and chop roughly. Add to a bowl with the lemon juice. Toss in the rest of the salad ingredients, except the za'atar, including the sprouted seeds, if using. Pile the salad on top of the grilled breads and sprinkle with za'atar. Serve at once. *Feeds 2—4.*

Chorizo, Crispy Chickpea & Avocado Toasts

A Middle Eastern take on avocados that makes a great lunchtime salad or light summer starter when watermelons line the fruit stalls.

3 cooking chorizo sausages
    (about 190g)
1 tbsp extra-virgin olive oil,
    plus extra to drizzle
240g cooked chickpeas
    (from a can or see page 301)
1 tsp sweet smoked paprika
3–4 slices sourdough
    or country-style bread
1 garlic clove
1 large or 2 medium Hass avocados
finely grated zest and juice of ½ lemon
small handful of parsley
    leaves, roughly chopped

Quarter the chorizo lengthways and then cut into dice. Add 1 tbsp of olive oil to a frying pan, put over a medium-high heat and fry the chorizo for 5–8 minutes until the fat has rendered out and it is looking nice and crisp. Remove with a slotted spoon and add the chickpeas and paprika to the chorizo oil, increasing the heat to its highest. Fry the chickpeas for another 5–8 minutes in the hot fat until deliciously crisp. Season generously with salt and pepper. Toss the chickpeas and chorizo together.

Toast the bread, rub it gently with the garlic clove and drizzle it with the olive oil.

Remove the flesh from the avocado and mash it up roughly with a fork with the lemon zest and juice. Season generously with salt and pepper, spread over the toast, top with the hot chorizo and chickpeas and scatter with the parsley. Eat at once. *Feeds 2–3.*

Crushed Avocado with Lemon-Tahini Dressing

Lots of us associate sesame with Asian cuisine, but sesame seeds are used throughout Mexican cooking. The combination of sesame in different forms – oil, tahini, black and white seeds – with citrus and green avocado is a fresh, nutty and zesty way to set you up for the day and it looks gloriously pretty. Make it for someone you love after a wild night out.

20g tahini paste, plus a
    drizzle of the tahini oil
2 tbsp lemon juice
1 tbsp extra-virgin olive oil
1 tsp toasted sesame oil
1 tsp each of white and
    black sesame seeds
2 tsp buckwheat (optional)
2 pieces of sourdough bread
1 small garlic clove (optional)
1 medium Hass avocado
pinch of Turkish chilli flakes

To Serve
handful of rocket
1 radish, finely sliced

Whisk the tahini paste and oil with the lemon juice until thoroughly combined, with no lumps left. Season well with salt and pepper and stir in the olive and sesame oils.

Toast the sesame seeds in a dry frying pan for a few minutes until the white sesame seeds turn a pale caramel. Repeat with the buckwheat, if using.

Toast the bread and, if you like, rub gently with the cut garlic clove. Remove the flesh from the avocado and mash roughly onto the toasts, season with a pinch of salt and drizzle with half the dressing. Sprinkle with the sesame seeds and chilli flakes. Serve with the rocket, topped with the radish, the rest of the lemon-tahini dressing and the toasted buckwheat, if using. *Feeds 1—2.*

Corn on the Cob with Charred Tomato Dressing

FEEDS FOUR

It is hard not to love a chargrilled stick of deeply yellow corn, steaming hot and dripping in butter, or doused in mayonnaise, crumbled cheese, lime juice and chilli as they eat it in Mexico. The corn season, from the end of August until the end of September, coincides perfectly with tomatoes at their best. This tomato dressing, inspired by the style of dry-roasting tomatoes and chillies used in Mexico, is both sweet and rich, and hot and smoky.

Make plenty of the tomato dressing to use throughout the week; it is truly wonderful over roast cauliflower, in the lentil salad below, or any other combination that occurs to you, such as in tacos with avocado and sprouting seeds.

First make the dressing. Put your oldest, most knackered heavy-based pan over a high heat. Once hot, add the chilli and tomatoes and, turning with tongs, dry-roast on all sides for 10–15 minutes, or until blackened all over. The blacker the fruit, the more flavour will come through in the dressing. After 10 minutes, add the garlic and roast on all sides too (it will cook much faster). Once roasted, peel the garlic and cut open the chilli lengthways and scrape away the seeds and membrane, trying not to touch the seeds or you will have very spicy fingers for several hours. Add the chilli, garlic and tomatoes to a blender, black skins and all, and blitz to a thick purée.

Add the vinegar, sugar and allspice, season generously with salt and, with the motor running, add the oil in a slow, steady stream until the dressing is emulsified. Season to taste; it will need quite a bit of salt. Set aside, or chill in the fridge for up to 2 weeks.

When almost ready to eat, place the corn cobs straight onto a hot barbecue and turn them for 10 minutes until the husks blacken and become like tissue paper. Alternatively, cook them in an oven preheated to 220°C/gas 7. Peel back the husks, so you can use them as handles. Brush with the melted butter, spoon over some of the tomato dressing and sprinkle with the feta, coriander and smoked sea salt, if using. If you are serving a larger crowd, cut the cobs into thirds. Devour at once!

Why not try lentil, smoky tomato & feta salad?

Place 200g Puy lentils, 1 bay leaf and 1 garlic clove in a pan and cover with water. Simmer for 25–30 minutes until the lentils are just tender, then drain. Discard the bay and garlic. Add 3 tbsp olive oil, season well and stir in a large handful of chopped parsley leaves (about 100g) and 200g crumbled feta. Toast 150g torn sourdough bread, then toss it in 3 tbsp Charred Tomato Dressing. Toss through the lentil salad, then spoon on more of the tomato dressing to serve. Feeds 4 as a side, or 2 as a main.

For the Corn

4 corn on the cob,
   still in their husks
50g butter, melted
50g feta, crumbled
small handful of coriander
   leaves, roughly chopped
1 tsp smoked sea salt (optional)

For the Dressing

1 Scotch Bonnet chilli
3 large, ripe plum tomatoes
1 garlic clove, unpeeled
2 tbsp sherry vinegar
½ tsp soft light brown sugar
few pinches of ground allspice
130ml olive oil

Lamb Meatball & Spicy Red Pepper Sauce Wraps

FEEDS FOUR

Ever since I did some judging on *MasterChef* and was forced to eat overcooked sea bass bathed in a thin, insipid red pepper sauce, I've avoided red peppers like the plague. The Tex-Mex obsession with bell peppers hasn't helped our relationship. Recently, however, I've been reading about brilliant young chefs across the Atlantic creating intensely flavoured reductions with red peppers. This sparked a memory of reading *Delia's Summer Collection* cover-to-cover as a girl and happily roasting and caramelising peppers. So I'm now back on the red peppers ... just as long as they are in this concentrated form.

Put all the different parts of the dish on the table and let people gather round and help themselves. I love the communal feel of everyone passing round huge trays of golden spicy meatballs, flatbreads, crunchy lettuce leaves, lemon or lime wedges and bowls of the scarlet sauce and cooling yogurt.

For the Sauce
3 medium red peppers
  (or use 190g roasted
  red peppers from a jar)
4 tbsp extra-virgin olive oil
1 tbsp breadcrumbs
1–2 tsp chilli flakes (depending
  how hot you like it, if at all)
2 tsp pomegranate molasses
  (or use balsamic vinegar)

Preheat the oven to 180°C/gas 4. Halve and deseed the peppers, rub the skins with 1–2 tablespoons of the olive oil and roast them, skin side up on a baking sheet, for 20–25 minutes until blackened and soft. Put them in a bowl, cover with cling film and leave for 10 minutes, then peel. Place the peeled peppers (or peppers from a jar) in a blender with the remaining sauce ingredients and blitz to make a sauce. Season to taste and warm gently in a pan.

For the Meatballs
500g minced lamb
½ onion, very finely chopped
¼ tsp dried oregano
½ tsp smoked paprika
½ tsp cumin seeds, freshly ground
juice of ¼ lemon
handful of parsley leaves,
  finely chopped
olive oil, to fry

Reduce the oven temperature to 140°C/gas 1 and warm the flatbreads, wrapped in foil.

In a bowl, mix the lamb with all the other meatball ingredients except the oil, then form the mixture into small walnut-sized balls; you should get about 24. Heat the oil in a large frying pan over a medium-high heat and fry the meatballs for 2 minutes on each side until golden. Meanwhile, mix the yogurt with the feta and dill in a bowl. Squeeze in a little lemon juice and season to taste.

For the Yogurt
100g yogurt
50g feta, crumbled
handful of dill fronds, chopped
squeeze of lemon juice

Take everything to the table in bowls to assemble into wraps.

To Serve
4 fresh flatbreads (for home-made,
  see page 125) or large pittas
Iceberg lettuce leaves, dressed
  with a little lemon juice

Why not try pomegranate & yogurt meatballs with cumin rice?
Cook the meatballs as above. Add 300g basmati rice and 1 tsp crushed cumin seeds to a pan with 700ml lightly salted cold water. Bring to the boil, then reduce the heat to low, cover and cook for 15 minutes until the rice has absorbed the liquid. Take off the heat but keep the lid on. Meanwhile, fry 3 onions in a knob of butter with another pinch of cumin seeds for 15 minutes until soft. Mix through the rice and season. Stir the meatballs into 100g natural yogurt and 1 tsp pomegranate molasses and serve with the rice, crushed pistachios, pomegranate seeds and chopped coriander leaves. Feeds 4.

Potato & Anchovy Soufflé with Buttermilk & Little Gem Salad

Despite their reputation, soufflés are surprisingly easy to make and, once you are confident, you will find them to be a brilliant standby supper, transforming the humblest of fruit or vegetables. Here, the silkiness of the potatoes marries well with the gutsy anchovies and Parmesan.

Preheat the oven to 200°C/gas 6 and butter 6 small ramekins or a 15cm baking dish (ideally with straight sides). Use about 2 tbsp of the grated Parmesan to dust over the butter to prevent the mixture clinging to the sides.

Place the potato in a pan with the salt. Cover with cold water, bring to the boil and cook until completely soft.

Meanwhile, melt the butter in a pan over a medium heat and gently fry the garlic and thyme for a minute or so until the garlic softens. Stir in the anchovy fillets and cook for a moment longer, squishing them into the pan until they melt into the butter. Stir in the flour and bay leaf, cook for another minute, then slowly stir in the milk, whisking continuously until it comes to the boil and begins to thicken. Reduce the heat and leave to simmer gently for 4 minutes, whisking occasionally. You want it to be the consistency of thick double cream.

While still warm (but not hot), whisk in the egg yolks and 30g of the remaining Parmesan. Drain the potato, mash until smooth and stir into the white sauce. Season to taste with salt and pepper and a little nutmeg and remove the bay leaf.

In a spotlessly clean bowl, whisk the egg whites until you have stiff peaks. Stir 1 tbsp of the egg whites into the potato mix to lighten it, then gently fold in the rest of the egg whites, being careful not to knock out too much air. Spoon into the ramekins so they are three-quarters full and smooth the top with a spoon. Sprinkle over the remaining Parmesan, then run a finger around the edge to create a little groove (this encourages rising).

Place in the oven for 10–12 minutes (15–20 minutes if you are cooking in a large dish) until risen and golden on top with only a slight wobble in the middle.

Meanwhile, whisk together all the salad ingredients, except the leaves, until combined. Toss the Little Gem leaves with this dressing in a large salad bowl. Serve with the soufflé as soon as you can, as even the best will sink in time.

For the Soufflé

30g butter, plus extra for the dish(es)
90g Parmesan, finely grated
1 large baking potato (about 300g), peeled and cut into chunks
1 tsp salt
2 garlic cloves, finely chopped
5 sprigs of thyme, leaves picked
10 anchovy fillets in oil, drained and chopped
30g plain flour
1 bay leaf
300ml whole milk
4 eggs, separated
pinch of grated nutmeg

For the Buttermilk Salad

½ garlic clove, crushed with a little salt
1 tsp Dijon mustard
6 tbsp buttermilk
1 tbsp olive oil
1 tbsp white wine vinegar or lemon juice
4 Little Gem lettuces, leaves separated

Serrano Ham & Lincolnshire Croquetas

Jo Ingleby is a brilliant nursery school teacher in Bristol who has pioneered teaching cooking to under-fives. She advised me against only baking biscuits and cakes and sweet treats with my daughters. Instead, she made me think carefully about something savoury we might cook together and this was our first recipe. I won't tell you what the kitchen looked like by the time we had finished rolling the little logs, but there were a lot of very happy faces after we'd eaten these golden fried nuggets of cheesy béchamel and strips of Serrano ham.

You can make these with leftover chicken, Serrano ham and peas, artichoke hearts and cheese or whatever other combination you can dream up.

Melt the butter in a large pan and add 150g of the flour. Stir well so the butter and flour are completely incorporated and fry for 2 minutes until nutty-smelling. Slowly pour in the milk, whisking all the time, until you have a thick roux. Season generously and stir in the ham and cheese. Allow to cool completely until firm enough to shape.

Put the remaining flour, the eggs and breadcrumbs into 3 separate shallow bowls. Take 1 heaped tbsp of mixture (about 25g) and, with wet hands, shape into a small log. Dry your hands then dip the croqueta into the flour then, with the other hand, dip into the egg; passing hands again, coat in the breadcrumbs. Repeat to coat all the croquetas, lay them all on a tray and freeze for 10 minutes to firm up. (You should get about 24.)

Fill a pan two-thirds full with oil. Heat to 180°C, measuring with a kitchen thermometer, or until a piece of bread turns golden in 40 seconds. Lower a batch of croquetas into the oil and cook for 2–3 minutes until golden and crisp. Transfer to a plate lined with kitchen paper and repeat to fry them all. Serve hot, scattered with salt.

Kitchen Note:
You can freeze the croquetas before frying for up to 3 months; simply fry straight from frozen, adding an extra minute to the cooking time.

Why not try broad bean & jamón salad?
Heat a griddle pan over a high heat. Top, tail and half lengthways 250g unshelled young broad beans and toss with 1 tbsp olive oil, ¼ tsp chilli flakes and ½ crushed garlic clove. Sprinkle them with water and griddle – still in their pods – on both sides until the pods blacken slightly. Remove from the pan, squeeze over the juice of ½ lemon and season. Transfer to a bowl and mix with 300g warm shelled cooked broad beans, 100g thinly sliced Serrano ham, 2 tbsp shredded mint leaves, 1 finely sliced banana shallot, 3 tbsp good-quality sherry vinegar and 6 tbsp extra-virgin olive oil. Feeds 2–4.

80g butter

225g plain flour

450ml whole milk

75g Serrano ham, roughly chopped

40g Lincolnshire Poacher,
    Manchego or an extra mature
    Cheddar, coarsely grated

2 eggs, lightly beaten

125g fresh breadcrumbs
    (for home-made, see page 277)

groundnut or rapeseed oil, to fry

Cheat's Sunday Lunch: Bavette with Roast New Potatoes

FEEDS FOUR—SIX

Much to my husband's dismay, I rarely cook a whole joint of beef. Either it is the cost or the time commitment that puts me off (or maybe it is because I get my fill of beef through the steak and cheese tacos that we serve at Wahaca). However even I sometimes get a yearning for beef at weekends, either a roast rib, or a flash-roasted fillet, or a pot-roasted topside. Here I have created a quick fudge by taking a delicious cheap cut and serving it with all the classic trimmings, including some absurdly garlicky, crispy, golden potatoes that take half the time of proper roast spuds. It is important not to cut these new potatoes in half after par-boiling, but to crush them (with an old wine bottle or a can or whatever) once the skins are broken, as all the cracks soak up the garlic- and thyme-scented oil; therein lies their secret.

Although packed with flavour, both bavette and onglet steaks can turn tough and rubbery if over- or undercooked; they need to be medium rare. Season them generously with salt and pepper an hour before you cook them and let them come to room temperature. If you forget, then just give them as long as you can. Cook for 3 minutes a side but not much longer, this allows the tight proteins in these cuts time to relax. If in doubt, undercook first; you can always cut it open to check the doneness and pop back in the pan if it needs more time. Slice against the grain and serve with the potatoes and one or two of the sauces overleaf.

Season the steak with salt and pepper and set aside for at least 1 hour to come to room temperature. Preheat the oven to 210°C/gas 7.

Put the potatoes into a large pan of cold water, bring to the boil and par-boil for 7–10 minutes. Drain, then tip them into a roasting tin and crush lightly with another roasting tin, a masher or the back of a wooden spoon. Drizzle with the olive oil and toss with the rosemary sprigs and garlic cloves. Season generously with salt and roast for 25–30 minutes until golden and crisp.

Halfway through roasting the potatoes, rub the steak with olive oil. Heat a griddle or frying pan over a high heat and, when smoking hot, fry the steak for 3 minutes on each side, or until well browned on the outside and medium rare in the middle. Move to a board and leave to rest for 5 minutes before slicing thickly.

Serve with any or all of the sauces overleaf. The steak is also excellent the next day in a sandwich with Little Gem lettuce and any of the leftover sauces.

700g bavette steak, butterflied out to an even width (your butcher can do this for you)
500g baby new potatoes
4–6 tbsp extra-virgin olive oil
3 whole sprigs of rosemary
4 fat garlic cloves

Cheat's Sunday Lunch: Bavette with Roast New Potatoes (Continued)

Cheat's Béarnaise (see page 289 for the real McCoy)

Roughly chop a handful of tarragon leaves. Gently heat 150g full-fat crème fraîche, 1 tbsp red wine vinegar, 1 egg yolk and 1 tsp Dijon mustard and any resting juices from the steak in a pan. Whisk in 2 tbsp mayonnaise and the tarragon leaves and season well with salt. Also excellent with poached eggs or steamed asparagus.

Chimichurri

Blitz 3 garlic cloves, 1 shallot, 1 red chilli, a large bunch of parsley, 2 tbsp fresh oregano leaves, 3 tbsp red wine vinegar and 1 tsp salt in a food processor. Stir in 100ml extra-virgin olive oil and season with ½–1 tsp hot smoked paprika. Best made on the day. This Argentinian condiment is also great with roast chicken or slow-roasted lamb shoulder (see page 147).

Horseradish Cream

Finely grate 3 tbsp horseradish into 200g crème fraîche. Season with salt and pepper, the finely grated zest of ½ lemon, 1 tbsp lemon juice and 2 tbsp extra-virgin olive oil. Also delicious with hot-smoked trout, roast beetroot and watercress salad or on bruschetta (for home-made, see page 277).

Mojo de Ajo

This translates as 'dunked in garlic' or 'garlic gravy'. Peel and finely chop the cloves from 2 heads of garlic (if in a food processor, use the pulse button to avoid getting a paste). Add the garlic to a pan with 100ml rapeseed oil, 100ml extra-virgin olive oil, 1–2 tsp finely chopped chipotles en adobo or ½ tsp each sweet and hot smoked paprika, a few sprigs of stripped thyme leaves and lots of salt and pepper. Simmer very gently for 30 minutes so that bubbles are barely breaking the surface. If you cook over too high a heat the garlic will burn. You will have a sweet, slightly caramelised, garlic bath, delicious with roast chicken or chargrilled chicken thighs and lime wedges.

Spanish Tortilla with Chorizo & Alioli

FEEDS SIX

A memorable picnic in Northern Spain cured me of my teenage indifference to the simple spud. Long-cooked onions were sweet and silky, rich with extra-virgin olive oil, binding the waxy potatoes. It was an early lesson in how even the humblest of ingredients can become stars of the show with a good recipe.

Cut the potatoes into quarters, then slice about the thickness of a £1 coin. Heat the oil in a deep 25cm non-stick frying pan over a medium heat. Add the onions, plenty of salt and black pepper, reduce the heat to medium-low and cook until the onions are soft and golden, 30–35 minutes, stirring occasionally to prevent the onions from catching. Add the chorizo, potatoes, paprika and parsley and continue cooking and stirring for another 20 minutes or so until the potatoes are tender and broken up and the whole mass has turned into a deep brown mush. Taste for seasoning, adding more if needed. Using a slotted spoon, transfer everything to a colander or sieve standing over a bowl to drain away the excess oil. Transfer the chorizo and potato mixture to a bowl. Reserve the drained oil to cook the tortilla.

Whisk the eggs in a bowl with 2 tsp of water and plenty of salt and pepper, then stir into the potato and chorizo mix.

Clean the pan and put back over a high heat. When hot, pour in 1 tbsp of the drained oil, swirl around the pan and pour in the egg mixture. Reduce the heat to medium-low and gently shake the pan to distribute the egg mixture, patting down the filling to a flat, smooth shape. Cook for 4–5 minutes until the edges are cooked.

Gently move a spatula around the edges of the tortilla to loosen it and check that it isn't stuck, then place a large plate over the top and invert the pan, watching out for any wet egg sliding out. Add another 1 tbsp of the drained oil to the pan, heat for a minute, then carefully slide the tortilla back into the pan, uncooked side down. Continue cooking over a low heat for 2–3 minutes. Invert the tortilla again onto a serving plate and rest for 5 minutes while you prepare the alioli.

Put the egg yolks, garlic and a generous pinch of salt into a food processor and blitz briefly. With the motor running, very slowly drip three-quarters of the oil through the funnel until the alioli starts to thicken and emulsify, then pour in the remaining oil in a slow, steady stream. Add lemon juice and salt to taste and loosen with a few tbsp of water, then transfer to a bowl.

Serve the tortilla in slices or cubes, either warm or at room temperature, with a crisp green salad and the alioli on the side.

For the Tortilla

700g waxy potatoes, such as Charlotte or Desirée, peeled
150ml extra-virgin olive oil
4 large white onions (about 500g), finely sliced
225g spicy cooking chorizo, finely diced
½ tsp smoked paprika
small bunch of parsley leaves, finely chopped
6 eggs

For the Alioli

2 egg yolks
3 garlic cloves, finely chopped
250ml mild olive oil
few squeezes of lemon juice

Pomegranate-Glazed Chicken Thighs with Red Quinoa Salad

My children love nothing more than opening up pomegranates, to find the sparkling bright pink jewels hidden within. This is a cheering, colourful salad with a satisfying crunch.

Place the garlic in a pestle and mortar with a pinch of salt and crush to a paste. Add the cumin seeds and peppercorns and crush them too, then stir in the molasses, oil and lemon juice. Transfer to a large bowl, then add the chicken thighs and rub the marinade into them thoroughly. Cover and place in the fridge to marinate for 1 hour.

Meanwhile prepare the salad. Place the quinoa in a pan with a few pinches of salt and cover with 800ml boiling water. Cover with a lid and simmer for 15–17 minutes. Remove from the heat, drain in a sieve, then sit the sieve on top of the hot pan and cover it with a clean tea towel. Leave to steam-dry for at least 10 minutes.

Combine the remaining salad ingredients in a bowl (except for the oil and lemon juice) and lightly season. When the quinoa has steamed dry, fluff it up with a fork. While still hot, pour over the oil and half the lemon juice, mix well and season lightly. Combine with the other salad ingredients, squeeze over the remaining lemon and mix well. Set aside.

Add a small splash of oil to a lidded frying pan and place over a medium-high heat. Season the thighs with a little salt and add them skin side down to the pan when hot. Fry for 2 minutes on each side until golden and crisp. Turn them over once more, add the pomegranate seeds, any marinating liquid and a splash of water. Cover, reduce the heat to low and continue to cook for another 3 minutes until cooked through (the juices should run clear when you insert a skewer). Uncover and leave to rest for 3 minutes.

Cut the thighs into thirds and sit them on top of the salad, spooning over the cooking juices and cooked pomegranate seeds.

Why not try pomegranate cake?

Butter and line a 20cm sandwich cake tin. Preheat the oven to 180°C/gas 4. Melt 150g butter, 50g light muscovado and 100g caster sugar together, allow to cool, then beat in 3 eggs in turn. Stir in 2 tbsp pomegranate molasses. Sift 150g plain flour, ½ tsp bicarbonate of soda and a pinch fine salt into a bowl, then fold in the wet mixture. Stir in 50ml buttermilk, spoon the batter into the prepared cake tin and bake for 25–30 minutes until golden and a skewer comes out clean when inserted into the middle of the cake. Cool for 5 minutes in the tin, poke holes all over with a skewer, then pour over 75ml pomegranate molasses. Remove from the tin before slicing.

For the Chicken

1 garlic clove

½ tsp cumin seeds

pinch of black peppercorns

3 tbsp pomegranate molasses
   (for home-made, see page 298)

1 tbsp olive oil, plus extra to fry

squeeze of lemon juice

6 boneless chicken thighs

seeds from ½ small pomegranate

For the Quinoa Salad

125g red or white quinoa, rinsed

2 handfuls of gently toasted
   pistachios, roughly chopped

¼ red onion, finely chopped

seeds from ½ small pomegranate

1 celery heart, finely sliced

1 red pepper, deseeded
   and finely diced

½ bunch of parsley, leaves
   and stalks finely chopped

2 large handfuls of mint
   leaves, finely chopped

2 tbsp extra-virgin olive oil

juice of 1 lemon

Roast Carrots & Parsnips with Split Peas & Yogurt

FEEDS FOUR—SIX

Here warming, aromatic spices envelop the sweet root vegetables with a Middle Eastern flavour that is enhanced by roasting. The whole recipe is extremely simple to prep; as you roast the roots the lentils simmer until tender, leaving you time to make the garlicky, minty yogurt dressing, which adds a silky, fresh body to the dish. This would go beautifully with sausages or lamb chops but is just as tempting on its own.

Preheat the oven to 200°C/gas 6.

Rinse the split peas in cold water and transfer to a pan with the thyme and 2 of the garlic cloves. Cover with cold water and bring to the boil. Simmer gently for 35–50 minutes until tender but not falling apart (cooking times vary quite widely depending on the age of the peas). Take them off the heat, season with a few pinches of salt and leave to cool. Remove the thyme stalks and garlic.

Meanwhile, briefly warm the whole spices in a small pan until fragrant, then coarsely grind in a pestle and mortar. Add a garlic clove and crush into the spices with some salt. Finally, stir in half the olive oil.

Chop the carrots and parsnips or cut them in lovely long lengths. Pop into a large roasting tin with the spice paste. Season with salt and pepper, add a splash of water and roast in the oven for 30 minutes or until lightly coloured and just tender.

Wipe out the pestle and mortar with a damp cloth and use to crush the remaining ½ garlic clove with a pinch of salt. Stir into the yogurt with the remaining oil and a squeeze of lemon juice. Drain the split peas and transfer to a bowl. Toss in half the yogurt dressing and season to taste.

Place a large helping of split peas on each plate and spoon over the warm root vegetables, followed by a little more yogurt, the roughly torn mint leaves and a sprinkle of chilli flakes.

Kitchen Note:

I love to roast all sorts of roots in smaller chunks with these spices, then fold them through fat pearls of Palestinian or Israeli couscous for a warming bowl of root heaven. Try a mixture of celeriac, beetroots, Jerusalem artichokes, carrots and parsnips and serve with yogurt, coriander or parsley leaves and Rose Harissa (see page 296).

200g split peas
few sprigs of thyme
3½ garlic cloves
2 tsp coriander seeds
1 tsp nigella seeds
1 tsp cumin seeds
4–5 tbsp extra-virgin olive oil
300g carrots
300g parsnips
125g Greek yogurt
squeeze of lemon juice
handful of mint leaves, to serve
Turkish chilli flakes, to serve

Crispy Green Potato Cakes

These are perfect for eating on lazy weekends and also feel like they are doing you the world of good.

I love sorrel for its lemony sharpness. If you can't get hold of it, use spinach with a few squeezes of lemon juice. I usually double up when making the basil and sorrel oil, because it makes a great dressing for soups and salads, as well as a last-minute pesto for a midweek supper.

Cover the potatoes in cold salted water and bring to the boil, then cook until just beginning to fall apart. Drain and leave to steam dry. Meanwhile roughly chop the sorrel or spinach, shred the basil leaves and whizz them in a blender with the garlic. Stir in half the olive oil and the Parmesan and season with a little salt and pepper to taste.

Once the potatoes are cool enough to handle, pull off their skins (I sometimes bake them into crisps). Place the flesh in a large bowl and crush with a potato masher until just broken down. Stir through two-thirds of the green sauce and season generously to taste; you want it packed with flavour. Shape the potato mixture into 8–10 peach-sized balls, flatten out between your palms and chill in the fridge for at least 1 hour.

Stir the rest of the olive oil into the rest of the green sauce and set aside.

Melt half the butter in a large frying pan over a high heat with a splash of oil and add half the cakes, making sure they've got a bit of room. Immediately reduce the heat to medium and cook for 1½–2 minutes each side until a golden crust has formed. They can break up with rough handling, so treat them gently. Repeat with the remaining butter and potato mix.

To serve put a couple of the cakes on each plate and top with a fried or poached egg. Spoon over the remaining green sauce and, if you like, a little extra grated Parmesan and a few sorrel or spinach leaves.

Why not try a sweet potato rösti?

Coarsely grate 500g peeled sweet potato and 1 small onion, toss with 1 tsp of salt and leave to drain. Meanwhile put ½ small garlic clove, 2 large handfuls of parsley and a squeeze of lemon juice in a food processor and whizz to a smooth purée with 75–100ml extra-virgin olive oil. Season. Beat an egg, season and mix into the squeezed-out sweet potato; the mix will be very delicate so if this frightens you beat in 2 tbsp white spelt flour and ¼ tsp baking powder. Divide into 4 and pat out into discs. Fry gently in olive oil until crisp and golden on both sides. Serve with poached eggs, sliced avocado, the parsley oil and, if you like, fried slices of chorizo. Feeds 4.

800g floury potatoes, such as
  Maris Piper, unpeeled and cut
  into even chunks
100g sorrel leaves (or use spinach and
  lemon juice, see recipe introduction)
bunch of basil, leaves picked
1 garlic clove
8 tbsp olive oil, plus extra to fry
4 tbsp Parmesan, finely grated
  plus extra to serve (optional)
20g butter
poached or fried eggs,
  to serve (see page 18–9)

Black Pudding Ragú with Parmesan Polenta

Black pudding has a mixed reputation but I adore it and it is packed with goodness. Find a good-quality pudding from Ireland or a Spanish supplier like Brindisa and you will find the flavour is wonderfully sweet and mellow.

This dish was inspired by a memorable morcilla and chickpea dish I had many years ago at a stand called Pinocchio in La Boqueria, the famous market in Barcelona. Tiny pieces of black pudding had melted into a sauce that bathed the chickpeas. Here the black pudding similarly collapses and dissolves into a ragú of tomatoes, cinnamon and thyme that you heap onto piles of silky Parmesan polenta.

Heat the olive oil in a large pan and add the onions. Cook over a medium heat for 15 minutes until they are softened but not too coloured. Add the garlic and fry for a minute more.

Stir in the spices then add the black pudding, breaking it into small pieces with a wooden spoon. Stir in the chopped tomatoes, vinegar and thyme and increase the heat to bring the sauce to the boil. Reduce to a gentle simmer and cook for 45 minutes. Season to taste.

While the ragú is simmering, bring 1 litre of water to the boil in a pan. With a whisk at the ready, pour in the polenta and begin to whisk so that there are no lumps, being careful of spitting. Reduce the heat to low and cook for according to the packet instructions, stirring occasionally with a wooden spoon. Add the butter and Parmesan and season with plenty of salt and pepper.

Toast the pine nuts gently in a dry pan until lightly golden. Serve the polenta in shallow bowls, topped with ragú and a sprinkling of toasted pine nuts and Parmesan, if you like.

Why not try black pudding & chicory salad with roast pear & sticky walnuts?
Quarter and core 3 ripe pears and drizzle with 2 tbsp olive oil and 1 tsp sweet paprika. Season with a pinch of sugar, salt and pepper and roast in a preheated 200°C/gas 6 oven for about 20 minutes. Toast 60g walnut pieces in the same oven until pale golden, about 5 minutes. Whisk together 75ml extra-virgin olive oil and 2 tbsp red wine vinegar with 2 tsp Dijon mustard and 1 tsp honey and add 1 finely sliced banana shallot. Slice 300g black pudding into 2cm-thick pieces and fry in 1 tbsp oil for a few minutes on each side until browned and crisp. Drain on kitchen paper. Toss 3 heads of red chicory leaves and 2 large handfuls of watercress in one-third of the dressing. Top with the pears, walnuts and black pudding, drizzle with more dressing and serve while the pears and black pudding are still warm. Sweet and crisp, mellow and earthy. Feeds 4.

For the Ragú
good glug of olive oil

2 onions, finely chopped

1 large garlic clove, chopped

1 tsp hot smoked paprika

½ tsp ground cinnamon

250g good-quality soft
   black pudding (I like Brindisa
   or Laverstoke Park)

2 x 400g cans chopped tomatoes

1 tsp red wine vinegar

3 sprigs of thyme, leaves picked

25g pine nuts

For the Polenta
200g quick-cook polenta

25g butter

25g Parmesan, finely grated,
   plus extra to serve (optional)

Kamut Flour Soda Bread with Potted Shrimps

FEEDS FOUR

I grew to love soda bread at the Ballymaloe Cookery School, it is fast to prepare and has a deliciously crumbly texture. When made with kamut flour it manages to taste both sweet and earthy. It needs no kneading and can be baked in 1 hour, or 30 minutes if you make it into smaller scones instead. The important thing is to mix the wet ingredients away from the dry, then stir them together briefly and deftly into a wet, sticky dough and bake immediately for a beautifully light, crusty loaf.

Kamut or khorasan flour is an ancient Egyptian wholegrain wheat that an American farmer chanced upon at a market in the 1960s. Fascinated by the unusual looking grains, he started growing it. His son discovered that people who were intolerant to conventional wheat flours could easily digest this flour and it is now sold worldwide.

Preheat the oven to 200°C/gas 6 and oil a baking sheet with the vegetable oil.

Mix together the flour, salt and bicarbonate of soda and separately combine all the wet ingredients in a measuring jug. When the oven is up to temperature, pour the wet mixture into the dry and mix briefly and deftly with your hands. Form into a wet ball then place on the oiled baking sheet. Using a sharp knife, score a deep cross into the top of the dough. Sprinkle with flour and the pumpkin seeds and caraway seeds, if using, then bake on the middle shelf of the oven for 50 minutes–1 hour until the base sounds hollow when tapped. Allow to cool (it'll continue to cook out of the oven).

Meanwhile, prepare the shrimps. Melt the butter in a pan, then add all the ingredients apart from the shrimps. Simmer for a couple of minutes, being careful that the butter doesn't burn, then remove from the heat. When the butter has cooled a little, but not completely, add the brown shrimps and season generously with salt and pepper. Stir, then place the pan in the fridge, stirring every 3 minutes for 15 minutes until the butter starts to firm up. Before it hardens, pour into 4 x 150ml ramekins and leave to set for 20 minutes in the fridge. If not serving immediately, pour a layer of melted butter on top and keep covered in the fridge, removing 20 minutes before serving.

Serve the potted shrimps with thick slices of the soda bread and lemon wedges.

Kitchen Note:
If you can't find kamut flour, substitute with spelt or plain white flour but remember that kamut takes a little more liquid than other flours.

For the Bread
vegetable oil, for the baking sheet
500g kamut/khorasan flour,
   plus extra to dust
1 tsp fine salt
1 tsp bicarbonate of soda
200ml natural whole milk yogurt
300ml whole milk
150ml buttermilk
1 tbsp pumpkin seeds
½ tsp caraway seeds (optional)

For the Potted Shrimps
200g butter, plus more
   to seal if needed (optional)
1 blade of mace
1 bay leaf
¼ tsp paprika
juice of ½ lemon
200g peeled brown shrimps
lemon wedges, to serve

Mexican-Style Pizzas

There are two streets in Oaxaca City, Mexico, where you can find late night *tlayudas* made for the revellers crawling out of cantinas, mezcalerias and salsa bars. Although the originals are made with 100 per cent corn flour, I find it hard to make the texture work with the quality of corn flour we get here, so I compromise with a mixture of flour and fine cornmeal. Other than that I cook it straight over the charcoal of the barbecue, just like they do in Mexico. It is a real weekend treat and magic when we have families over; everyone just goes mad for them. Don't be afraid to let the dough char a little! The black bits are pure flavour.

Dissolve the yeast in the warm water with the sugar in a large mixing bowl. After 5 minutes stir in the salt, cornmeal, wholemeal flour and olive oil. Sift in the flour, stirring it in with a wooden spoon as you go until you have a stiff dough (you might not need all of it).

Lightly oil a work surface and turn the dough out onto it, oiling your hands too. Knead the dough for several minutes and, when it is smooth and shiny, transfer it to a clean, oiled bowl. Brush the dough with more oil, cover with a damp tea towel and leave it to rise in a warm place for 1½ 2 hours. Punch down the dough and knead again, using more oil on the work surface to prevent the dough sticking. Now divide into 4 balls (you can freeze them at this point, they will prove as they defrost), cover them in cling film and let them rise for about 45 minutes while you light the barbecue.

Brush a flat baking sheet with olive oil and put down 1 of the balls on it, turning it in the oil. Once well coated, use your hands to spread the dough out to a roughly 30cm rectangle or circle. Allow the dough to rest if it keeps shrinking back, before stretching out once more. Once the fire is hot, grab the 2 nearest corners of the dough and drape it over the grill. After a minute it will have puffed up and cooked on the underside. Flip it and transfer to a cool part of the barbecue while you brush it generously with olive oil and add 1 of the toppings overleaf. Give it a final drizzle of oil, pull half of it back over the hot part of the grill and slowly rotate the pizza so it evenly cooks all the way around, moving it to a cooler spot if it looks like it is burning. It is cooked when the top is bubbling and the cheese is melted.

If cooking these on the barbecue feels like a stretch too far, you can cook the pizzas on a chargrill or on a pizza stone in a very hot oven.

1 x 7g sachet active dry yeast

240ml warm water

pinch of sugar

2 tsp fine salt

50g fine cornmeal

3 tbsp wholemeal flour

1 tbsp extra-virgin olive oil,
    plus more to knead and grill

360–380g white flour

Mexican-Style
Pizzas (Continued)

Sobresada, Avocado & Pecorino

Sobresada is spreadable cooking chorizo but, if you can't get hold of it, use slices of ordinary cured chorizo. Dot the top of each pizza with 25g grated pecorino, 25g grated Parmesan and drizzle with 30g sobresada that you have warmed in a small pan. Season well and grill. Top the finished pizza with avocado and rocket and serve.

Sautéed Mushrooms, Chilli Oil, Thyme & Mozzarella

For every pizza try 100g mixed wild mushrooms in 2 tbsp olive oil, 2 finely chopped garlic cloves and some shredded thyme leaves for 10 minutes over a high heat until most of the moisture has evaporated. Use to top the pizza along with ½ large ball of sliced mozzarella and 25g grated pecorino. Drizzle with chilli oil (for home-made see page 295), season and grill.

Courgettes, Courgette Flowers, Chervil & Pecorino

For every pizza shave ½ courgette (yellow or green) with a peeler to get long, thin strips. Place on top of the pizza with 25g pecorino and ½ large ball of sliced mozzarella and strew with chervil and, if you can find any, some torn courgette flowers. Season well with salt, pepper and a drizzle of truffle oil (if you have some to hand) and grill.

Charred Tomatoes, Chipotle, Sautéed Onion & Mozzarella

For every 2 pizzas, dry-roast 1 punnet of cherry tomatoes in a dry frying pan for about 10 minutes until blackened all over (see page 104 for method). Meanwhile, sweat 1 finely sliced red onion in olive oil and thyme leaves until soft and translucent. Dot each pizza with half the tomatoes and onions and ½ large ball of sliced mozzarella and top with 25g grated pecorino and dollops of puréed chipotle in adobo. Season and grill.

Kitchen Note:

For a simpler, faster dough, mix together 200g white flour and ½ tsp fine sea salt with 100ml warm water and 3 tbsp olive oil in a large bowl. Turn out onto a lightly floured work surface and knead for 2 minutes until you have a very smooth, silky ball of dough. Leave to rest for 1 minute. Divide the dough into 2, then roll into circles about the size of your frying pan or barbecue. Heat a large frying pan with a drizzle of olive oil over a high heat, then add the rolled dough and fry for 2–3 minutes on each side until puffed and charring.

Chapter FIVE

FEEDING THE TROOPS

FEEDING THE TROOPS

For me, there is little more pleasing than seeing and feeding family or friends. Our friends are like an extension of family, but it is hard to see them for more than snatched moments unless we are in one another's homes, when time seems to slow down. Any excuse to meet up is a boon and – invariably – our dinners grow because I keep adding people to the guest list. My husband Mark is quite used to discovering that a lunch planned for six has turned into a party for 15.

There is something happy and soothing about spending a few focused but relaxed hours chopping, bashing and mixing ingredients to create something delicious that you know will give pleasure, but I don't think you have to be a perfect hostess with everything pristine and ready; more often than not a few friends end up mucking in. Those who want to, gather around the large island in my kitchen, which is essentially one giant wooden chopping board. I'll set them up with a stool and a fat drink and arm them with a knife for chopping, greens for washing, herbs for picking or beans for podding. I fear I am quite bossy in this environment, giving people clear instructions on exactly how I want things to be, but mostly they seem to come back!

When throwing parties and entertaining, I strongly believe that perfection shouldn't be your goal and that if you are relaxed about when dinner hits the table, then people will have fun. Just make sure that the drinks flow, there is something delicious to nibble on and music in the background. And make life simple for yourself if you are short on time. If you are cooking quite an involved main course for a large gang, give yourself a break by buying cheese and a few dates for pudding, or by prepping stuff the day before. It will make the world of difference to how you enjoy your evening. If people realise that you are thrilled to be with them, they will be as thrilled to be with you.

Roast Chicken & Other Stories

Very often our lunches or dinners are last-minute arrangements, where we are suddenly expecting a mass of people who need to be fed, but with next-to-no-time to cook. Roast chicken is my fallback recipe on these occasions; you can always be creative with how you cook it. Given that the chicken is the star of the show here, I'd advise buying something of good quality from a farmer's market, a brilliant online seller such as www.fossemeadows.com, or at the butcher. Buy the chicken with the gizzards and livers inside; stash the livers in the freezer until you have enough to make a pâté and use the gizzards for a stock (see pages 74 and 46).

My Ultimate Roast Chicken with Lemon, Caramelised Garlic & Thyme

Preheat the oven to the highest setting. Season the chicken inside and out, then stuff with the lemon half, half the herbs, plus 1 onion half. Roughly slice the rest of the onions, spread them over a roasting tray and scatter in the garlic and the rest of the herbs. Rub the chicken with the oil and season generously with salt and pepper. Pull the legs slightly away from the body and then sit the chicken, breast side down, on top of the onions and place in the oven. Immediately reduce the oven temperature to 190°C/gas 5 and cook for just over 1 hour (30 minutes per kilo plus 15 minutes for good measure). The chicken is cooked when the juices run clear when the thickest part of the thigh is pierced with a skewer (if in doubt you can also cut the thigh away from the body and see if it is cooked in that crevice). For the most succulent meat, it is very important to rest the chicken in a warm place, covered in foil, for 15 minutes while you make the gravy.

Meanwhile, pop the potatoes in a large baking tray with the garlic and herbs. Pour over the oil, season well with salt and pepper and give everything a good toss. Roast in the same oven as the chicken, occasionally stirring and adding a little more oil if they look dry. They will be crisp and golden in about 1 hour.

Skim off most of the fat in the chicken roasting tray, leaving behind a few tbsp, then put it over a medium heat. Crumble in the stock cube and whisk in the flour. Let it cook over the heat for a few minutes, to cook out the raw flavour. Pour in the wine, a little at a time, allowing to bubble for a minute between each addition. Allow to boil for a few moments, then pour in enough boiling water to thin to your desired consistency (anything between 200–400ml). Simmer for 5–10 minutes and check for seasoning; I like plenty of salt and pepper in my gravy. Discard any herbs but save the delicious onions and garlic to serve with the chicken and pour the gravy through a sieve (though if it's just family I don't bother). Pour into a warm jug, carve the chicken and dish up!

For the Chicken
1 whole chicken, about 1.6kg
½ lemon
8 sprigs of thyme or
    2 sprigs of rosemary
4 bay leaves
2 white onions, halved
5 garlic cloves
1 tbsp olive oil

For the Potatoes
1kg baby new potatoes,
    scrubbed and halved
5 garlic cloves
handful of sprigs of thyme,
    oregano or rosemary
4 tbsp olive oil

For the Gravy
½ chicken stock cube
1 tbsp plain flour
150ml dry white wine

Brilliant Sauces
with Chicken

Green Tahini

Crush 1 garlic clove with salt in a pestle and mortar, and stir in 2 tbsp tahini. Whizz a bunch each of tarragon, basil and parsley with 6 tbsp oil in a food processor, then stir into the tahini with a small tub of Greek yogurt and the juice of 1 lemon. Season well.

Green Aioli

Blitz 1–2 garlic cloves with 1 tsp salt, 1 jalapeño chilli and a bunch each of basil and coriander in a food processor. Stir in the finely grated zest and juice of 1–2 limes and 300g good-quality shop-bought or home-made mayonnaise (see page 288).

Muhammara

Place 2 roasted and skinned red peppers (see page 73) in a food processor with 30g fresh breadcrumbs, 1 tbsp pomegranate molasses (see pages 277 and 298 for home-made), 1 tsp ground cumin, 1 tsp Aleppo chilli flakes, 1 finely chopped garlic clove and 30g walnuts. Blitz roughly until coarse, then stir in 3 tbsp olive oil and a squeeze of lemon juice.

Four More Chicken Feasts

California Roast Chicken with Citrus, Oregano & Chilli

Fry 75g pancetta until it begins to release its fat, then add 2 chopped garlic cloves and 1 chopped banana shallot and cook until everything is softened. Stir in 2 handfuls of fresh white breadcrumbs (see page 277 for home-made), 1 tbsp dried oregano, ½ tsp chilli flakes, the finely grated zest of ½ orange and ½ lemon and 1 beaten egg. Season generously, then take off the heat and leave to cool. Stuff into the cavity of the chicken, making sure you don't stuff the chicken too tightly, as it needs to cook evenly. Cook (see page 129), but deseed 3 peppers (2 red and 1 orange), cut into wedges and add to the roasting tray with the potatoes. It will need about 10 minutes more in the oven. I love this with Guacamole (see page 222).

The Most Luscious Roast Chicken with Tarragon Butter

Combine 75g softened butter with a large handful each of chopped parsley and tarragon leaves, 1 crushed garlic clove and the finely grated zest of 1 lemon. Season well. If you like, peel a celeriac and chop into walnut-sized pieces (or try a few bulbs of fennel in summer). Throw into a roasting tin with some garlic and thyme. Season well. Pop one-third of the butter inside the chicken with ½ onion and ½ lemon and rub the rest all over it. Cook as on page 129, stirring the vegetables a few times during cooking.

Coriander Seed and Miso Roast Chicken

Combine 60g miso paste with 60ml soy sauce, 1 tbsp olive oil, ½ tsp chilli flakes and 1 tbsp crushed coriander seeds. Smear all over the chicken and marinate for 1 hour. Sit on a bed of leeks and cook as on page 129, pouring 1 glass of dry sherry into the pan 30 minutes before the end.

Flattened Sweet Cinnamon Roast Chicken

Soak 250g basmati rice in water. Remove the backbone from the chicken with a pair of kitchen scissors and then push down on the breastbone to flatten it out (or ask a friendly butcher to do this for you). Grind the seeds from 10 cardamom pods, 1 tsp allspice berries and 1 tsp black peppercorns and mix with 1 tbsp ground cinnamon. Rub half this mix all over the chicken with 2 tbsp olive oil and season with plenty of salt and pepper. Roast the chicken skin side up in a 200°C/gas 6 oven for 25–30 minutes. Meanwhile fry 2 chopped onions in more oil and the rest of the spices. Once the onions are soft, stir in the drained rice. Pour in 500ml chicken stock (see page 46 for home-made), or water, add a few bay leaves, season and simmer for 20 minutes, covered. Turn off the heat and leave to steam-cook until tender. Serve with the chicken and lemon wedges.

Leftover Chicken Ideas

Croutons, Raisins, Pine Nuts & Chicory Salad

Rip up some sourdough or other coarse-textured bread, drizzle with oil and place in an oven preheated to 180°C/gas 4 oven for 10–12 minutes until golden. Meanwhile, make a dressing with a few tbsp plump raisins, 1 tbsp sherry vinegar, 4 tbsp olive oil and a handful of chopped parsley leaves. Shred the chicken and toss with chicory leaves, the croutons, toasted pine nuts and the dressing.

Devilled Chicken Salad

Combine 2 tsp mustard powder with 2 tsp cayenne, 2 crushed garlic cloves, 4 tbsp Worcestershire sauce, 1 tbsp brown sugar, 2 tbsp tomato purée and the juice of ½ lemon. Rub into cooked chicken and fry in butter until hot and crisp at the edges. Or use to marinate raw chicken thighs and fry until crisp. Serve with Cos lettuce dressed with 3 tbsp extra-virgin olive oil, capers, parsley and lemon juice.

Avocado, Watercress & Chicken Wrap

Warm up a tortilla wrap, smear it with Green Aioli (see page 130) then stuff the wrap with shredded chicken, sliced avocado and a handful of watercress. Roll up and eat up!

Smoky Chicken Tinga

Heat 2 tbsp olive oil in a pan with a knob of butter and sauté 1 large finely sliced onion with ½ tsp ground allspice, ½ tsp ground cinnamon and 2 tsp Demerara sugar. Season well and when the onion is soft add 2 crushed garlic cloves and continue to cook for a few minutes before adding 2 tbsp Smoky Chipotle Paste (see page 286) and 2 x 400g cans plum tomatoes. Cook for 10 minutes to develop the flavours and then stir in about 700g cooked shredded chicken. Serve in wraps, on rice or in baked potatoes with slices of avocado and soured cream.

Chicken Cacciatore Spaghetti

Fry 4 chopped anchovy fillets gently in oil with 2 chopped garlic cloves and a sprig of chopped rosemary until fragrant. Add ½ glass of white wine, a handful of pitted black olives and 1 x 400g can chopped tomatoes. Add 500g cooked shredded chicken and simmer for 5–10 minutes to warm through. Stir through hot spaghetti and sprinkle with a little finely grated Parmesan before serving.

Chicken & Shiitake Broth

Fry 200g chopped shiitake mushrooms with 1 chopped garlic clove and a thumb-sized piece of peeled and finely chopped fresh ginger in sesame oil until soft, then stir in some shredded chicken and a splash of soy sauce. Combine this with cooked soba noodles and shredded spring greens, then pour over hot chicken broth and serve.

Braised Oxtail with Saffron Risotto & Orange Gremolata

FEEDS SIX—EIGHT

For the Oxtail

olive oil, to fry

2 oxtails, cut into chunks

1 tbsp plain flour

2 onions, finely sliced

3 garlic cloves, finely sliced

3 bay leaves

2 sprigs of rosemary

1 star anise

1 cinnamon stick

pared rind of ½ orange

1 x 400g can plum tomatoes, drained

500ml red wine

500ml beef stock

6 carrots, halved lengthways

For the Saffron Risotto

150g butter

2 onions, finely chopped

2 celery sticks, finely chopped

500g Carnaroli rice

125ml dry vermouth

1.5–1.75 litres chicken stock
   (see page 46 for home-made)

1 tsp saffron threads,
   soaked in 2 tbsp hot water

100g Parmesan, finely grated

For the Gremolata

finely grated zest of 1 small orange

½ garlic clove, very finely chopped

½ bunch of parsley, leaves
   picked and finely chopped

The secret to making a great risotto is energetic stirring – almost beating – with a wooden spoon. This helps bind the starches and fat to create the famously creamy texture. The flavour of this oxtail improves immeasurably if you cook it a few days in advance.

Preheat the oven to 170°C/gas 3.

Heat 1 tbsp of oil in a heavy-based casserole over a medium-high heat. Dust the oxtail in well-seasoned flour and brown the pieces in batches, adding more oil as needed.

Wipe the pan clean, reduce the heat and add another 2 tbsp of oil. Sweat the onions for 5–10 minutes until soft and sweet, seasoning with salt and pepper and adding the garlic after 5 minutes. Add the herbs, spices, orange rind and tomatoes and return the oxtail to the pan. Pour over the wine and enough stock to just cover the meat and bring to the boil. Season generously, partially cover with a lid and pop in the oven for about 3 hours until the meat is falling off the bone. Add the carrots in the last hour. Leave the casserole to cool, when a layer of fat should have risen to the surface. Skim off the excess and, if the sauce is a little thin, remove the meat and simmer the sauce to thicken.

For the risotto, melt half the butter in a heavy-based pan, wider than it is tall, over a medium heat. Add the onions and celery and a pinch of salt and sweat for 10 minutes until soft, then add the rice and stir well so that every grain is coated in butter.

Pour in the vermouth and as soon as it begins to bubble start adding the stock a ladleful at a time. It is worth keeping the stock warm over a gentle heat. Beat the

rice well with a wooden spoon between each addition and make sure the stock is absorbed before adding more. Halfway through, add the saffron and continue adding the stock until most has been absorbed and the risotto has a light nutty bite to it, 15–20 minutes. You may need more or less stock, depending on the rice. Note that the risotto will keep on absorbing liquid after you have removed it from the heat. Stir in the remaining butter and the Parmesan and check the seasoning, adding a little more liquid if the risotto is too thick. Keep warm.

Chop all the gremolata ingredients on a board until very fine. Spoon generous dollops of risotto onto hot plates, top with the oxtail and lots of sauce and sprinkle the gremolata on top.

Why not try saffron arancini?

Allow the saffron risotto to cool, then roll into balls, poking a small hole in the centre and stuffing with mozzarella, blue cheese, meat ragu or sautéed mushrooms and finely chopped rosemary. Beat 1 egg with 170g plain flour and 170ml water to make a batter, then roll the balls in the batter, followed by breadcrumbs (see page 277 for home-made). Heat a pan of vegetable oil to 170°C and fry until golden. Sprinkle with salt and serve with aioli (see page 288) or a rich tomato sauce.

Duck Legs with Silky Rich Veracruzan Tomato Sauce

FEEDS FOUR—SIX

This unusual, bewitching dish is a good way to convince doubters of the subtleties of real Mexican food. It is from Veracruz, where Cortez first landed in the Americas. At that time Spain occupied Sicily, so traders brought capers and olives with them to Mexico and returned to Europe with cacao, tomatoes and gold.

The olives, capers and sherry lend a piquant savoury character to this slow-cooked tomato sauce; the jalapeños a light touch of heat; the spices a gentle warmth and complexity; the tomatoes acidity and sweetness, cutting through the rich flavour of the duck. I always prefer to cook the legs and breast of the duck separately; the breast needs to be eaten pink so is seared quickly over a high heat, whereas legs, with more flavour, need slow cooking.

Season the duck legs generously with salt and pepper and leave for 10–15 minutes to come to room temperature.

Heat the oil in a large heavy-based casserole and put in the legs, skin side down. Keep the heat on medium-high and brown the legs, rendering the fat for about 15 minutes, decanting as much fat as possible halfway through and adjusting the heat so that the skin crisps and browns but does not burn. Once they are a lovely golden colour, transfer them to a plate. You should have about 4 tbsp of duck fat in the pan.

4 large duck legs

1 tbsp olive oil

1 large Spanish onion, finely chopped

2 carrots, finely diced

½ fennel bulb, finely chopped

2 celery sticks, finely diced

4 fat garlic cloves, finely chopped

3–4 bay leaves (preferably fresh)

handful of oregano leaves, or thyme

1 large cinnamon stick

1 star anise

2 x 400g cans plum tomatoes

100ml Manzanilla sherry

200ml chicken stock
   (see page 46 for home-made)

40g pickled jalapeños

40g capers

120g good-quality green olives,
   pitted and roughly chopped

Add the onion, reduce the heat to medium and sweat gently for 5 minutes before adding the carrots, fennel, celery and garlic. Season generously and allow the vegetables to soften in the fat for about 10 minutes, stirring occasionally.

Now add the herbs, spices, tomatoes, sherry and stock and cook for about 5 minutes, breaking up the tomatoes with a wooden spoon and bringing everything up to a gentle simmer. Put the duck legs, plus any duck juices, back into the casserole and put a lid on the pan, slightly askew to allow some gentle evaporation of the sauce. Stew very gently over a low heat, so that the sauce is barely bubbling, for about 1½ hours or until the duck meat is tender and falls away from the bones.

About 10 minutes before the end of the cooking time, stir in the jalapeños, capers and olives. Check and adjust the seasoning and serve with brown basmati rice and some sautéed greens. I also love it with Smashed Courgette Salad (see page 227).

Kitchen Note:

Make more of the ragu than you need. You can eat the leftover sauce over steaming bowls of polenta or wide noodles such as pappardelle.

Beef Rendang with Cucumber Relish

FEEDS FOUR—SIX

This is sensationally easy to cook once you have gathered together all the exotic spices and seasonings. I like to get all the ingredients organised in various small bowls beforehand. Then all you have to do is cover the meat in the paste that you have whizzed together and cook it slowly for a few hours. The dish is a fiery riot of flavour.

For the Beef

1.5kg chuck or feather blade
   steak, cut into chunks
2 x 400ml cans coconut milk
2 tsp soft light brown sugar
2 tsp salt

For the Spice Paste

2 tamarind pods
1 tbsp coriander seeds
1 tsp cumin seeds
1 cinnamon stick
4 cloves
2 star anise
1 tbsp cardamom pods
6 dried Kashmiri chillies,
   stalks removed
thumb-sized piece of fresh ginger,
   peeled and finely chopped
6 garlic cloves, finely chopped
1 lemon grass stick,
   outer layer reserved,
   the rest roughly chopped
1 onion, roughly chopped
1 tsp ground turmeric
1 tbsp chopped galangal (optional)

For the Cucumber Relish

1 cucumber
1 tsp salt
2 bird's eye chillies, deseeded
   and very finely sliced
1 small red onion, very finely sliced
3 tbsp lime juice
2 tsp caster sugar
1 tsp fish sauce

Cover the tamarind pods for the spice paste with about 70ml boiling water and leave to sit for 10 minutes. Heat the coriander seeds, cumin seeds, cinnamon, cloves, star anise, cardamom pods and dried chillies in a dry frying pan for a few minutes. When they are smelling aromatic and wonderful, tip into a spice grinder and grind to a fine powder. Put the ginger, garlic, chopped lemon grass, onion, turmeric and galangal, if using, in a food processor, with the ground spices. Work the tamarind pods into the hot water in which they have been steeping, dissolving as much of the fruit pulp as possible. Push through a sieve, add 2 tbsp of the tamarind water to the food processor and blend everything to a smooth paste.

Tip the paste into a large, heavy-based pan and add the reserved outer lemon grass layer, the beef, the rest of the tamarind water, the coconut milk, sugar and salt. Bring to a simmer and cook, uncovered, for about 2½ hours, stirring every now and then. Stir more frequently towards the end of cooking to stop it from sticking. Eventually the oil from the coconut milk will start to separate from the sauce, but continue to cook for a minute or so longer, to allow the meat and its coating to fry lightly in the oil. Remove and discard the lemon grass and check the seasoning.

For the cucumber relish, peel the cucumber, cut it in half lengthways and scoop out the seeds with a teaspoon. Cut across into thin, half-moon slices and toss in a colander with the salt. Leave for 15 minutes, then rinse with cold water and dry on a tea towel. Mix with all the remaining ingredients.

Serve the rendang with the cucumber relish, some sesame oil-tossed greens such as pak choy and steamed rice.

Why not try lemon grass vichyssoise?

Strip the leaves from a large handful of coriander. Trim 3 thick lemon grass sticks and remove the outer layers. Do the same with 5 spring onions. Take all the trimmings, wash and put in a pan with the coriander stalks and 800ml of water and simmer, covered, for 30 minutes. Melt 50g butter in a large pan, add the chopped lemon grass inners, 2 chopped onions and 300g new potatoes, cut into small chunks. Sweat for 10 minutes then pour in the strained stock. Add 160ml whole milk and most of the coriander leaves and season generously. Simmer for 20–25 minutes. Cool, add half a chopped cucumber, blitz and strain. Adjust the consistency to your liking with water. Serve chilled, with the remaining coriander leaves and a squeeze of lime juice. Feeds 4, or 8 as a starter.

Braised Beef Short Ribs with Dried Mexican Chillies

FEEDS SIX

For the Braised Beef

about 2½ kg beef short ribs,
    cut into 10–15cm lengths
4 ancho chillies
3–4 chipotle or Pasilla
    de Oaxaca chillies
2 onions, roughly chopped
1 carrot, chopped
2 celery sticks, chopped
2 star anise
1 cinnamon stick
1 tsp allspice berries
1 bay leaf
½ head of garlic
2 beef tomatoes, chopped
250ml red wine
750ml good-quality chicken stock
   (see page 46 for home-made)
100g raisins

For the Polenta

300g quick-cook polenta
75g butter
75g Parmesan, finely grated

Short ribs are a very fashionable cut of meat from the States, previously known over here as 'Jacob's Ladder'. I first came across them many years ago when I did some cooking with Enrique Olvera, who was trying to find the cut in London ... not a single butcher knew what he was talking about! Now they seem to be a feature on every cool street food menu.

Here I give them a very Mexican treatment, slow-cooking them for several hours with dried Mexican chillies, which give a rich, subtle background heat to the sauce as well as immense flavour.

Season the ribs generously with salt and pepper and leave them to sit for a few hours, preferably overnight. Preheat the oven to 230°C/gas 8.

Put the ribs in a large roasting tray and roast for 25 minutes until golden and some of the fat has rendered out. While the meat is roasting, tear open the chillies, empty out and discard the seeds and the stalks and tear the flesh into large pieces.

Once the meat has had its initial sear in the hot oven, remove the tray and reduce the oven temperature to 160°C/gas 3. At this stage if you want a less rich, lighter sauce you can pour out some of the excess fat. Remove the ribs temporarily from the tray and fill with the remaining ingredients, including the torn chilli pieces, which you should try to submerge underneath the liquid. Put the ribs on top of the vegetables, cover tightly with foil and roast for 3–4 hours until the ribs are tender and falling apart. Remove the ribs, strip the meat from the bones and set the meat aside. Empty the remaining contents of the roasting tray into a deep pan and top up with 200ml water. Whizz it all with a stick blender until smooth.

To make the polenta, bring 1.25 litres of well-salted water to the boil in a deep pan. Pour in the polenta in a steady stream, stirring continuously with a wooden spoon for 5 minutes (you might want to wrap your stirring hand in a kitchen paper as the polenta will bubble up). Remove from the heat and stir in the butter and Parmesan.

Gently heat up the sauce, adding more stock to get it to the desired consistency. To serve, pour the polenta into shallow bowls, put the ribs on top and pour over the sauce. Alternatively use the ribs to fill tacos, burritos or with noodles or rice.

Kitchen Tip:

If you want to introduce yourself to cooking with Mexican chillies this is an ideal recipe; the ancho chillies lend sweetness and the chipotles a wonderful smokiness. If you can get hold of the rare Pasilla de Oaxaca chillies even better, as their smoky flavour is in another league. Mexican chillies are now widely available in larger supermarkets (where they are more expensive) and online: try the South Devon Chilli Farm or Cool Chile Co). They keep for at least a year in the cupboard, so buy lots to keep.

Braised Pork in Cider with Celeriac & Apple Mash

FEEDS EIGHT

The classic, soothing flavours of this slow-cooked joint are a dream and it is very undemanding to make. The children love the hint of apple in the mash, which gives it sweetness and sharpness, in fact the combination of celeriac and apple is so good that I have also turned it into a soup, laced with toasted hazelnuts (see page 50).

Rub the pork skin in 1 tsp of the salt and place uncovered in the fridge to dry out.

Preheat the oven to 150°C/gas 2. In a pestle and mortar, bash the fennel and caraway seeds and the peppercorns with the remaining 2 tsp of salt.

Heat the olive oil in a large, deep casserole over a medium-high heat. Brown the pork on all sides, then remove and set aside.

Scatter the onions, celery, garlic and bay leaves in the casserole, then rub the spice mix into the pork and sit it on top of the vegetables. Pour over the cider, then cover and place in the oven for 3½–5 hours (cooking times for pork shoulder vary wildly), turning, basting and checking it every hour or so. You know it's done when the meat is soft and pulls apart easily. Remove and keep warm.

Increase the oven temperature to 220°C/gas 8 and place the pork skin on a rack over a roasting tray. Place in the oven for 20–30 minutes until it has crisped up and is golden. (You can always put it under the grill for a few minutes if it needs a final push.)

Meanwhile, cut the celeriac and potatoes into small chunks, aiming to make the celeriac smaller than the potatoes. Place in a large pan, cover with water and add plenty of salt. Bring to the boil and cook until tender, approximately 15 minutes.

While the celeriac and potatoes are cooking, cut the apples into small cubes, cover with boiling water and return to the boil. Cook for 5 minutes or until the apples are just tender. Pour everything into a large colander, then return to the large pan and, using plenty of elbow grease, roughly mash everything together, stirring in the butter and crème fraîche as you go. If you prefer super-smooth mash you can always use a potato ricer, if you have one. Season to taste.

Pull the pork apart with a couple of forks and chop up the crackling. Serve with a dollop of mash and plenty of cooking juices and anything green, either salad or a steamed leafy vegetable.

For the Braised Pork

2kg boneless pork shoulder, skin removed and scored by the butcher

3 tsp salt

2 tsp fennel seeds

1 tsp caraway seeds

½ tsp peppercorns

2 tbsp olive oil

3 onions, thickly sliced

2 celery sticks, cut into quarters

6 garlic cloves

5 bay leaves

250ml cider

For the Celeriac Mash

1kg celeriac, peeled

500g floury potatoes, peeled

2 apples, peeled and cored

50g butter

100g crème fraîche

Picadillo with Lettuce Tacos

FEEDS FOUR—SIX

For the Picadillo

300g minced beef

300g minced pork

1 large onion, finely chopped

4 tbsp olive oil

2 garlic cloves, finely chopped

1 large apple, peeled,
    cored and chopped

2 chipotle chillies

½ tsp ground cinnamon

½ tsp ground cumin

¼ tsp ground cloves

70g raisins

2 x 400g cans plum tomatoes

60g green olives, pitted
    and roughly chopped

2 tbsp red wine vinegar

350ml beef stock
    (see page 47 for home-made)

pinch of brown sugar

60g blanched almonds

large handful of chopped
    chervil or parsley leaves

To Serve

4–6 Baby Gems, washed
    and separated into leaves

lime wedges

hot sauce

Sweet Cucumber Relish
    (optional, see page 300)

Picadillo is a classic Mexican dish and is the inspiration behind the Texan Chile con Carne. In Mexico it is made with sautéed plantain, pineapple and apple, but for simplicity I use just apple, or apple and plantain. It is a great delicacy in Veracruz, used to stuff little deep-fried smoked meco chillies, while in other parts it is stuffed inside ancho chillies or poblanos to make the national dish, *chiles en nogada*.

When you start out you can't believe that the minced meat and various ingredients are going to taste that special but as you continue to layer the spices, fruits and seasonings, the flavours build to make an utterly wonderful dish. Here I serve it in light refreshing lettuce cups, Asian-style.

Mix the meats together in a bowl and season generously with salt and pepper.

Sweat the onion in half the oil over a medium heat for 5 minutes before adding the garlic, apple, chillies, spices and raisins. Cook for another 5 minutes until the onions look translucent, then add the rest of the oil to the pan with some of the meat. Keep frying, increasing the heat a little and breaking up the meat with a wooden spoon into the smallest crumbs possible, then adding more meat until it is all browned.

Add the tomatoes, olives, vinegar and stock, bring up to heat and simmer gently for 20–25 minutes. Taste and season again with salt and pepper and a pinch of brown sugar. Toast the almonds in a dry frying pan and roughly chop. Stir them into the picadillo, transfer it to a hot dish and sprinkle with the chervil or parsley.

Lay out the lettuce leaves on plates, spoon over the picadillo and serve with lime wedges, hot sauce and the Sweet Cucumber Relish, if using.

Kitchen Note:

This picadillo is very easy to scale up. I once made it for a dinner of 50, you just need a pan big enough. You can also serve the picadillo inside rehydrated ancho chillies (soak the deseeded chillies in boiling water seasoned with 2 tbsp brown sugar and 2 tbsp cider vinegar for 15 minutes) or in jacket potatoes, with rice, with spaghetti or in burritos.

Ten-Hour Porchetta with Borlotti & Pea Salsa

Porchetta is the Italian equivalent of a hog roast, only in my opinion it is infinitely better with its filling of herbs and garlic. The borlotti and pea salsa is a wonderful vivid green partner to the succulent pork. It is ideal party food, especially as you can do most of the prep the night before. You could also serve the porchetta the traditional way and stuff it into crusty bread rolls.

For the Pork

3.5kg boneless pork shoulder

1 tsp salt

1½ tbsp fennel seeds, toasted

1 tsp chilli flakes, toasted

1 whole head of garlic, cloves crushed

large bunch of parsley leaves

handful of sage leaves

2 tbsp each of rosemary
   and thyme leaves

2 large slices of stale bread
   (preferably from a dense
   loaf such as a sourdough)

large handful of wild fennel leaves
   or the fronds from 3 fennel
   bulbs, chopped (optional)

4 tbsp olive oil

200ml white wine

For the Beans

300g dried borlotti
   (or cannellini) beans

2 tsp bicarbonate of soda

For the Pea Salsa

500g peas (frozen or fresh)

handful each of basil, mint and tarragon
   leaves, washed and shaken dry

100ml olive oil

2 tbsp capers

4 anchovy fillets in oil, drained

juice of 1 lemon

Ask your butcher to butterfly the pork shoulder to a fairly even thickness of about 2.5cm; you want a large rectangular sheet that you are going to stuff and roll. Lay the shoulder skin side down on a large chopping board or work surface and season generously with the salt. Meanwhile preheat the oven to 110°C/gas ¼.

Grind the fennel seeds and chilli in a pestle and mortar, then tip into a food processor with the rest of the ingredients for the porchetta, except the wine, and pulse to make a vivid green paste. Spread all over the pork, wrap up tightly into a long roll and tie up with butcher's string at intervals along the length of the pork. Now wrap up tightly in foil, so as not to allow any steam to escape, and bake ion a tray n the oven for 8–10 hours until completely tender (I do this overnight).

Soak the borlotti beans overnight in plenty of cold water with the bicarbonate of soda. The next day remove the pork from the oven and allow to cool. Drain the beans, add to a pan and cover with at least 10cm of fresh cold water. Bring to the boil and cook for 30–60 minutes, or until tender. Drain, reserving half a cup of the cooking liquid.

About an hour before you are ready to eat, preheat the oven to its highest setting, unwrap the pork and roast in the oven until the skin is crisp and golden brown, about 30 minutes. Once golden, remove from the oven and allow to rest while you pour the wine into the juices and herbs in the pan and stir over a medium-high heat, scraping all the bits at the bottom of the pan. Strain through a sieve and keep warm.

Meanwhile blanch the peas for 2–3 minutes in boiling water, drain and rinse briefly under a cold tap. Blitz with the rest of the salsa ingredients and fold into the beans and reserved cooking liquid, warming the whole lot gently and seasoning to taste with salt and pepper. Serve slices of the pork with the salsa and the gravy.

Kitchen Note:

The leftovers make amazing banh-mi sandwiches. Spread baguettes with Delicious Chicken Liver Pâté (see page 74) or a good shop-bought pork pâté. Stuff with sautéed pork slices, some Pickled Carrot (see page 164) and a hot chilli sauce.

Lamb Shoulder Three Ways

I love the texture and flavour of a shoulder of lamb (or mutton), slow-cooked until so soft that you can pull it apart with a spoon. The cooking is incredibly forgiving, allowing you to bung the lamb in the oven and forget about it for several hours (ideal if you have crammed the weekend with children, outings, errands and other things). I love the way lamb can take on the flavours of so many different continents; with a few well-chosen spices you can be transported to the Mediterranean, the Levant, the sub-continent or the Americas. Here are a few of my favourite recipes.

Slow-Roasted with Anchovies, Rosemary & Potatoes

A classic for a reason.

Preheat the oven to 150°C/gas 3.

Prepare the potatoes first. Cut them into very thin slices (a mandoline is best, but the slicing attachment on a food processor will also do). Layer the potatoes with the sliced onions, rosemary and garlic in a deep roasting tin that's large enough to take the lamb, seasoning each layer with plenty of salt and pepper. Pour over the wine and stock.

Mix together the garlic, anchovies, capers and oil, then make shallow slashes all over the lamb before rubbing in the anchovy mixture. Season the outside with salt and pepper. Lay the lamb on top of the potatoes and cover the pan tightly with foil. Roast for 3 hours, then remove the foil, pour the cream into the pan and cook for a further hour until the lamb is tender enough to pull apart with 2 forks.

Transfer the meat to a carving board, and shred or carve it as you like. Serve with the potatoes and some greens on the side.

For the Potatoes

1.25kg floury potatoes, such as Maris Piper or King Edward, peeled
2 large onions, finely sliced
2 sprigs of rosemary, leaves stripped and finely chopped
2 garlic cloves, finely sliced
200ml white wine
500ml chicken stock (see page 46 for home-made)

For the Lamb

4 garlic cloves, crushed with a little salt
8 anchovy fillets in oil, drained and finely chopped
1 heaped tbsp capers, finely chopped
1 tbsp olive oil
1 bone-in lamb shoulder (about 2kg)
200ml single cream

Lamb Shoulder Three Ways (Continued)

Lamb Shoulder Braised with Dried Mexican Chillies & Borlotti Beans

Preheat the oven to 160°C/gas 3. Pour boiling water over 2 ancho chillies and 1 chipotle chilli and leave to soften for 10 minutes. Remove the stem and seeds and place in a food processor with 4 chopped garlic cloves, 2 tbsp redcurrant jelly, 1 tsp ground cumin and 2 tbsp olive oil. Whizz until smooth, then make lots of shallow slashes all over the lamb before rubbing in the chilli mixture. Season well, then place in a deep roasting tin with 100ml water, stock or red wine, 2 x 400g cans drained borlotti beans, 1 x 400g can chopped tomatoes and a few fresh bay leaves. Season well with salt and pepper, cover with foil and roast for 3 hours, then remove the foil and cook for a further hour until the lamb is tender enough to pull apart with 2 forks. Serve with tortillas and Guacamole (see page 222). *Feeds 6–8.*

Souk Lamb Shoulder Braised with Tomatoes, Chickpeas & Moroccan Spices

Preheat the oven to 160°C/gas 3. In a pestle and mortar, bash the leaves from 4 sprigs of thyme and 2 sprigs of rosemary, then add 2 garlic cloves, and a little salt and bash until you have a rough paste. Stir in 1 tsp each of ground cumin, coriander, paprika and cinnamon, ½ tsp ground fennel and 2 tbsp olive oil. Make lots of shallow slashes all over the lamb shoulder, then rub in the spice paste and season well with salt and pepper. Place in a deep roasting tin with 100ml stock or water, 2 x 400g cans rinsed and drained chickpeas, 1 x 400g can plum tomatoes and 1 tsp dried oregano and cover with foil. Roast for 3 hours, then remove the foil and cook for a further hour until the lamb is tender enough to pull apart with 2 forks. Serve with a saffron-laced couscous and raisin salad and Roast Carrots & Parsnips (see page 117). *Feeds 6–8.*

Thai Green Sea Bass with Galangal, Lemon Grass & Coconut

I made this for a group of very old friends who all happened to be in London between Christmas and New Year. I had no idea what I was going to cook, but when I got to the supermarket I realised that it had all the ingredients to make a really delicious Thai paste, including galangal and lemon grass. I called the fishmonger and, as luck would have it, he had wild sea bass. The paste took about 20 minutes to make from start to finish, which was just as well, given how last-minute my arrangements were. We feasted like kings that night on the succulent sea bass flesh, almost melting into the sweet, hot, aromatic paste.

For the Fish

1 whole sea bass (1.5–2kg in weight)

a few lime leaves (optional)

a few slices of lime (optional)

100ml water, fish or vegetable stock
   (see page 47 for home-made)

lime wedges, to serve

For the Thai Paste

2 star anise

½ cinnamon stick

1 tbsp black peppercorns

thumb-sized piece of fresh galangal,
   peeled and roughly sliced

thumb-sized piece of fresh
   ginger, peeled and roughly sliced

4 garlic cloves, bashed
   to remove the skin

3 banana shallots, roughly chopped

3 lemon grass sticks, outer
   layer removed and kept aside,
   the rest roughly chopped

6–8 bird's eye chillies, or to taste

2 tbsp fish sauce

juice of 2–3 limes

2 tbsp Demerara sugar

large bunch of coriander, leaves
   and stalks chopped separately

1 x 400ml can coconut milk

First make the Thai paste: grind the spices in a spice grinder or pestle and mortar. Put in a food processor with the galangal, ginger, garlic, shallots, lemon grass (reserving the outer layers), chillies, fish sauce, lime juice and sugar. Blitz to a rough paste.

Add the chopped coriander stalks and coconut milk to the paste with ½ teaspoon salt and blitz again until all the ingredients are combined. At this stage taste the paste, it will taste hotter before baking so if you want to add more chillies do so at this stage (when the paste is baked the chilli heat will reduce dramatically). The paste will last for a week in the fridge, or for a month in the freezer.

Preheat the oven to 200°C/gas 6. Lay out the bass in a deep roasting tin large enough to fit it comfortably. Make a few slashes in both sides of the body and cover with enough paste, inside and out, so that it is well coated. If you have any lime leaves you could stuff them inside the cavity of the bass at this stage with the lemon grass outer layers and, if you like, a few slices of lime. Mix the rest of the paste with the water or stock and pour into the roasting tin. Bake for 25–30 minutes or until a thin metal skewer can slide easily all the way into the thickest part of the fish.

Scatter with the chopped coriander leaves and serve with lime wedges, Coconut Rice (see page 81) and some steamed or stir-fried pak choy laced with 1 tbsp of toasted sesame oil.

Why not try baked sea bass with layered potatoes, fennel & salsa verde?
Layer 1kg peeled and sliced floury potatoes in a large roasting tin with 2 bulbs of thinly sliced fennel (use a mandoline for both ease and speed). Drizzle with Salsa Verde (see page 290), 100ml extra-virgin olive oil and the juice of 1 lemon. Stuff a whole sea bass with lemon slices and fresh herbs and season inside and out with salt and pepper. Lay on top of the potatoes and fennel and bake as above. Feeds 6.

Seafood Paella

I learned to cook a truly authentic paella at a farmhouse outside Valencia, when I was filming *A Cook's Tour of Spain*. My twinkly-eyed teacher was adamant on several points: a real paella must be cooked in a paella pan, outside, over a wood fire and eaten at lunchtime. She also taught me never to stir the rice. There should be a crust on the bottom of the pan, this is the *socarrat* or 'singed bit' and is the best part of the paella. If you don't have a paella pan use the widest and thinnest pan you have. I don't worry too much about the rest of the rules.

Place the stock and saffron in a large pan, simmer for 5 minutes, then set aside. Halve the tomatoes and grate coarsely with a box grater, discarding the skins and reserving the flesh.

Pour half the olive oil into the paella pan and put over a medium heat until the oil starts to smoke. Sear the monkfish on all sides for a minute, seasoning lightly with salt. Remove and set aside and repeat with the squid, cooking for about 2 minutes until tender.

Pour in the rest of the olive oil and add the peppers. Fry for a few minutes before pushing out to the less hot sides and adding the garlic. Cook for about 30 seconds until fragrant, then add the grated tomatoes and paprika. Reduce the heat to low and cook the tomatoes for 5–10 minutes until reduced to a thick paste. Stir the rice into the paste, season generously with salt and pepper and pour in 1 litre of the stock. Put the pan over 2 low burners, stir in half the parsley and shake to spread out the rice evenly. Cook for 10 minutes over a medium heat, then reduce the heat to low, cover with foil and cook for another 5 minutes.

Return the monkfish and squid to the pan and dot with the clams and prawns. Cover tightly with kitchen foil and continue to cook for another 10–15 minutes until the rice is cooked and the clams have opened. If the rice looks dry at any stage pour in more stock, but resist the temptation to stir as you want a lovely, slightly charred crust on the bottom of the pan.

Once the rice is cooked, turn off the heat and let stand for 5 minutes. Uncover the dish and serve at the table with the lemon wedges and a big bowl of alioli.

Why not try brown jasmine rice with spring vegetables?

Put 300ml lightly seasoned chicken or veg stock in a pan (with a lid), add 200g brown jasmine rice, bring to boil then cover, reduce the heat to a very gentle simmer and cook for 15 minutes. Trim and slice 12 asparagus spears. Bring a separate pan of salted water to the boil and blanch the asparagus with 80g each petit pois and broad beans (fresh, or frozen and thawed) for 30 seconds. Mix through the cooked rice with a knob of butter and 1 tbsp soy sauce, or to taste. Feeds 2.

For the Paella

1.5 litres fish or shellfish stock
(see page 47 for home-made)
large pinch of saffron strands
3 large, very ripe tomatoes
6 tbsp extra-virgin olive oil
300g monkfish,
cut into large chunks
200g squid, cleaned and cut
into equal-sized pieces
1 red pepper and 1 green pepper,
deseeded, halved lengthways
and cut into thin strips
½ head of garlic, cloves crushed
1½ tsp sweet smoked paprika
600g Bomba or Calasparra
rice (Spanish short-grain
rice), rinsed in cold water
large bunch of parsley
leaves, finely chopped
100g clams
12 large prawns

To Serve

2 large lemons, cut into wedges
Alioli (see page 113)

Indian
Baked Egg
& Pea Curry

This is a vegetarian feast that even my meat-loving friends rather enjoy. There are masses of recipes in this book that are either vegetarian or can be adapted (see the index on pages 306–315). The eggs look pleasingly like flowers as they open out on top of the curry. Serve with nutty, steamed pilau rice and another curry such as the Chard, Cauliflower & Paneer Curry (see page 200).

Melt the ghee or butter and oil in a wide frying pan over a medium heat. Once melted and beginning to bubble, add the mustard seeds. Once they start to pop stir in the curry leaves (if you have them) and almost immediately stir in the onion, garlic, ginger and a pinch of salt. Reduce the heat to low and cook gently for 5 minutes or so until the onion is soft, then add the ground black pepper, garam masala and turmeric. Cook for a minute longer, then stir in the tomatoes and a pinch of sugar. Season well and leave to simmer for 15 minutes.

Stir in the peas, cover and leave to cook for another 15 minutes, stirring occasionally, until the peas are completely soft and sweet. Stir in all but a few of the coriander leaves and adjust the seasoning to taste. Make 6 small indentations in the sauce and crack an egg into each. Cover with a lid and simmer for about 5 minutes until the whites have just set.

Scatter over the remaining coriander leaves and a sprinkle of nigella seeds. Serve with a spoonful of yogurt and naan or chapati.

Why not try curried egg sandwiches?

Boil 6 eggs in boiling water for 8 minutes, run under cold water, then peel and roughly chop. Mix with 6 tbsp good shop-bought mayo, a squeeze of lemon juice, ½ tbsp mango chutney and 1 tsp garam masala. Add a little finely chopped parsley or coriander leaves. Season and stuff into granary bread rolls with cress or sliced cucumber. Feeds 4.

30g ghee or butter

splash of olive oil

1 tsp black mustard seeds

small handful of curry
    leaves (optional)

1 small onion, finely chopped

3 garlic cloves, finely chopped

small thumb-sized piece
    of fresh ginger, peeled
    and finely chopped

½ tsp ground black peppercorns

2 tsp garam masala
    (for home-made see page 293)

½ tsp ground turmeric

2 x 400g cans chopped tomatoes

pinch of sugar

250g frozen peas

large handful of coriander leaves

6 eggs

few pinches of nigella seeds

yogurt and naan or chapatti, to serve

Olive Oil Poached Sea Trout with Shaved Fennel Salad

FEEDS FOUR

For the Sea Trout

500ml extra-virgin olive oil,
   plus extra to roast
pared rind of ¼ lemon,
   plus a little of the juice
4 coriander seeds
4 fennel seeds
1 bay leaf
4 sea trout fillets
   (about 150g each), pin-boned

For the Dressing

1 tsp brine from a jar of capers
1 tsp white wine vinegar
⅛ tsp finely grated garlic
1 tsp sugar
3 tbsp extra-virgin olive oil
squeeze of lemon juice
¼ small preserved lemon, flesh
   removed, rind finely chopped
2 tbsp chervil or parsley
   leaves, finely chopped, plus
   a few whole leaves, to serve

For the Salad

1 large fennel bulb
200g radishes, half finely
   sliced, half quartered
2 tbsp capers, drained

This recipe feels like the height of luxury, but most of the work is done in advance so it makes a great feasting dish. You poach fillets of sea trout in an aromatic bath of extra-virgin olive oil, re-using the oil as many times as you want. It is a beautifully light but filling summery dish. I like to serve it with a steaming bowl of minted, buttery new potatoes or a fresh summery buckwheat or couscous salad, flecked with masses of summery herbs such as chervil, mint, parsley and thyme.

Gently heat the olive oil, lemon rind, coriander and fennel seeds and bay leaf in a pan large enough to fit the 4 fillets neatly, or cook the fish in 2 batches (you will need less oil). When the oil starts to shimmer slightly and the lemon starts to bubble, add the fish. If you have a kitchen thermometer you should aim to keep the oil at 55–65°C. Gently swirl the pan occasionally or spoon the oil over the fish as it cooks. After 7–10 minutes, when the fish is opaque and a beautiful pale pink throughout, lift each fillet with a fish slice onto a plate lined with kitchen paper. Allow to rest until cooled.

Make the dressing in the bottom of a serving bowl. Whisk together the brine, vinegar, garlic and sugar until the sugar dissolves, then whisk in the olive oil and lemon juice until emulsified. Stir through the preserved lemon rind and chervil or parsley leaves and season to taste.

Just before serving, very finely slice the fennel and radishes, using a mandoline if you have one. Toss through the dressing with the quartered radishes, capers and any fronds from the fennel bulbs. Serve the salad with the cooled trout fillets.

Kitchen Note:

You can cook as many fillets as you want in this oil and re-use it to cook salmon or mackerel later on in the week. These are transformed into a silky treat by poaching in oil and are great in a classic salad Niçoise. Save what oil is left to make an aioli (see page 288).

DATE NIGHTS

Chapter SIX

DATE NIGHTS

This chapter is dedicated to those occasions when there are just the two of you. Perhaps you are spoiling yourself with a date night at home or having a meal with a best mate while you catch up on months of gossip.

There are some wonderfully luxurious recipes here for just such moments, when you want to open a bottle of wine and take time to savour the evening. Whether it is a Friday night in or just a random midweeker, you can treat yourselves to individual cuts of meat – such as pork or lamb chops – far more affordable when cooking for two. With any luck you will have had time to pick up something from a butcher on the way home. Friday night in might mean a delicious T-bone steak as a treat. We always have oven chips in the freezer ready to whip out, drizzle in olive oil, salt and pepper and throw in the oven for date nights in a rush, but home-made are the ultimate luxury when you have more time on your hands. Some steamed broccoli, a salad and a fast Hollandaise Sauce or Home-Made Mayonnaise (see pages *289* and *288*) will complete the feast: a steak supper costing less than a takeaway and taking no longer.

There are also recipes here for when there is no one to impress other than yourself. There's something absurdly luxurious about turning on the radio, some music or the TV and having time to slow down and just be by yourself, allowing the tensions of the day to slowly seep away. I like to fix myself a drink, alcoholic or not depending on my mood. I have a tried-and-tested core of 'cocktails' that I drink while I cook, made with apple juice from the market, vinegars, angostura, fizzy water, tonics, hibiscus and more besides. Drink in hand, I can then stand in front of the fridge deciding what to cook. Usually something delicious and uncomplicated such as the Welsh Rarebit or Crispy Egg you'll find in this chapter. Sitting down and eating alone is a rare pleasure and gives me a chance to think about the day and plan the next.

Gnocchi with Courgette & Hazelnut Butter

Silky, feather-light and with an other-worldly texture, home-made gnocchi is one of the most spoiling things you can make for someone, yet it is surprisingly simple to put together, especially when just for two. A luxurious plate of food.

Preheat the oven to 200°C/gas 6. Pierce the unpeeled potatoes with a fork a few times then thread onto a skewer. Bake for 1¼ hours or until tender when poked with a sharp knife. (You can also boil them for 30 minutes with their skins on, then drain and replace over the heat to steam and dry before removing their skins.) Allow to cool, then peel.

Coarsely grate the courgettes, sprinkle with salt and set aside in a sieve. Mash the potato well or, better still, push through a ricer until you have a completely smooth mash. Stir in the egg yolk, flour and salt until combined, then turn out onto a lightly floured surface. Cut the dough into 4 and roll each piece into a sausage about 2cm thick, then use a sharp knife to cut each into 3cm pieces. Move each piece onto a floured baking tray as you work, then set aside (for up to 6 hours in the fridge if well-covered, or frozen on trays, then transferred to labelled freezer bags).

Bring a large pan of lightly salted water to the boil, then melt the butter in a large frying pan over a medium heat. Add the thyme and hazelnuts, season generously with salt and fry until the butter starts to bubble and turn a deep golden brown. At first, the bubbles will be large, then they die down. Watch carefully at this point as it can suddenly go from brown to black; swirling the pan around helps you to see how brown the solids are becoming. As soon as they turn a deep nut brown, take the pan off the heat and squeeze in the lemon juice, to arrest the cooking. Add the courgettes and stir to coat in the butter. Sprinkle over the Parmesan, stir very briefly and set aside.

Now add the gnocchi to the pan of boiling water and cook for 2–3 minutes or until they float to the top. Drain and gently toss into the courgettes. Spoon into shallow bowls and serve with extra toasted hazelnuts on top.

Why not try golden baked gnocchi with sausage & mozzarella?

Squeeze the meat out of 2 good pork sausages and fry in a pan until crisp. Add 10 halved cherry tomatoes and 10 finely chopped sage leaves. Fry for a minute more before adding 100ml double cream. Cook 300g gnocchi in boiling water until they float to the top, then drain. Mix into the sausage and tomatoes and tip into a 1-litre baking dish. Season and then top with 4 slices of buffalo mozzarella. Bake in a preheated 180°C/gas 6 oven for 25 minutes until golden and bubbling. Rest for 10 minutes before tucking in. Feeds a hungry 2.

For the Gnocchi

600g floury potatoes,
  such as Maris Piper
1 egg yolk
85g plain flour, plus extra to dust
¾ tsp fine salt

For the Sauce

500g courgettes (about 3)
50g butter
6 sprigs of thyme, leaves picked
25g roughly chopped hazelnuts,
  plus extra to serve
squeeze of lemon juice
75g Parmesan, finely grated

Grilled Indian Lamb Cutlets with Carrot Purée

FEEDS TWO

For me lamb chops are special, for when you really have a hankering for a fine cut of meat and Welsh lamb is particularly delectable. When grilled for a few minutes with salt, pepper, a knob of butter and a sprinkle of chopped mint leaves they are in a league of their own.

This is a vibrant dish you might find in any Michelin-starred Indian restaurant: full of clean, distinct flavours but without leaving you too full. You could push the boat out and make a raita, marinate the chops overnight and barbecue them, then serve with a mezze of other Indian-inspired dishes.

Dry fry the cumin seeds, mustard seeds and coriander seeds together in a small pan until the mustard seeds start to pop and the spices are fragrant. Grind in a pestle and mortar, then tip into a bowl and add the turmeric, yogurt, oil or melted ghee and lemon juice; season well. Add the lamb cutlets and mix them well in the spiced yogurt. Leave to marinate, covered in cling film, for 20 minutes.

Steam the carrots over boiling water for 15 minutes or until tender. Transfer them to a food processor and add the butter or ghee and chilli flakes, then whizz until smooth. Push through a sieve into a pan if there are still lumps. Season to taste and keep warm over a gentle heat.

Heat a griddle pan over a high heat, add the lamb and fry for 4 minutes on each side until medium rare. Rest the cutlets for 5 minutes then transfer to warm plates with the carrot purée. Scatter with shredded mint leaves and nigella seeds and finish with a squeeze of lemon juice.

For the Lamb

1 tsp cumin seeds

½ tsp mustard seeds

1 tsp coriander seeds

½ tsp ground turmeric

100g thick Greek yogurt

1 tbsp olive oil or melted ghee

juice of ¼ lemon, plus extra to serve

4 lamb cutlets (about 75g each)

handful of mint leaves, shredded, to serve (or home-made Mint Sauce, see page 290)

1 tsp nigella seeds, to serve

For the Carrot Purée

4 large carrots, cut into large chunks

30g butter or ghee

½ tsp chilli flakes

Kitchen Note:

This purée is delicious with baked pitta crisps. Cut 10 pitta breads into triangles and rub with a raw garlic clove. Scatter with 1 tsp ground cumin and a pinch of salt and drizzle with olive oil. Place on a baking sheet and bake in a preheated oven at 180°C/ gas 4 for 5 minutes until crisp. Warm the carrot purée and loosely stir through a little yogurt and some shredded mint leaves. Serve with the pitta crisps. Feeds 4.

Pan-Fried Duck Breast With Plum Sauce

FEEDS TWO

We planted a plum tree outside our house a few years ago and every summer there is great excitement as we wait for the fruit to grow. Plum sauce is the perfect foil for the gamey duck and it is seasoned with the aromatic, warm flavours of Chinese five-spice.

Use a sharp knife to score the duck skin in a criss-cross pattern. Rub the breasts all over with the Chinese Five-Spice and salt, then leave to marinate in the fridge for at least a few hours, or overnight.

Meanwhile make the sauce: throw the plums into a pan with 3–4 tbsp of water and the remaining sauce ingredients. Season with salt and bring to the boil. Reduce the heat and simmer gently for 10–15 minutes, stirring occasionally until the plums have collapsed and the sauce has darkened and turned syrupy. Taste, season generously with salt and pepper and a little more vinegar if it is needed. Push the sauce through a sieve to get rid of the stones (I find this much easier than pitting the plums beforehand) and put back into a clean pan, ready to warm gently later.

Take the duck breasts out of the fridge about half an hour before you are ready to eat and allow them to come to room temperature. Preheat the oven to 180°C/gas 4.

For the Duck

2 duck breasts

2 tsp Chinese Five-Spice
  (for home-made, see page 293)

½ tsp salt

20g butter

100ml red wine or port

For the Plum Sauce

450g plums

4 tbsp soft light brown sugar

½ tsp Chinese Five-Spice
  (for home-made, see page 293)

2 tbsp soy sauce

1 tbsp rice wine vinegar,
  plus extra to taste

thumb-sized piece of fresh
  ginger, peeled and sliced

Heat a frying pan over a medium heat and, when the pan is hot, add the butter, swirl it around and then add the duck breasts, skin side down. Cook the duck for 8–9 minutes until the skin is golden and crisp, pouring out the fat it releases as you cook (you can save it for roast potatoes). Briefly turn the breasts over, transfer to an oven dish and roast in the oven for 5 minutes. Turn off the oven, pull the oven door ajar and leave the duck to rest for 10 minutes.

Meanwhile, with the heat high under the duck pan, pour in the red wine or port and allow to simmer and reduce by half (you are deglazing the pan). Pour these juices into the plum sauce, while it is gently reheating.

Slice the breasts as thinly as you can and serve with the plum sauce. This is great with mash and greens, or in Chinese pancakes with strips of cucumber and spring onion.

Kitchen note:

If you are prone to panicking about whether the meat is cooked, worry not. Stick in a skewer after 10 minutes of resting and if the juices that come out are bloody you can always pop it back in the pan for a few more minutes. The plum sauce is delicious with ham or any other rich meat. Leftover duck is wonderful in an Asian beansprout salad.

Juniper Pork Chops with Grilled Hispi Cabbage

FEEDS TWO

Gloriously juicy chops are perfect with these sharp, tangy caper-dressed grilled cabbage wedges. Almost more than any other, a pork chop is a cut that needs a bit of money spent on it. A chop from a well-reared animal is juicy, full of flavour and a real treat ... but from some factory-reared animal it tends to be dry, insipid and scarcely worth the money. Without the chops, the cabbage makes a meat-free dish good enough to spoil any food-lover, especially when served with a Crispy Egg (see page 169) and steamed potatoes (floury or waxy) cooked until tender and seasoned with butter, salt and pepper.

Take the chops out of the fridge to allow them to come up to room temperature and season well with salt and pepper.

Put a heavy-based griddle pan over a high heat, or preheat a grill to high. Drizzle the cabbage with a little oil and season with salt and pepper. Griddle or grill, turning regularly, for 10 minutes until lightly charred and tender, sprinkling with the sugar towards the end of the cooking. Remove from the heat and keep somewhere warm.

Meanwhile, place a large frying pan over a medium-high heat. When it's very hot, add a splash of oil and place the chops in the pan fatty edges down, holding them there with tongs for a few minutes until golden and some of the fat has been released. Then put them down flat in the pan and cook for 2–4 minutes each side (depending on thickness) until golden brown, pressing down with a spoon to get maximum contact with the pan. Transfer to a plate and rest somewhere warm for 5 minutes.

In the same pan, melt the butter over a medium heat and add the juniper, sage and capers, frying them for a minute or so until the sage leaves are slightly crisp. Squeeze in the juice of half the lemon and season with a little salt and pepper. Add the grilled cabbage and toss in the caper and sage butter. Cut the remaining lemon half into wedges and serve with the chops. Some mash would be good, too...

Why not try pork chop with rhubarb & onion salsa?

Finely slice ½ stick of rhubarb (about 125g) and chop ½ red onion. Heat 1 tsp olive oil in a pan and fry the onion, rhubarb, a pinch of sugar, 1 crushed juniper berry and ½ small garlic clove; season with salt and pepper. When they have softened, pour in the resting juices from a fried pork chop. Serve the salsa on top of the chop.

2 bone-in free-range pork chops
2 Hispi cabbages, cut into
    quarters through the stem
olive oil, to cook
¼ tsp caster sugar
40g butter
4 juniper berries, crushed
handful of sage leaves,
    roughly shredded
2 tbsp baby capers
1 lemon

Vietnamese-Style Crab Pancake

FEEDS TWO

I'm fairly new to South East Asian food; my eyes were opened to it when I went to the Melbourne Food Festival in 2011. It is so extraordinarily light, full of explosions of fresh flavour from chilli and herbs.

There are a few ingredients in this recipe but most of them are easy to find in larger supermarkets. I ordinarily find recipes like this intimidating because they are so unfamiliar, but when I saw it being cooked in Melbourne it seemed so easy that I couldn't resist including it. Just get all the ingredients chopped and ready in ramekins and give yourself time to read the recipe first.

It is a wonderful, brightly fragrant gluten-free supper dish. I often double up the pickle quantities as it keeps for several weeks in the fridge and makes the most delicious Vietnamese sandwiches (see page 146). Any leftover beansprouts and herbs make a great salad with rice noodles, toasted peanuts and grilled chicken.

For the Pancake

50g brown crab meat

150g white crab meat

30g beansprouts

juice of ½ lime

½ tbsp fish sauce

50g rice flour

75ml coconut cream

50ml water

¼ tsp ground turmeric

4 spring onions, 2 finely
    chopped and 2 finely sliced

1 tsp coconut oil

1–2 red chillies, finely chopped

handful of coriander leaves, torn

handful of Thai basil leaves, torn
    (or use regular basil)

handful of mint leaves, torn

For the Pickled Carrot:

½ tbsp caster sugar

2 tbsp rice vinegar

½ tbsp fish sauce

juice of 1 lime

1 carrot, finely shredded

First prepare the pickled carrot: bring the sugar, vinegar, fish sauce and lime juice to a simmer until the sugar dissolves. Take off the heat, add the carrot and leave to lightly pickle for 10 minutes.

Mix the crab meats and beansprouts and season to taste with lime juice, fish sauce and salt and pepper. In another bowl beat together the rice flour, coconut cream, water, turmeric and the 2 finely chopped spring onions and season.

Melt the coconut oil in a frying pan over a medium-high heat. Ladle in half the batter, quickly swirling the pan to make a very thin pancake. Cook for a minute and, when it starts to bubble a little, top with the crab meat mixture. Cover with a lid and cook for 3–4 minutes or until golden on the underside. Make sure you let the batter properly fry before you try to fold the pancakes.

Remove the lid, add half the chillies, sliced spring onions, herbs and some pickled carrot. Fold the pancake over itself and slide onto a plate. Be gentle when handling the pancake as gluten-free rice flour can be brittle. Serve immediately while you repeat to make a second pancake, offering more pickled carrot in a bowl.

Why not try Asian sea bass ceviche?

Shave a carrot with a vegetable peeler into ribbons. Pickle as above and, when cool, stir through 2 x 100g sea bass fillets, skinned, pin-boned and chopped. Gently stir through 30g beansprouts and cover and chill for at least 30 minutes and up to 2 hours. Before serving, stir in finely chopped coriander and mint leaves, lime juice and a finely chopped red chilli. Feeds 2 as a starter.

Chicken Dumplings with Sesame Avocado Rice

FEEDS TWO WITH SOME
LUNCHBOX LEFTOVERS

Familiar ingredients can be transformed with a little inspiration. The *Nanban* cookbook by Tim Anderson has made me more entranced with Japanese home cooking than ever before. These dumplings were adapted from Tim's book and are much raved about in our house.

The Californian-inspired sesame rice here is really tempting as well as healthy but it's the sticky, glazed dumplings that really lift the whole dish. A butcher should be able to mince chicken thighs for you.

Rinse the rice in clean water a few times and leave to soak while you prepare the rest of the ingredients.

Mix the minced chicken with the ginger, garlic and half the spring onions. Season with salt and pepper, white if you have it. With clean hands, pat the mixture into oblong patties about the size of a small madeleine, or 2 walnuts side by side. You want to get about 4 patties per person. As you pat them into shape, put them onto a baking sheet lined with baking parchment and, once done, pop them in the fridge to firm up.

Meanwhile put all the marinade ingredients into a small pan and bring to the boil. Simmer gently for 10–15 minutes until it is rich, glossy and slightly sticky.

Cover the rice in double its volume of water, season generously with salt and bring to simmering point. Simmer for 15 minutes, then cover, reduce the heat to its lowest setting and leave to finish cooking in its own steam.

Peel, pit and dice the avocado and toss in the sesame oil, seeds and lime juice.

Heat 1 tbsp of oil in a large frying pan. Brush the patties with the soy marinade and fry in batches for about 4 minutes each side until they are golden and just cooked through (you can keep them warm in a low oven). Repeat to glaze and fry them all. Add the remaining 1 tbsp of oil to the pan and fry the mushrooms over a high heat for 5 minutes until cooked through and golden, sprinkling in the chilli, if using, and seasoning with a touch of salt and pepper.

Drain the rice (if there is still any water left in the pan) and then toss with the mushrooms, the rest of the marinade, the avocado and sesame mixture and the rest of the spring onions. Serve with the golden chicken dumplings.

For the Dumplings and Rice

150g brown rice

4 chicken thighs, minced
(or about 350g minced chicken)

15g fresh ginger,
peeled and finely grated

1 fat garlic clove, finely chopped

2 small spring onions, finely chopped

1 ripe Hass avocado

1–2 tbsp sesame oil

1 tbsp sesame seeds (I like to
use both black and white)

juice of 1 lime

2 tbsp sunflower oil

100g shiitake, Portobello or chestnut
mushrooms, roughly sliced

pinch of chilli flakes (optional)

For the Marinade

50ml chicken stock (for
home-made, see page 46)

50ml soy sauce

50ml mirin

15g brown sugar

1 garlic clove, crushed

5g fresh ginger,
peeled and finely sliced

'Nduja, Plum Tomato & Clams with Casareccia Pasta

FEEDS TWO

This recipe is inspired by a bowl of pasta my husband and I ate on honeymoon in Sicily, with clams that had just been pulled from the sea. I think of it as a romantic, gutsy dish, perfect for an anniversary or Valentine's Day. Casareccia, meaning 'home-style', is a hollow, tube-like pasta from Sicily that has the knack of holding onto sauces (fusilli or orecchiette are also good) while the 'nduja (pronounced en-doo-ya) is a spicy Calabrian spreadable cured meat with a rich, fiery taste that adds depth and punch to the simplest of foods. The garlic and tomatoes collapse in the warm olive oil and 'nduja-rich sauce that coats the clams and pasta, while the garlicky breadcrumbs lends a pleasing crunch.

Buy the 'nduja in delis, supermarkets or online (Ocado sells it via the Italian supplier Natoora). Its heat varies wildly and a little goes a long way so add it bit by bit, tasting as you go, or leave it out and add lots of fresh thyme to the sauce as well as more basil at the end. If the clams are a step too far for you, leave them out and you will have with a wonderfully homely, comforting bowl of pasta.

First, make the breadcrumb topping. Heat a frying pan over a high heat and toast the breadcrumbs until golden. Drizzle over the olive oil and add the lemon zest and garlic. Fry for 2 minutes and then toss in half of the parsley and set aside.

For the pasta, warm the olive oil in a frying pan and add the garlic and tomatoes. Fry for a few minutes until the skin of the tomatoes begins to soften and the juices are released. Add the 'nduja and stir through.

Add the clams to the tomatoes and turn up the heat. Pour in the white wine, cover the pan with a lid and steam the clams for 2–3 minutes, or until they have all opened. Discard any that are still firmly closed, then add the basil leaves. Season generously.

Meanwhile, bring a pan of salted water to the boil and add the pasta. Cook for 2 minutes, or according to the packet instructions, then drain and add to the clams. Serve with all the juices and a scattering of the remaining parsley leaves. Finish by sprinkling over the garlicky breadcrumbs.

Why not try ricotta & 'nduja toasts?

Griddle 6 spring onions for 10 minutes until softened and blackened. Mix together 100g soft goat's cheese with 100g ricotta and a handful of chopped basil and mint leaves, then spread on 2 thick slices of sourdough toast. Fry 1 tbsp 'nduja with a drizzle of olive oil and spoon over the toasts. Top with the spring onions, grate over some lemon zest and serve. Serves 2.

For the Pasta

3 tbsp olive oil

1 garlic clove, finely chopped

250g baby plum tomatoes, halved

2 tbsp 'nduja

200g fresh clams, cleaned

175ml white wine

small bunch of basil leaves

250g fresh egg casareccia pasta,
   or a similar shape such as trofie
   or orecchiette, or even fusilli

For the Breadcrumb Topping

50g soft white breadcrumbs
   (for home-made, see page 277)

drizzle of extra-virgin olive oil

finely grated zest of 1 lemon

½ garlic clove, crushed

handful of parsley leaves,
   finely chopped

Crispy Egg with Chorizo, Parsley & Tomatoes

FEEDS TWO

Eggs are such a wonderful standby to have in the house, ready for anything from impromptu weekend pancakes, to spur-of-the-moment cakes or fast, nourishing suppers. We buy them from the market and they sit in a spiral contraption on our work surface nestled around two hidden, bouncing 'eggs' that provide endless amusement to the children.

In this recipe the whites turn golden and crispy in the oil and the yolk runs into the quick tomato sauce, made spicy, rich and garlicky by the cooking chorizo. It is definitely worth buying a good chorizo; I get mine online from Brindisa and always have a packet in the freezer, but do try different brands and find one that you like.

If you are vegetarian, give your sauce a zing with a few exotic, warming spices such as cardamom or star anise, coupled with cinnamon, allspice and chilli. The dish is wonderful with yogurt stirred through (add tahini if going without the chorizo) and a sprinkling of lemon zest.

Heat 1 tbsp of oil in a deep frying pan or casserole dish and fry the chorizo over a high heat until crispy and golden and the juices have been released. Transfer to a bowl using a slotted spoon and keep warm. Reduce the heat, add the onion and fry for 5 minutes until it is soft and red from the chorizo juices. Add the garlic and chilli or paprika, fry for a minute, then pour in the canned tomatoes and bring to a simmer. Season and cook for a further 15 minutes. If you think the sauce needs a little more liquid during cooking, add a few tbsp of water. Stir through most of the parsley.

Just before you want to eat, heat about 1cm of oil over a medium heat in a large frying pan. Fry the eggs so that the whites bubble and turn slightly golden. Once the whites are cooked, remove the eggs with a slotted spoon and place directly onto the chorizo. Scatter with the remaining parsley and a little more chilli. If you have a good olive oil, a drizzle would be great here. Serve with yogurt and lemon wedges.

Why not try black bean & chorizo soup?

Dry fry 50g finely chopped cooking chorizo for 10 minutes until crisp. Remove with a slotted spoon onto kitchen paper. Meanwhile, heat 25g butter and 1 tbsp oil in a large, heavy-based pan, then add 1 chopped onion, 2 chopped garlic cloves, and 1 tbsp finely chopped oregano leaves. Sweat for 5–10 minutes until soft, then add 600g cooked black beans and 1 tbsp chipotle en adobo if you want some smoky heat. Add 1 litre of stock (for home-made, see pages 46–7) and simmer gently for 10–15 minutes. Whizz briefly, season with salt, pepper and the juice of a lime, then top with soured cream, coriander and the crispy chorizo. Feeds 4–6 and freezes well.

rapeseed or olive oil, to fry

225g cooking chorizo
(or 3 small sausages), chopped
into hazelnut-sized cubes

1 large red onion, finely sliced

1 garlic clove, finely sliced

¼ tsp chilli flakes or ½ tsp hot
smoked paprika, plus extra to serve

1 x 400g can plum tomatoes

handful of parsley leaves, chopped

4 eggs

extra-virgin olive oil, to serve (optional)

yogurt and lemon wedges, to serve

Globe Artichokes with Burnt Butter

I am delighted that today's health czars have finally woken up to the joys of butter and that naturally occurring, saturated fats are no longer considered the devil incarnate. My grandmother, a glamorous former model, ate butter with everything and burning it was one of her tricks. When you cook butter in a pan over a medium to medium-high heat the milk solids turn a deep, dark brown. This is a classic *beurre noir* and is deliciously nutty. I think I could eat it on almost anything, but it seems particularly suited to the slightly sweet, enigmatic flavour of globe artichokes.

So I always make a little extra of the butter, it is good on bread and will transform any vegetable. I particularly like it with bubble and squeak or gnocchi (see page 159).

Cut off the stalks and remove the toughest outer leaves from the artichoke bases.

Put the artichokes in a large stainless steel pan (aluminium pans will taint the' flavour) and add the bay leaves, lemon juice and salt. Cover with cold water and place a heavy pan lid on top of the artichokes to keep them submerged (they have a tendency to bob up and down). Bring to simmering point and cook for 20–25 minutes, or until the outer leaves pull away easily. Drain and keep warm.

Meanwhile melt the butter in a small pan, seasoning generously with salt and pepper, and cook over a medium heat until the solids start to darken. Now reduce the heat a little and continue to cook until the butter is a rich nut-brown, being careful not to burn it. The moment you think it is done, squeeze in the lemon juice to stop it cooking further and remove from the heat.

Put the warm artichokes onto large plates and place a large bowl in the middle of the table for the leaves. Pour the butter into 2 small warmed ramekins and place them beside each artichoke, so you can dip in the leaves. When you reach the heart of the choke, cut it in half and ensure that you slice away all of the hairs. Cut up the hearts and dunk in the rest of the salty, nutty butter; the best bit saved for last!

Kitchen Note:

Artichokes are also excellent with grilled with cheese. Preheat the grill to high. Toss 700g drained chargrilled artichoke hearts (those sold in oil) with 1 tbsp of their oil, 1 finely chopped garlic clove, 6 tbsp full-fat Greek yogurt and the finely grated zest of ½ lemon in a wide ovenproof dish; you don't want them to overlap much. Season well then grate over 50g Parmesan. Place under the grill for 6–7 minutes until golden and bubbling. Sprinkle with a little sweet smoked paprika or chopped parsley and serve as they are, or whizz into a dip and serve with crostini (for home-made, see page 277).

For the Artichokes

2 globe artichokes

2 bay leaves

juice of ½ lemon

1 tsp salt

For the Beurre Noir

150g butter

juice of ¼ lemon

Pan-Fried Hake with Swiss Chard & Lemon Aioli

FEEDS FOUR

Chard with this bright, fresh aioli is just stunning. The sweet, citrusy tones of the sauce bring alive the soft flavours of the chard and hake. If you cannot find chard, try slow-cooked courgettes or marrow instead.

Put a pan of water on to boil, separate the leaves of the chard from the stalks and slice the stalks into 2cm-wide pieces. Put the stalks in the boiling water and cook for 3 minutes before adding the leaves and cooking for a further 2–3 minutes until soft. Drain and leave to steam-dry.

Meanwhile make the aioli: put the yolks, garlic, mustard and a generous pinch of salt into a food processor and briefly blitz. Very slowly drip the oil through the funnel of the processor with the motor still running until the mayonnaise starts to thicken and emulsify, then pour in the remaining oil in a slow, steady stream. Loosen with the lemon juice and a few tbsp of water. Season to taste and transfer to a bowl.

Back to the chard. Heat 4 tbsp of the olive oil in a large frying pan over a medium heat and fry the spring onions, garlic and coriander stalks with a pinch of salt until softened, about 3–4 minutes. Squeeze out any excess water from the cooled chard and add to the frying pan. Season with a little salt and pepper and fry until warmed through and all the flavours have mingled. Stir in the coriander leaves so they wilt and squeeze in the lime juice. Keep warm.

Pat the hake dry on both sides with kitchen paper and season well with salt and pepper. Heat the remaining 2 tbsp of oil in a large frying pan over a medium-high heat and fry the fish for about 3 minutes each side (depending on its thickness) until golden. Cover the pan if you want it to cook faster. Serve on top of the chard with a dollop of mayonnaise on each fillet.

Kitchen Note:

In no time at all you can transform the aioli above into a vivid green coriander aioli that is delicious with grilled fish, leftover Ten-Hour Porchetta (see page 146) or pork or in tacos (particularly if accompanied by some pickled jalapeños). Blitz 200ml olive oil with 2 large bunches of coriander, the juice of ½ lime and 2 garlic cloves. Season generously with salt and fold into the aioli.

For the Hake and Chard

2 bunches of Swiss chard (about 1kg)

6 tbsp extra-virgin olive oil

6 spring onions, finely sliced

2 garlic cloves, finely sliced

½ bunch of coriander,
    leaves roughly chopped
    and stalks finely chopped

juice of ½ lime

4 hake fillets (about 150g each)

For the Lemon Aioli

2 egg yolks

1 garlic clove, crushed
    to a paste with a little salt

1 tsp Dijon mustard

500ml mild olive oil

juice of ½ lemon

Chickpea Pancakes with Potato & Savoy Cabbage Curry

These dosa-inspired chickpea pancakes are perfect for sharing with someone you love. The gently-spiced potato curry is simple to prepare and, when wrapped in nutty, gram flour paper-thin crepes, is perfect for eating with your hands.

Make the chickpea batter by placing the flour in a large bowl with the salt and whisking in 400–450ml cold water until the batter is the consistency of single cream. Leave to rest in the fridge while you prepare the curry.

Put a large, heavy-based pan over a medium heat and when hot add the oil, followed by the cumin and mustard seeds. When the mustard seeds begin to pop add the onions, chilli and bay leaves and reduce the heat a little. Add a pinch of salt and fry until the onions are soft, sweet and coloured, about 10 minutes.

Now add the ground coriander and fennel seeds and cook until they smell fragrant. Stir in the garlic and ginger and cook, stirring, for a further few minutes. Add the cabbage, tomato and a splash of water and stir well. Season generously with salt and pepper, then cover and leave to cook for 10 minutes until the cabbage is tender.

Meanwhile, place the potatoes, turmeric and another heaped tsp of salt in a small pan and cover with cold water. Bring to the boil and cook for 8–10 minutes until the potatoes are completely tender and bright yellow. Drain, keeping a cup of the cooking liquid, and leave to steam-dry.

Stir the potatoes into the cabbage, breaking them up a bit with your spoon. Stir in the chopped coriander and lime juice and check the seasoning. Add at least half the reserved potato cooking water so that you have a nice, wettish curry (or more if you like lots of sauce). Keep warm while you cook the pancakes.

Place a large frying pan over a medium heat and add a splash of oil. Swirl it around to coat the pan, then pour off any excess into a cup. When the pan is hot add a small cup (3–4 tbsp) of batter and swirl around the pan so that it coats the base. Cook for about 15 seconds until bubbles start appearing and the pancake turns golden at the edges. Use a palette knife to lift the pancake and turn it over. Cook on the other side for a few moments until golden, then keep warm in a low oven while you make a few more. Serve with the potato curry, some yogurt and chutneys.

Kitchen Note:

The curry lasts beautifully: reheat as a side dish to other curries, or eke out and feed more people with it by adding a can of chickpeas, rinsed and drained, another Savoy cabbage, 2 cans of tomatoes and twice as many of those wonderful spices.

250g gram (chickpea) flour

1 tsp salt

4 tbsp vegetable oil, plus more to fry

1 heaped tsp cumin seeds

1 heaped tsp brown mustard seeds

2 onions, thinly sliced

1 red chilli, deseeded
    and thinly sliced

2 bay leaves

2 tsp ground coriander

1 tsp fennel seeds

2 garlic cloves, crushed with a little salt

thumb-sized piece of fresh ginger,
    peeled and finely grated

1 head of Savoy cabbage, core
    discarded, leaves shredded

1 large beef tomato, roughly chopped

650g floury potatoes, peeled
    and cut into 3cm chunks

1 tsp ground turmeric

large handful of roughly
    chopped coriander

juice of 1 lime

yogurt and chutneys, to serve

Welsh Rarebit

FEEDS TWO

This is a classic Sunday night supper in our house. The texture of the crisp green salad dressed with the nutty walnut oil dressing works well against the oozing smooth cheese.

I am an unapologetic cheese fiend. Cheese, like bread, is life-affirming, with its savoury, complex flavours. The quality of your cheese will make all the difference in this recipe; we will often splash out on a wedge of Lincolnshire Poacher or hard goat's cheese from the market or a great Cheddar from the cheese shop at the weekend, but you can also use up odds and ends from the fridge. In fact, the combined flavours of different types of blue and hard cheeses can make a miraculous rarebit.

If you splash out on proper walnut oil (beware of cheaper, flavourless supermarket imitations), make sure you store it in the fridge or it will go rancid, which would be a sad waste.

For the Rarebit

20g butter

2 tbsp plain flour

1 tsp English mustard powder

½ tsp cayenne pepper

good splash of
   Worcestershire sauce

220ml strong ale

500g extra-mature Cheddar,
   or other good-quality
   hard cheese, grated

4 slices sourdough or other
   coarse-textured bread

For the Salad

3 Baby Gem lettuces

½ tbsp cider vinegar

½ tsp caster sugar

1 tbsp olive oil

1 tbsp walnut oil

squeeze of lemon juice

small handful of walnuts,
   toasted and chopped

Melt the butter in a heavy-based pan and, when sizzling, stir in the flour and cook for a few minutes until it smells toasted but hasn't browned. Add the mustard powder, cayenne pepper and Worcestershire sauce before stirring in the ale, bit by bit. Add the cheese and stir to melt until you have a smooth, fairly thick sauce.

Pour the sauce into a shallow container and transfer to the fridge or freezer for at least half an hour to set. You want it to be a completely firm paste the texture of playdough by the time you are ready to cook.

When ready to eat, preheat the grill to high and toast the bread. Scoop out some cheese mix and mould into a paddle the same shape as the bread slices and about ½–1cm thick, depending on how hungry you are. Cover the toast with the cheese paddles and grill until the cheese is golden, blistered and bubbling.

Separate the lettuce leaves into a bowl. Whisk the dressing ingredients together, add the toasted walnuts and toss with the lettuce. Serve with the toasts.

Why not try little crab rarebit bites?

Stir 100g mixed white and brown crab meat into half the cheese paste, preferably made with a mix of Parmesan and Cheddar. Use to top dark rye sourdough, grill and eat as is or cut into small squares as a pre-dinner snack. Or fill sourdough sandwiches with the rarebit, alone or mixed with sautéed leeks or mushrooms. Fry on both sides until crisp and golden and serve with chilli oil or tomato chilli jam (for home-made versions of both, see pages 295 and 285).

EVERYDAY EXPRESS

EVERYDAY EXPRESS

When I'm in during the week I start thinking about dinner at about 7.30 or 8.00 after I've put the children to bed. At this point it is easy to cop out of the cooking; my husband never expects dinner to 'arrive' on the table and we both usually have things to do, whether making plans for the weekend or catching up on some work. The very thought of messing up the kitchen is a turn-off. And yet mostly I am too greedy to make do with a takeaway, and too impatient. I know instinctively that in the time it would have taken for a takeaway to arrive I can have rustled something up that tastes great and makes me feel good. And the very act of chopping an onion or warming oil in a pan gives me a meditative moment, an instant of pleasure that a takeaway box never can. The recipes in this chapter aim to take less than 45 minutes, often fewer and are designed to be cooked with absolute ease.

These recipes were generally inspired by last-minute suppers I've cooked up with what I've found in the kitchen. During the week the hero ingredients of my meals tend to be the vegetables I've bought at the weekend; vegetables are quick to cook and full of possibilities, easy to weave an exciting recipe around.

A well-stocked kitchen is the key to express cooking. My vegetable drawer always has carrots and celery plus maybe a cauliflower or cabbage, a head of broccoli or a few stray courgettes. There are fresh herbs in window boxes. I try to have a few cans of tomatoes, chickpeas, black beans and lentils in the cupboards. Packets of peas and sweetcorn nestle in the freezer, plenty of onions and garlic are on hand and I would never be without anchovies, Parmesan or yogurt. I find garam masala, dukkah, harissa and tamarind paste super-useful to have in the house, they add flavour to otherwise perfectly ordinary ingredients (you can buy these or make your own, see the Store Cupboard chapter). I also cheat a bit with short cuts such as Spice Tailor's wide range of curry pastes which help make brilliant quick dinners when combined with sweated onions and different vegetables, as do good-quality Thai pastes. Life is too short to be overly fussy and anything that helps you to make fast and great-tasting food is good in my book, especially if it doesn't cost a fortune.

There's a bonus here too. Once you get into the rhythm of cooking these quick recipes you will find that entertaining in the week becomes much less daunting. It is so easy to go without seeing people for months, even if they live a couple of miles away. Dishes such as Tamarind Prawns with Noodles & Coconut Rice or Crab Linguine are speedy yet simple midweek suppers that will knock your friends' socks off, so get in touch and get them round.

Conquering
the Fear of Fish

When I started cooking at university, fish always caused me undue panic. It seemed like an expensive luxury and one I couldn't afford to mess up. We didn't eat it at home much either, so it felt quite alien to me, all glistening skin, slimy scales and shiny eyes. And how on earth was one to tell when it was cooked? Over the years I have picked up some basic tricks through friends in the food industry. I have also discovered how inexpensive it can be when buying direct from fishermen at local markets. It has revolutionised the way I think about this delicately textured, delicious food.

When there are just two of us at home and we want a fast, fuss-free dinner, fish is perfect. A mackerel fillet cooks in less than five minutes in a hot oven, a whole mackerel takes less than fifteen and, even when you are cooking a big meal for friends, a large whole fish (or two) will rarely take longer than half an hour to roast. And what could be more spectacular than delivering a whole baked fish (or even a giant Seafood Paella, see page 153) to a table full of friends? Just make sure you check what you are buying. There is a brilliant guide to species under threat of extinction on the Good Fish Guide website (*goodfishguide.org*). If – when you buy it – you always ask where fish has come from and if it was sustainably caught, the people you buy from will soon realise that we really do care about how many fish there are left in the sea.

Tips:

— Generally fish should be cooked over a very high heat, whether in a pan on the hob or in the oven.

— If you're baking a whole fish, you can tell when it is cooked when a thin metal skewer slides easily through the thickest part, bones and all, meeting no real resistance.

— When pan-frying fish, check to see if it is done by inserting a sharp knife deep into the thickest part. If cooked, the flesh will flake away easily; if undercooked it will still cling to the bones.

— Thin fish fillets such as mackerel or sea bass can be fried or baked quickly and easily. When cooking thicker fillets such as monkfish, salmon or hake, try starting them in a pan to get a crisp crust and finishing in a hot oven (this creates a perfect texture without burning the skin).

— If a fish starts oozing a milky residue, take it off the heat immediately. This is a classic sign of overcooking.

The Fastest Fish,
Several Ways

FEEDS FOUR

Simple Flash-Baked Mackerel

Mackerel is one of my favourite fish: affordable, versatile and packed with good Omega oils. However, it is less sustainable than was previously thought, so do check that your fish is line-caught.

Preheat the oven to 200°C/gas 6.

If using whole mackerel, season inside and out with plenty of salt and pepper and stuff the cavity with lemon slices. Put on a baking tray, drizzle with the olive oil and roast for 10–12 minutes. If using fillets, put on a baking tray and squeeze over the juice of the lemon instead, season generously with salt and pepper and drizzle over the olive oil. Bake on the top shelf of the oven for 4–5 minutes until sizzling and just cooked so that the flesh is opaque and easy to flake. Serve immediately with …

Beetroot & Horseradish Cream
Mackerel and beetroot is a beautiful match. Take the borani dip (see page 89) but make it with shop-bought beetroot instead of roasting your own and season it with crème fraîche instead of yogurt plus a heaped tsp grated fresh horseradish. This is delicious with boiled new potatoes or couscous flecked with mint and parsley.

Tomato, Olive & Parsley Salad
Combine a large bunch of roughly chopped parsley leaves, 3–4 ripe plum tomatoes, cut into 1–2cm dice, 50g roughly chopped finest-quality Kalamata black olives and 2 tbsp finely chopped red onion in a bowl. Add a squeeze of lemon juice to taste and a sprinkle of ground cumin.

Fennel, Orange, Pine Nut & Raisin Salad
Very finely slice 2 large fennel bulbs and toss with 1 tbsp sherry vinegar and the fennel fronds. Segment 2 oranges over the bowl, letting any juices drip in. Drizzle over 6 tbsp extra-virgin olive oil and season. Toast 40g pine nuts in a little oil and, when golden, toss through 50g raisins over the heat for 1 minute. Toss with the fennel, a handful of chopped mint leaves and ¼ tsp caster sugar.

4 very fresh line-caught mackerel,
    gutted and cleaned, or 8 fillets
1 lemon
very good-quality extra-virgin olive oil

The Fastest Fish, Several Ways (Continued)

FEEDS FOUR—SIX

For the Mackerel

4 very fresh line-caught
   mackerel (about 300g each),
   gutted and cleaned
45g coriander seeds
1 tbsp cumin seeds
½ tsp black peppercorns
½ tsp yellow mustard seeds
½ tsp chilli powder
½ tsp fine salt
1 garlic clove
2cm piece of fresh ginger,
   peeled and finely grated
½ tbsp cider vinegar
2 tbsp groundnut,
   vegetable or olive oil

For the Sambal

300g cherry tomatoes
½ red onion, finely sliced
50g coconut cream
1 red chilli, finely chopped
1½ tsp cumin seeds, toasted
small handful of mint
   leaves, roughly chopped
juice of ½ lemon
2 tsp vegetable oil

Madras Mackerel with Sambal

When you want something with a bit more oomph, this exotically and richly spiced mackerel is utterly delicious. Serve with couscous or Coconut Rice (see page 81).

Preheat the oven to 220°C/gas 7. Slash the mackerel 3–4 times on each side and place on a roasting tray.

Grind together the dry spices in a pestle and mortar or spice grinder then add the salt, garlic and ginger and grind until there are no big lumps. Stir in the vinegar and oil until you have quite a dry paste. Push the paste into the slashes in the mackerel and any leftover into the cavity of the fish. Bake for 10–14 minutes until the flesh of the mackerel is just cooked and flaky.

Meanwhile, make the sambal by combining all the ingredients and seasoning generously with salt and pepper. Serve with the roast mackerel.

Miso-Smoked Mackerel with Avocado Salad

FEEDS TWO

Omega-3 oils are supposed to be fantastic, so I try to keep a packet of smoked mackerel in my fridge or freezer. I recently learned a neat and simple trick: warm a smoked mackerel fillet under a hot grill for a minute and the flesh turns soft and almost molten: delicious.

This discovery had me running round my kitchen trying different butters on top of the mackerel just before grilling, to add an extra level of moisture and flavour. The result is a butter with a mellow, roasted flavour of Turkish chilli flakes intensified by the savoury taste of miso. The flavours of the mackerel are complemented by the nutty, fresh avocado and sprout salad. It takes 15 minutes from start to finish and is an ideal healthy midweek meal. If you are avoiding bread just flake the mackerel into the salad and add some toasted pumpkin seeds.

For the Salad
120g mixed sprouted seeds
1 large, ripe avocado,
    peeled and diced
juice of 1 lime
2 tbsp sesame oil
2–3 smoked mackerel fillets
2 slices of sourdough toast
small handful of parsley leaves,
    finely chopped
lime wedges, to serve

For the Butter
50g miso paste
30g butter, softened
2 tsp Turkish chilli flakes

First make the butter by beating the three ingredients together and seasoning to taste with salt and pepper if needed (go easy as both the miso and fish are salty). At this point you can roll the butter into a log and chill in the fridge or freezer if you have time. Don't worry if you don't, you may get a little messy but it won't affect the recipe!

Put the mixed sprout seeds in a sieve and rinse well under cold, running water. Drain and dry thoroughly with a tea towel. Toss the avocado with the sprouts, lime juice and sesame oil and season lightly with salt and pepper.

Preheat the grill to high. Line a baking sheet with foil and place the smoked mackerel on top. Put a slice of butter on top of each fillet and grill for a minute or so until the butter is melted and bubbling.

Toast the bread and spread with a little more of the miso butter. Top with the mackerel, sprinkle with the parsley and serve with a pile of the avocado and sprout salad, with lime wedges on the side.

Flash-Roasted Cod with Chickpeas & Kale

FEEDS FOUR

Cod has been endangered for some time, but stocks have now been significantly revived after a successful collective international effort. Here I roast it on a bed of wilted kale with really soft chickpeas and a punchy, citrusy basil and caper oil.

For quick recipes, I use the Napolina brand of canned chickpeas, which are plump and yielding, unlike the hard bullets you can often find (if you do only find hard chickpeas, simmer for 10–15 minutes to soften them). You could add some chopped and sautéed, good-quality cooking chorizo to the mix to glam up this recipe.

Heat half the butter in a large frying pan over a medium-high heat and fry the onion and fennel seeds until golden. Add the garlic, chickpeas, flour and sugar and fry for about 5 minutes until the chickpeas begin to crisp up. Turn off the heat, season with salt and pepper and lightly squash with the back of a wooden spoon.

Place another large pan over a high heat and add the half the olive oil. Fry half the kale until it starts to wilt and colour and catch, then squeeze over some of the lemon juice and season. Tip onto a serving platter, leaving a gap in the middle for the chickpeas, cover with foil and repeat with the remaining oil and kale. Meanwhile put the basil leaves, capers, extra-virgin olive oil, lemon zest and the remaining lemon juice into a small food processor, season and blitz to a purée.

Wipe the pan clean with a piece of kitchen paper. Return it to a high heat and add the remaining butter. Season the fish on both sides. Place the fillets skin side down in the pan and fry for 3–4 minutes on each side until the skin is crisp. Turn the fish a third time and check if the flesh is starting to flake. If not, fry for a further 2–3 minutes until flaking. Remove from the heat.

Gently reheat the chickpeas and spoon onto the kale. Top with the fish, flaking it and discarding the skin if you prefer, or keeping the fillets whole. Spoon over the basil and caper oil and serve.

Why not try kale & pumpkin seed salad?

Shake 1 tsp Dijon mustard, 1 tsp honey, 1 tbsp cider vinegar, 2 tbsp extra-virgin olive oil, 1 tbsp walnut oil and a squeeze of orange juice in a jar with a tight-fitting lid until emulsified. Season, adding a little more of any of the dressing ingredients to your taste. Toast 50g pumpkin seeds in a pan for 2 minutes. Tip into a bowl but keep the pan over the heat. Wash 200g trimmed kale and transfer – still wet – to the hot pan so it sizzles and steams. When wilting, remove from the hob, give a quick squeeze over a colander then dress with the vinaigrette and pumpkin seeds in the warm pan. Feeds 4 as a side.

For the Cod, Chickpeas & Kale

30–40g butter

1 red onion, sliced

½ tbsp fennel seeds

1 garlic clove, finely chopped

2 x 400g cans chickpeas, rinsed and drained

½ tbsp plain flour

¼ tsp sugar

3 tbsp olive oil

200g kale, coarse stalks removed, well washed

finely grated zest and juice of 1 lemon

3 x 300g skin-on cod, coley or dab fillets (fresh and sustainably sourced)

For the Basil & Caper Oil

large handful of basil leaves

50g capers in brine, drained and rinsed

3 tbsp extra-virgin olive oil

Crab Linguine

When crab is in season it is fresh and sweet; for me it conjures up memories of idyllic summer holidays. If you can't be by the seaside for fresh crab then dressed crab will more than do the job. It makes for terrific fast food. When buying crab try to ensure you get some brown meat; it is much cheaper, more savoury and just a little of it accentuates the sweetness of the white flesh. The quantities given here are approximately what you would get from 1 large fresh crab.

Here the crab dissolves into a sauce of olive oil, garlic (which is at its gentlest in the summer, when crab is at its best) and watercress. It is such a simple dish that each of the individual flavours gets to shine. I often give this to friends as a starter in the height of the summer in tempting, small scoopfuls with delicious, chilled white wine. There is no finer way to start a meal.

Bring a pan of salted water to the boil and cook the pasta according to the packet instructions.

Meanwhile crush the garlic with a little salt until you have a paste. Transfer to a large bowl and stir in the white and dark crab meat, the chilli and lemon zest and juice. Season well with salt and pepper, then slowly stir in the oil.

Drain the pasta, reserving a cup of the cooking water. Pour the pasta into the bowl with the crab meat, adding the watercress. Stir and toss it all, adding a few good splashes of the cooking water to loosen the sauce, until the watercress has just started to wilt and every strand of pasta is coated. The pasta will continue to absorb the water as it is tossed so you might need to add a few splashes more. Serve immediately with an extra drizzle of oil.

Kitchen note:

Whizz leftover crab with mayonnaise or aioli (see page 288 for home-made versions of both), finely chopped cucumber, chervil, finely chopped Granny Smith apple and chopped spring onion for a delicious baguette or croissant filling.

400g spaghetti or linguine

1 garlic clove

200g white crab meat

100g dark crab meat

pinch of chilli flakes

finely grated zest of 1
    and juice of 2 lemons

150ml extra-virgin olive oil,
    plus extra to serve

100g watercress

Sweet Potato & Watercress Salad with Quick Labneh

FEEDS FOUR—SIX

Dukkah is a Middle Eastern mix of nuts, herbs and spices. I think of it as magic dust that you can sprinkle over the simplest dish to transform it into something extraordinary. It adds crunchy texture to vegetables and a toasty, earthy, warming flavour to dips.

In this recipe dukkah is paired with another Middle Eastern stalwart, labneh or strained yogurt. In this speedy version you strain the yogurt while the sweet potatoes are roasting; it becomes thick and luscious (but is even better if you can start the night before).

Preheat the oven to 180°C/gas 4. Toss the sweet potatoes in a roasting tin with the vinegar, oil, coriander seeds, herbs and a good sprinkling of salt and pepper, then roast in the oven for 25 minutes.

Meanwhile, spoon the Greek yogurt into the centre of a muslin set over a bowl with half the lemon zest and some salt and pepper. Stir briefly to combine. Tie a string to close the muslin around the yogurt and hang it over the bowl so that the whey can drip out. Leave to drain, squeezing the muslin occasionally, while the sweet potatoes are roasting. For a really firm labneh, leave to drip overnight. If muslin is too much of a faff, you could try using a fine-mesh sieve or even a very clean sock.

Put the roast sweet potato into a bowl with the watercress and season, then toss with the lemon juice and an extra 1 tsp of red wine vinegar. Make a gap in the potatoes and turn out the labneh from the muslin into the hollow you have made. Scatter over the rest of the lemon zest and sprinkle with the dukkah and extra oregano. Serve with crusty bread. This is also delicious with leftover roast lamb, lamb burgers or spicy merguez sausages.

Why not try flash-roast cauliflower with cherry tomatoes, dukkah & feta?
Break up a whole head of cauliflower, toss in a roasting tray with 2 punnets of cherry tomatoes, 4 tbsp olive oil and 3 tbsp dukkah (for home-made, see page 294) and sprinkle with 100g feta; season. Roast in a preheated oven at 230°C/gas 8 for about 25 minutes until the cauliflower is blackened. Transfer to a serving dish, or blitz and serve as a dip. Feeds 4.

For the Salad
1kg sweet potatoes, unpeeled
    and cut into 3cm chunks
1½ tbsp red wine vinegar,
    plus extra for the salad
3 tbsp sunflower or light olive oil
½ tbsp coriander seeds,
    crushed in a pestle and mortar
small handful of oregano leaves,
    plus extra to serve
small handful of rosemary needles
50g watercress
50g good-quality dukkah
    (for home-made, see page 294)

For the Labneh
300g Greek yogurt
finely grated zest and juice of 1 lemon

Tamarind Prawns with Noodles & Coconut Rice

FEEDS FOUR

If I have friends for supper but no time to cook, this is one of my standby recipes. The combination of flavours is fantastic: sour tamarind, fiery chilli heat, sharp lime, umami-rich soy, nutty toasted coconut and sweetness from the prawns and sugar. Despite it being Asian, I first discovered tamarind when I was living in Mexico, where it is mixed with smoky chipotle chillies and lime in seafood dishes such as the salmon below.

Tamarind paste is easy to make (see page 298) but I also always keep a jar of the ready-made paste in the cupboard. It tastes a little tinnier than home-made but when you are in a hurry it is great!

Cook the rice noodles according to the packet instructions, then drain and toss them in the oil.

Meanwhile, toast the rice and coconut flakes in a dry pan until most of the grains have turned a lovely nutty brown colour. Give it a brisk grind in a pestle and mortar to break up the rice and grind the coconut.

Put a small frying pan or wok over a gentle heat, add the sugar, soy sauce, lime juice, chilli flakes and tamarind paste. Warm through until the sugar melts. Increase the heat, add the prawns and fry for 2 minutes until just pink and golden; if you fry them for any longer they will become tough and rubbery.

Open up the leaves – 2 on each plate – and top with the cooked rice noodles. Spoon the prawns on top, pouring over the sauce. Sprinkle with the chopped chilli, coriander and toasted rice. Serve with lime wedges.

Why not try flash-baked salmon with a smoky tamarind glaze?
Blitz together 1 tbsp vegetable oil, 1 tbsp honey, 2 tbsp soy sauce, 2 tbsp tamarind paste, 1 tsp chipotle paste, if you have it (for home-made versions of both, see pages 298 and 286) and 1 tbsp sesame seeds, then rub over 2 salmon fillets. Bake in a preheated oven in a shallow roasting tin at 220°C/gas 7 for 12–14 minutes until golden on the outside, but pink in the middle. Serve with Coconut Rice (see page 81). Feeds 2.

For the Prawns & Noodles

200g rice noodles (I love black
     noodles; you can find them online)
1 tsp peanut or groundnut oil
30g white basmati rice
15g coconut flakes
1 tbsp soft light brown sugar
     (or use palm sugar or Indian
     jaggery if you can find it)
2 tbsp soy sauce
1 tbsp lime juice
½ tsp chilli flakes
2 tbsp tamarind paste
     (for home-made, see page 298)
300g raw king prawns,
     preferably MSC-certified
     (see page 78), peeled and deveined
8 large leaves from a bunch of spring
     greens, Chinese cabbage leaves
     or Cos lettuce, washed and dried

To Serve

1 red chilli, very finely sliced
bunch of coriander leaves,
     roughly chopped
1 lime, cut into wedges

Sprout, Anchovy, Chilli & Pine Nut Pasta

I recently discovered a new vegetable called Rosetta, or flower sprouts. They look like mini Savoy cabbages when they are cooked and have a gentler flavour than the traditional Brussels sprout. They are quick to prepare and I love them in stir-fries or this pasta dish. Shredded Brussels sprouts work just as well if you can't find them.

This beautifully rich and rounded pasta sauce uses the gutsy flavours of rosemary, chillies and anchovies to add layers of flavour, but is softened and tamed by the mascarpone and Parmesan sauce.

Finely shred the sprouts; this can be done by hand but to save time, use a food processor. Set aside.

Heat the olive oil in a pan and gently fry the anchovies, rosemary and chilli flakes for 3 minutes. Toss in the sprouts and the garlic and fry for 1 minute. Increase the heat and add the wine. When the wine has almost evaporated, stir in the mascarpone, Parmesan and lemon zest, then season and remove from the heat.

Dry fry the pine nuts for 30 seconds until just golden.

Meanwhile, bring a large pan of salted water to the boil and cook the pasta according to the packet instructions. Drain, reserving 2 small ladlefuls of the pasta water to add to the sauce. Tip the pasta straight into sprouts along with the toasted pine nuts and a splash or so of the pasta cooking water. Toss gently and grate extra Parmesan over the top.

Why not try Parma ham & shredded sprout salad?

Slice 200g Brussels sprouts as finely as possible then place in a bowl. Make a dressing with the juice of 1 lemon plus the same amount of extra-virgin olive oil, a pinch of sugar, and ¼ grated garlic clove and season generously. Toss with the sprouts, 50g roasted, bashed hazelnuts, 10 slices of Parma ham or speck, 50g Parmesan shavings, a Granny Smith apple, cut into fine batons and finely chopped parsley and tarragon. Feeds 4–6.

400g Rosetta sprouts or
   Brussels sprouts, topped

2 tbsp olive oil, plus extra to serve

6 anchovy fillets in olive oil, drained

2 sprigs of rosemary needles,
   stripped and finely chopped

½ tsp chilli flakes (depending
   on how much heat you enjoy)

1 garlic clove, finely chopped

140ml white wine

60g mascarpone

100g Parmesan, finely grated,
   plus extra to serve

finely grated zest of 1 lemon

70g pine nuts

400g fusilli

Salmon & Toasted Pumpkin Seed Stir-Fry

FEEDS TWO—FOUR

A few days a week I work from home, writing. Invariably at about 2pm I realise that I am starving and need some lunch. I made this dish up on one of those occasions when I was desperate for some food, and fast.

It is worth making a large batch of the spiced seed sprinkles, they make a great snack and add a delicious crunchiness to salads and stir-fries, or are even good for scattering over fried eggs for supper.

Preheat the oven to 160°C/gas 3.

To make the seeds, mix all the ingredients together in a bowl, then spread the mixture on a baking sheet lined with baking parchment. Roast for 15–20 minutes, stirring the seeds every now and then, until dry and toasted. Allow to cool.

Wash the kale in plenty of cold water and drain, the residual water on the kale will help to cook it. Put a large wok over a medium-high heat and add 1 tbsp of the sesame oil. When hot add the kale plus 1 tbsp of water, stir, season and cover with a lid, steaming for 3–4 minutes until tender. Stir halfway through and add another splash of water if needed. Once wilted down, remove from the heat and transfer to a bowl.

Cut the salmon fillet into thick slices, then cut each slice in half. Put the wok back over a high heat and add 2 tbsp of sesame oil followed by the chilli flakes. Stir-fry for a minute or so to flavour the oil and fry the chilli until it blackens a little, then add the onion, garlic and ginger. Stir-fry, stirring continuously, until the onions have softened and turned translucent. Increase the heat, add another splash of oil and the salmon and stir-fry for a minute or so until the salmon pieces have started to colour. Now add the greens, soy sauce and sherry and stir for another minute or so to heat through the greens. Scatter with the spiced seeds and serve with rice noodles.

Why not try crab & ginger soup with crispy kale?

Warm 2 tbsp olive oil in a large casserole and add 1 onion and 2 garlic cloves, both peeled and finely chopped, and a 5cm piece of fresh ginger, finely grated. Cook for 10 minutes over a medium heat until soft, then pour in 2 tbsp brandy. Simmer for a few minutes over a higher heat, before adding 2 tbsp tomato purée. Cook for a minute, add 750ml fish stock (for home-made, see page 47), bring to the boil and add 140g salmon or white fish fillet and the meat from 1 dressed crab. Simmer very gently for 10 minutes, then whizz until smooth and season to taste. Serve with extra white crab meat on top, a scattering of Spiced Seeds and kale that you have drizzled with olive oil and roasted in your hottest oven for 5 minutes. Feeds 2–3 for a starter or light lunch.

For the Stir-Fry

350g kale or spring greens, coarse stalks removed and leaves cut into 2–3cm ribbons

3–4 tbsp sesame oil

1 large organic or wild salmon fillet (about 250g)

1–2 pinches of chilli flakes

1 large onion, finely chopped

3 fat garlic cloves, finely sliced

5cm piece of fresh ginger, peeled and finely chopped

3–4 tbsp soy sauce

3 tbsp sherry

For the Spiced Seeds

50g almonds (skin on), roughly sliced

50g pumpkin seeds

100g sunflower seeds

50g sesame seeds

1 tsp olive oil

1 tsp soy sauce

1 tsp maple syrup

1 tsp white miso paste

1 tsp chilli flakes

¼ tsp salt

Warm Tortillas with Toasted Black Beans & Charred Jalapeño Hummus

I always, always have a mass of cartons and cans of pulses and beans in my store cupboard. Whether it is the depths of winter and I am making baked beans or refried beans with eggs and warm tortillas, or I am throwing together light, healthy impromptu salads studded with lentils, chickpeas or beans in the height of summer, I find pulses an essential part of my cooking repertoire. They are deliciously nutty, richly filling and cost almost nothing. Of course, cooking any pulse from scratch does wonders for their flavour (see page 301), but in times of hurry, cans of pulses are a saviour. Here classic hummus is given a Mexican makeover, adding delicious, piquant heat. It makes a wonderful filling for the warm tortillas with the charred black beans and citrusy, sweet salad.

Prepare the tomato salsa first: finely chop and put into a mixing bowl with the garlic, herbs, chilli, if using, lime juice and oil. Season to taste, then set aside to marinate.

To make the hummus, put a dry frying pan over a medium-high heat and add the jalapeño chilli. Char all over, turning occasionally, for 10 minutes until completely blackened. Leave to cool, then discard the stalk and seeds and transfer to a food processor or blender with the pickled jalapeño, chickpeas, garlic, tahini, oil, lemon juice and coriander. Blitz until coarse, then add 2–3 tbsp of cold water to loosen the dip, season to taste and blitz again until smooth.

Place a large, non-stick frying pan over a medium-high heat. Give the drained black beans a quick rub with kitchen paper to remove any excess water, then add to the hot pan and cook for 5–8 minutes, shaking the pan occasionally, until the skins begin to split open and the beans crisp up. Season lightly, then transfer to a plate. Return the pan to the heat and warm up the tortillas, wrapping them in a tea towel to keep them warm (or you can warm a pile of them in the microwave, wrapped in cling film).

Put the hummus on the table and let everyone make their own tacos with the warm tortillas wrapped in a basket, toasted beans, hummus, tomato salsa and lime wedges. If you like, serve with Lancashire, feta or pecorino cheese to crumble over the top.

For the Tortillas

150g sweet cherry tomatoes

½ garlic clove, crushed
    with a little salt

small handful of coriander
    leaves, roughly chopped,
    plus extra to serve

small handful of mint
    leaves, roughly chopped,
    plus extra to serve

½ red chilli, finely chopped (optional)

juice of 1–2 limes

2 tbsp extra-virgin olive oil

1 x 400g carton black beans,
    rinsed and drained

8 small corn tortillas,
    or 4 large tortillas, halved

lime wedges, to serve

For the Hummus

1 jalapeño chilli and 1 pickled jalapeño

1 x 400g can chickpeas,
    rinsed and drained

1 garlic clove

1 tbsp tahini

60ml extra-virgin olive oil

juice of 1 lemon

small bunch of coriander
    (leaves and stalks)

Kitchen Note:

Make a quesadilla by heating a flour tortilla in a pan, sprinkled with 60g grated Monterey Jack or mature Cheddar. When melted, dollop on 3 tbsp Jalapeño Hummus (see above), 6 slices of pickled jalapeño, ½ carrot shaved with a vegetable peeler and a handful of coriander. Season and roll up. Eat while the cheese is still oozing.

Chard, Cauliflower & Paneer Curry

I once went on a food trip to Kerala, southern India, where we barely ate meat for 10 days. I came back feeling fresher, lighter and healthier although I had eaten as much as I wanted. The beauty of a vegetable curry is that you can get home in the evening, grab a few vegetables and make a delicious supper in half an hour.

Here I have used chard, which keeps producing throughout the summer and early winter. It is packed full of iron and has a beautifully sweet and delicate flavour. It is a common sight at farmer's markets but less so in supermarkets; you could use spinach or any other gentle-flavoured green. Cauliflower lends body to the curry, while the coconut and paneer add a lovely richness.

1 tbsp ghee (butter is fine too)

1 large onion, sliced

5cm piece of fresh ginger (about 25g), peeled and finely grated

1 garlic clove, finely chopped

1 tsp ground turmeric

1 tsp medium chilli powder, or to taste

1 tsp garam masala (for home-made, see page 293)

225g paneer

3 curry leaves (optional)

500g Swiss chard, washed, leaves separated from stalks, both roughly sliced (or use spinach)

300g cauliflower or romanesco, chopped into small florets

100g natural yogurt

60g coconut cream

50g double cream

1 tsp nigella seeds

Heat the ghee (or butter) in a frying pan and, when sizzling, fry the onion and ginger until the onion is almost soft. Stir in the garlic and spices. Add the paneer, curry leaves, if using, the sliced chard stalks and the cauliflower. Fry for 5 minutes.

Add the chard leaves or spinach, yogurt and coconut cream and cover with a lid for 5 minutes or until the leaves have wilted down. Season and add the double cream and nigella seeds, then simmer again for another 5 minutes until all the vegetables are tender. Serve with boiled or pilau rice.

Why not try crispy fried paneer with Indian tomato sauce?

This was inspired by a bowl of tomato rasam that I ate on the shores of the Arabian Sea. Rasam is a form of Indian consommé spiced with curry leaves and mustard seeds. Chop 225g paneer into large cubes, soak in water for 10 minutes, then dry out on kitchen paper. Dust in 25g plain flour and fry in 2 tbsp ghee until golden and beginning to crisp. Heat 1 tsp cumin seeds in a pan, then add 2 punnets of cherry tomatoes, ¼ tsp chilli flakes and 1 tbsp olive oil over a high heat until the tomatoes burst. Whizz then season to taste. Scoop into a bowl and serve with the paneer and some fresh naan. Feeds 2–4.

Sausages,
Roast Tomatoes
& Bean Mash

FEEDS TWO

Bangers and mash may be a great British comfort food but I have a real blind spot when it comes to mashed potatoes. They are a real faff to make and lumpy mash is gross. My father makes a three-hour Heston-inspired version that is wonderfully smooth and creamy, but I just don't have that sort of time to commit to something that doesn't set my world on fire in the first place.

This creamy textured bean mash is much more my thing: full of protein, scrummy and great for the children. When we are going meat-free we eat this bean mash with just the roast tomatoes, but doubled in quantity. Mash with more olive oil and no cream if you are avoiding dairy.

For the Sausages & Tomatoes

2 tbsp olive oil

4–6 Italian pork sausages, or merguez

500g vine-ripened cherry tomatoes

4 garlic cloves

2 sprigs of rosemary

2 tbsp oregano leaves

200ml beer

2 tbsp cider vinegar

For the Bean Mash

750g Home-Cooked beans
(see page 301) or 3 x 400g cans
cannellini beans, rinsed and drained

50ml hot chicken stock (for
home-made, see page 46) or water

2 tbsp extra-virgin olive oil

100g Parmesan, finely grated

100ml double cream

Preheat the oven to 200°C/gas 6. Pour the olive oil into a roasting tin and place over a medium-high heat on the hob. Add the sausages and brown them all over. Add the tomatoes, garlic and herbs followed by the beer and vinegar. Roast in the oven for 25 minutes until the tomatoes are puckered and sizzling and the sausages cooked.

Meanwhile, simmer the beans with the stock. Take the garlic cloves from the sausage pan and squeeze out the mellow cooked flesh from their skins into the beans. Add the extra-virgin olive oil and mash; how smooth is up to you. Stir in the Parmesan and cream and season to taste. Serve the mash with the sausages and tomatoes, pouring over any roasting juices.

Why not try cannellini beans with Moroccan-spiced tuna?

Heat 2 tbsp olive oil in a pan and add 1 finely chopped onion and 3 sliced garlic cloves, and sweat for 10 minutes until soft. Stir in 2 tsp ras el hanout, 1 x 200g can of tuna in oil, drained, 1 x 400g can drained cannellini beans, 1 finely chopped tomato and 100ml water or vegetable stock. Simmer for 5 minutes and season with extra-virgin olive oil, a pinch of chilli flakes, the juice of 1 lemon and a splash of wine. Serve in bowls scattered with chopped parsley and pile onto crusty bread, warm couscous or over bruschetta. Feeds 2–3 as snack or light lunch.

Grilled Tandoori Chicken with Mango Chutney

FEEDS FOUR

This recipe has always been a winner. Chicken thighs are one of the quickest cuts of meat to cook during the week and the fast tandoori marinade here turns them into something pretty special. I love them with sweet mango chutney, either in these baguettes or with the fast couscous salad below.

I often turn this recipe into a weekend meal for friends. If you cut out the backbone of a whole chicken and press down on the breastbone to flatten it (ask a friendly butcher if the idea puts you off) you can rub the marinade all over and leave overnight. The next day chargrill or barbecue the chicken until crispy, fragrant and delicious and serve with the Mango & Coconut Rice Salad (see page 81). A feast by anyone's standards.

For the Chicken

6–8 chicken thighs, deboned
 (or skinless and boneless chicken
 thighs, if you can find them)
4 seeded crusty bread rolls
 or small baguettes
1 jar of good-quality mango chutney
butter, for the rolls
2–3 heads of Baby Gem,
 leaves separated
juice of 1 lemon,
 plus more to serve (optional)
handful of coriander leaves,
 roughly chopped
½ cucumber, finely chopped (optional)

For the Tandoori Marinade

3 garlic cloves, finely grated
½ small thumb-sized piece of fresh
 ginger, peeled and finely grated
1 small red chilli,
 finely chopped (deseeded if
 feeding chilli-averse children)
½ tsp ground turmeric
2 tsp garam masala
 (for home-made, see page 293)
½ tsp cayenne pepper
250g natural yogurt

First make the marinade. Mix the garlic, ginger, chilli, turmeric, garam masala, cayenne and half the yogurt in a large bowl and stir to combine.

Flatten the chicken thighs between sheets of cling film by bashing with a rolling pin until roughly 1cm thick. Transfer to the bowl and rub the marinade into the chicken so that it is thoroughly covered.

Preheat the grill to high. Season both sides of the chicken, then place on a wire rack over a foil-lined baking tray and place under the hot grill for 10–12 minutes, turning the chicken over halfway. When it's brown on the edges and cooked though (check by cutting into a piece) remove from the oven to rest.

Split the rolls and spread a side of each with 1 tbsp of mango chutney; butter the other sides. Slice the thighs into thick fingers and cram into each roll, along with the lettuce, any leftover cooking juices and an extra dollop of mango chutney. Squeeze over the lemon juice, season to taste, then top with coriander. Serve at once with the extra yogurt in a bowl on the side, seasoned with some salt and pepper, a squeeze of lemon, and if you like, the cucumber.

Why not try fragrant cucumber couscous salad?

Heat 150ml seasoned chicken stock or stir a stock cube into 150ml just-boiled water. Pour the stock over 150g barley couscous in a bowl and cover with a tea towel. Leave for 5 minutes, uncover, then fluff with a fork. Make a dressing with 2 tbsp good mango chutney, 2 tbsp natural yogurt, ½ tsp grated fresh ginger, 2 tbsp groundnut oil, 1 tbsp water and the juice of ½ lemon. Season. Finely chop ¼ cucumber and a large bunch of coriander and stir through the couscous with the dressing. Sprinkle over ½ tsp garam masala, 1 tsp nigella seeds and serve. Add shredded chicken if you like. Feeds 2–3.

Poached Eggs with Melted Leeks & Chipotle-Tahini Dressing

This is for those evenings when it is late and you are shattered, but crave something healthy and not too heavy. This recipe came from a moment like that when I had a few leeks and some chipotles that were left over from recipe testing. Some tahini added a richness and nuttiness to the dressing and a good dose of calcium and protein to our supper. It is now a firm favourite that we make often.

In a way this dish is a tour of my culinary life; my glamorous granny lived in Wales and always made her leek quiche when we came to stay. The smell of sautéing leeks takes me back to the warmth of her kitchen and that quaking, cheesy tart of hers. The tahini and za'atar make me think of my time pottering among the Middle Eastern food shops of Shepherd's Bush. The chipotle in the dressing – one of the classic ingredients of Mexico – is the final touch.

Top and tail the leeks and peel away their outer layer. Cut them in half lengthways and wash them thoroughly under a cold, running tap. Slice them into finger-width rounds.

Put a large, heavy-based frying pan over a high heat and after a few minutes add the butter. When it is melted and sizzling add the chopped leeks, reduce the heat to medium, season generously with salt and pepper and sauté for 5–10 minutes, stirring from time to time, until collapsed and soft.

Meanwhile put the tahini, garlic and half the lemon juice in a small bowl with the chipotle and beat with a fork until smooth. Stir in the yogurt, taste and season with salt and pepper and more lemon juice if needed to brighten the flavours.

Poach the eggs and toast the bread, drizzling it with a little olive oil. Top the toast with the leeks, eggs and a sprinkling of za'atar. East with great dollops of the dressing.

Why not try charred leeks with goat's curd & warm raisin dressing?

Soak 30g raisins in 30ml just-boiled water (or sherry) for 10 minutes, then mix with 2 tsp red wine vinegar and the leaves from a sprig of thyme and boil in a pan until the liquid has evaporated. Add 2 tbsp extra-virgin olive oil. Heat a griddle pan to high. Rub 2 halved leeks (washed and trimmed) or 4 baby leeks in olive oil, salt and pepper. Griddle the leeks, turning, for 20 minutes until blackened and wilted, then remove from the pan. Put 100g goat's curd on each plate and lay a leek on top. Drizzle the raisins over, scrunch over a handful of walnuts and eat with warm flatbreads. Feeds 2 as snack or light lunch.

3 large leeks

40g butter

25g tahini

I small garlic clove, crushed

juice of 1 lemon

1 heaped tbsp chipotle en adobo, finely chopped

75g natural yogurt

2 poached eggs per person (see page 18 for Poached Perfection)

2–4 slices of sourdough or rye bread

olive oil, to serve

za'atar, to serve

Summery Green Herb Omelette

I love seeking out different varieties of eggs, as I am always pleased when I crack into them and see the deep ochre colour of the yolks. In the winter I like to fry eggs on sourdough toast for a filling, comforting supper, but in the summer I err towards a fast omelette, which I normally eat with a thrown-together crisp green salad. Soft summery herbs abound and when thrown into eggs they become a miraculously vibrant supper. This is where you can get as inventive as you like – add a mixture of your favourite soft herbs into the omelette, whether coriander, chives or oregano, or stick with a simple parsley filling – just be careful to treat herbs carefully; if you are too rough with them they become muddy and bruised.

Never waste leftover herbs, just whizz them into a green sauce which – when covered with a thin layer of oil – will last for several weeks in the fridge.

Whisk together the eggs and milk in a jug and season generously. Stir through most of the finely chopped herbs.

Heat the butter in a non-stick frying pan. When the pan is hot, pour in the egg mixture and swirl around the pan. Using a spatula, pull the sides of the omelette into the middle then swirl the pan again so you have a large, even circle, filling the gaps in the pan with the uncooked egg and spreading out the herbs with the back of the spatula. Loosen the edges of the omelette every now and then with the spatula. Cook for 2–3 minutes until the underside is golden and the top is just cooked. The omelette should be thick and fluffy.

Scatter the top with the remaining herbs then fold the omelette in half. Slide out of the pan and onto your plate.

Why not try a comforting ham & cheese omelette?

Whisk together 3 eggs, 2 tbsp milk and the leaves from a few sprigs of thyme (or dried oregano) in a jug; season generously with salt and pepper. Heat a non-stick frying pan until smoking. Add a knob of butter and, once melted and sizzling, pour in the egg mixture and swirl around the pan. Using a spatula, tip the pan towards you and pull the sides of the omelette into the middle, letting the wet egg run down. Repeat twice, swirling the pan again so you have a large, even, circle shape. Scatter over chopped ham and grated cheese and cook for a minute or so longer, so the underside is golden and the top still a little wet (it always carries on cooking). Fold the omelette in half then slide onto your plate. Warming, gooey and nourishing. Serve with a crisp green salad. Feeds 1.

3 large eggs

2 tbsp milk

handful of chervil or tarragon leaves, half finely chopped, half roughly chopped

handful of dill fronds, half finely chopped, half roughly chopped

handful of mint leaves, half finely chopped, half shredded

handful of basil leaves, roughly torn

knob of butter

Asian-Roast Cauliflower with Quick Kimchi & Sticky Rice

I have become increasingly fascinated by fermented foods. So much of what we eat is sterilised and does no good for our guts and digestive systems. The benefits of fermented foods such as home-made vinegars, kombuchas, sourdoughs, yogurts and pickles are now becoming apparent; they team with good bacteria that are amazing for gut health, aiding digestion and supporting our immune systems. Kimchi is an important (and trendy) member of this family.

This recipe takes the idea of kimchi and applies it to those crisp outer leaves of the cauliflower; they form such a large part of the vegetable and are so deliciously sweet and crunchy. I roast the main part of the cauliflower in sesame and soy until dark and caramelised and toss the leaves in a kimchi-inspired dressing, making a tangy, bright and spicy topping. Every bit of the vegetable is used and it only takes half an hour to make.

For an extra-express meal, use shop-bought kimchi.

Preheat the oven to 220°C/gas 7.

For the Cauliflower
1 large cauliflower head (pick one
    with as many leaves as possible)
1 tsp fine salt
2 tbsp sesame oil
2 tbsp soy sauce
300g sushi rice

For the Kimchi Dressing
1 red chilli, deseeded and finely sliced
1 garlic clove, finely chopped
very small thumb-sized piece of fresh
    ginger, peeled and finely chopped
1½ tbsp fish sauce
2 tsp soy sauce, or to taste
1 tbsp rice wine vinegar, or to taste
juice of 1 lime
2 tsp caster sugar, or to taste
3 spring onions, finely sliced

Throw away any very tired outer leaves from around the cauliflower, reserving the inner perky ones. Cut the florets from the core. Slice the core and leaves all into 1cm pieces and place into a large bowl. Sprinkle the cauliflower leaves and core with the salt. Massage the salt into the leaves with your hands for 3 minutes or so until they begin to wilt, then transfer to a sieve and rinse away all the salt. Place in a bowl and add all the kimchi dressing ingredients. Adjust the sugar, soy or vinegar to your liking and set aside while you prepare the cauliflower florets and rice.

Break the cauliflower into smallish florets (about 5cm) then place in a large roasting tray. Pour in the sesame oil, soy sauce and a generous pinch of salt. Mix well to coat, then roast for 20 minutes, shaking the tray every 5 minutes or so.

Meanwhile, prepare the rice by rinsing it under cold water until the water runs clear. Transfer to a pan with a pinch of salt and cover with approximately 480ml boiling water. Return to the boil, then cover and simmer for approximately 15 minutes until the rice is tender. Take off the heat and keep covered.

Spoon the rice onto plates and top with the roast cauliflower florets and kimchi mixture, spooning over the remaining dressing.

Rapid Ravioli with Walnuts, Goat's Cheese & Cavolo Nero Sauce

FEEDS FOUR

In the autumn, Tuscan kale (or cavolo nero) sticks upright from the ground, looking dark, feathery and showy, like the tails of a glamorous nightshade peacock. It has a rich, mineral flavour and inky colour that makes a stunning silky sauce.

The fresher the walnuts are, the sweeter they will be, so it is often worth buying them in their shells and cracking them yourself.

First make the sauce. Bring a large pan of lightly salted water to the boil then add the cavolo nero. Cook for a minute or so until the kale turns bright green and softens in the water. Lift out with tongs into a colander, keeping the cooking water to boil the pasta. Run cold water over the kale in the colander, squeeze out any excess water, then transfer to a food processor. Add the olive oil, garlic, lemon juice and salt and blitz to a fine pesto. Taste and season again if necessary and transfer to a small pan. Gently warm over a medium-low heat.

Clean the food processor and make the goat's cheese paste: add the walnuts, sage, goat's cheese, a good squeeze of lemon juice and the olive oil and blitz to a paste. Taste and season well then gently warm in another small pan over a medium-low heat, stirring occasionally.

Bring the pan of cavolo water to the boil again, adding more water if needed. Add the pasta sheets and simmer according to the packet instructions: roughly 3 minutes for fresh pasta, a little longer for dried. Drain, keeping a cup of the pasta water back to add to the cavolo sauce. Cut the pasta sheets in half and toss in a little olive oil. Stir the reserved pasta water through the cavolo sauce and keep on a low heat. If the sauce still looks thick, thin down with a little more water, or increase the heat a little if too thin; it should be pourable like double cream.

Put a pool of the vivid green cavolo sauce on each plate. Layer the lasagne sheets on top with spoonfuls of the goat's cheese paste in between each layer. Top with the last sheet of pasta and ladle over a little more cavolo sauce. Serve, with a wedge of pecorino or Parmesan to grate over.

Why not try white risotto with cavolo nero sauce?

Very finely chop 1 onion and fry in 1 tbsp each of butter and olive oil until softened. Add 200g risotto rice and fry for 3 minutes. Increase the heat and add 100ml white wine. Once evaporated, ladle in 750ml warmed good-quality chicken stock a little at a time, stirring until it is absorbed by the rice before adding the next ladle. When cooked, add a knob of butter and 30g finely grated Parmesan and season well. Loosely stir through the cavolo nero sauce above. Feeds 2 as a main, 4 as a starter.

For the Sauce

400g cavolo nero

150ml olive oil, plus extra
    to toss the pasta

2 small garlic cloves

juice of 2 lemons

1 tsp salt

8–12 fresh or dried lasagne
    sheets, depending on size

finely grated pecorino
    or Parmesan, to serve

For the Goat's Cheese Paste

140g walnuts

handful of sage leaves,
    finely chopped

120g goat's cheese

lemon juice, to taste

50ml olive oil

Purple Sprouting Broccoli with Ricotta on Toast

FEEDS FOUR—SIX

Purple sprouting broccoli is a welcome arrival to the winter market stall in late January, a constant friend amongst the roots and brassicas; it remains in season until the arrival of the spring. Once you learn how to trim and cut the stalks to match the size of the heads, it is a brilliantly easy vegetable to cook. I often steam it until just cooked and toss with olive oil and lemon as a side dish, but here it is the main ingredient in this perfect thrown-together supper.

Cut the stems from the broccoli, peeling away any tough outer skin with a speed peeler or sharp knife. Cut the stems into halves or quarters lengthways so that they are the thickness of your finger. Put into a steamer, stems first, then the florets on top and steam for 5–10 minutes or until the stalks are tender.

Warm the olive oil with the garlic in a pan and when smelling fragrant, after a few minutes, add the broccoli and stew gently for a further 10 minutes, stirring every now and then, until the broccoli has collapsed gently into the garlicky oil. Season to taste and squeeze over the lemon juice.

Toast the bread and drizzle with extra-virgin olive oil. Top with the broccoli and crumble the ricotta over. Drizzle with chilli oil (or sprinkle with chilli flakes), grate over the lemon zest and serve drizzled with more extra-virgin olive oil for flavour.

Kitchen Note:

Home-made Hot & Fiery Chilli Oil (see page 295) takes about 10 minutes to make and is gorgeous drizzled over pizzas, tarts and into the bases of soups and stews, but you can buy lots of delicious ready-made oils from delis, supermarkets and Asian grocers.

250g purple sprouting broccoli

5 tbsp olive oil

1 large garlic clove, finely chopped

juice of ½ lemon

4–6 slices of sourdough bread

extra-virgin olive oil, to serve

225g fresh ricotta

chilli oil (for home-made, see page 295) or a few good pinches of chilli flakes

finely grated lemon zest, to serve

Chapter
EIGHT

KIDS' FOOD (YOU'LL LOVE TOO)

KIDS' FOOD (YOU'LL LOVE TOO)

A love of good food starts early. We were in Mexico when I was weaning my first child and wherever we ate we'd ask the chefs if they had anything for a baby. They would make purées of poached chicken, fish, fresh herbs and vegetables. I can't help but think that adventurous start must have had a positive effect, as she'll try almost anything now, unless, of course, she is in a real strop.

I later read that scientists believe that exposing children to diverse food in the first thirty months helps them to become 'good' eaters. As they grow to be more independent, children become suspicious of many foods, especially those they've never seen before. Studies suggest this pickiness in toddlers may have evolved to keep them safe: rejecting unfamiliar food prevents the risk of poisoning. A wide range of foods and a balanced diet is key in my experience. As they grow up, even 'good eaters' have fussy fads, but I've found they pass quickly if they've started off with a variety of foods.

Some children, of course, are fussier than others: my youngest is a carb queen who I feared would only ever eat pasta and potatoes. When she rejected something outright, I would try weaving it subtly into other foods she enjoyed; in the end familiarity bred acceptance! She now adores beans in all guises, having grown to love them in the ketchup-laced Bean Salad, and polishes off vegetables when they come with Cheesy Polenta Wedges with a shaving of Parmesan on top.

Rather than ask the girls what they want, I give them meals as a fait accompli. But for special occasions or at weekends they can choose what to have for supper or we might cook it together. If I hit a brick wall on a meal and they are refusing to eat it, then I'm afraid it's tough luck. If I can remain calm and firm, I find toddlers' food tantrums (and food 'hates') soon dissipate; then if they've had a 'proper go' they can have their next course: some fruit, yogurt, or cheese and crackers.

Healthy food is important to me, too: we tend to opt for brown rice and pasta rather than white and fruit juice doesn't get a look in, except for high days and holidays when we make 'cocktails' with fizzy water. I try to avoid processed spreads in favour of butter, ditto sugary yogurts for natural ones. I'm a big believer in full-fat products, as low-fat foods are often pumped with dubious ingredients; I do season the children's food with a little salt as I know that they have very little coming from other sources. If we sometimes dive into burgers and fries, or spoil ourselves with pain au chocolat, then I'm relaxed about it; the majority of their diet is made up of fresh fruit and vegetables and home-cooked food. In any case I try to make mealtimes fun. If I can give my girls a love of good food and a healthy attitude towards eating, then I'll be thrilled.

Summer Spaghetti

This is more like a fresh dressing than a pasta sauce and it is my children's favourite summertime recipe. The warm juices trickle out of the tomatoes and run down their chins as they suck up the long strands of soft, slippery spaghetti. The garlicky breadcrumbs add a satisfying crunch.

Quarter the tomatoes, keeping every last drop of juice that you can, and add to a bowl. Smash the olives with the flat of your chopping knife, discard the stones and roughly chop. Add the olives to the bowl of tomatoes.

Crush the garlic to a paste with a pinch of salt and add half to the tomatoes along with at least 1 tsp sea salt, plenty of freshly ground black pepper and the sugar to taste. Pour in 4 tbsp of the olive oil and leave to steep for at least 10 minutes (but no longer than 1 hour), to allow the flavours to develop before you eat.

Heat the remaining oil in a frying pan and add the rest of the garlic paste. Cook over a medium heat for a minute or so before adding the fennel seeds and breadcrumbs. Fry for 5–10 minutes until the crumbs are toasted and golden. If you like add a pinch of sugar (I do). Transfer to a bowl.

Finally, cook the pasta in plenty of well-salted boiling water. Transfer the tomatoes to the frying pan in which you cooked the crumbs and place on top of the pan of water so that the sauce gets a chance to warm through (alternatively place the tomatoes over a low heat; you don't want to cook the sauce, just warm it).

Once the pasta is al dente, drain, keeping back a few tbsp of the cooking water. Toss the pasta thoroughly in the tomatoes, crumbs and cooking water. Check for seasoning and serve at once.

Why not try a simple pomegranate & tomato salad?

In the winter, when tomatoes are not at their best, pomegranate seeds add some much-needed sweetness to tomato salads. Roughly chop 3 beef tomatoes. Roll 2 pomegranates across a work surface before cutting open and removing the seeds. Stir them into the tomatoes, discarding any white pith. Add ½ finely sliced red onion, a handful of chopped parsley leaves, 2 tbsp good-quality sherry vinegar and 1 tbsp pomegranate molasses. Stir in 6 tbsp of your best olive oil and season with ½ tsp caster sugar and plenty of salt and pepper. Leave for at least half an hour at room temperature for the flavours to infuse. Feeds 4–6 as a side dish.

450g cherry tomatoes

60g Kalamata or other black olives,
   preferably stone-in for flavour

2 garlic cloves

a few pinches of sugar

5 tbsp extra-virgin olive oil

½ tsp fennel seeds, ground

60g breadcrumbs
   (for home-made, see page 277)

200g spaghetti

large handful of basil leaves

Pesto Perfection

This is a great children's cooking activity; it's action-packed and they can taste and see the vivid green results immediately. My kids love to pick and smell the herbs and press the buttons on the blender.

Dollop it on a bowl of pasta, in leftover mash or add to a fishcake mixture; stir it through goat's cheese or mayonnaise for crudités or arancini (Italian stuffed rice balls, see page 135). A handful of frozen peas thrown in here (give them small bowls of frozen peas for snacks), some softly steamed broccoli forked through there, sautéed courgettes or leeks or a rinsed and drained can of borlotti or cannellini beans all make fine additions and will give your children a boost of vitamins and fibre. Hand round Parmesan cheese at the table, and dress their pasta with extra drizzles of olive oil; both make them feel grown up and teach them about taste.

Pesto keeps well under a layer of oil for a week or two in the fridge, so do consider making a double batch.

Classic Basil Pesto

Put the garlic, pine nuts and basil leaves into a food processor or blender and pulse to a rough purée. Stir in the Parmesan (or Grana Padano) and then gradually pour in the extra-virgin olive oil.

Season to taste after adding the Parmesan, as it is a naturally salty cheese.

1–2 fat garlic cloves
50g toasted pine nuts
100g basil leaves
50g Parmesan, or Grana Padano, finely grated
120ml extra-virgin olive oil

Pasta & pesto tip:
Always keep half a cup of the pasta cooking water back from the drained pasta. Cooked pasta absorbs moisture after cooking, so a previously shiny, glossy pesto can quickly become dry and mealy. Bring it back to its former glory by loosening the mixed pasta and pesto with as much of the cooking water as you need to moisten it and make it glossy again, adding a dash of extra-virgin olive oil for good measure.

Below are some delicious alternatives that my kids love. If you run low on pine nuts try substituting in hazelnuts, walnuts or almonds or even seeds and use any other combination of basil, tarragon, parsley or mint leaves; whatever happens to be growing in your garden or on your kitchen windowsill.

Pumpkin Seed & Parmesan Pesto

Crush 1 garlic clove and add to a blender with 100g pumpkin seeds, 100g finely grated Parmesan and 100ml extra-virgin olive oil and blitz until smooth but still with a little texture. Transfer to a bowl and stir through 1 tsp cider vinegar, 3 tbsp water (or more to loosen further). Season with salt and pepper to taste.

Spread onto oven-baked chicken thighs for their last 5 minutes of cooking and cook until bubbling; stir into a white garlic soup; or spread onto Crostini (for home-made, see page 277) and top with smoked anchovy fillets.

Pea, Feta, Dill & Almond Pesto

In a dry pan toast 25g blanched almonds. Crush in a large pestle and mortar, then grind a little more with 200g peas (fresh or defrosted from frozen), gradually pouring in 75ml extra-virgin olive oil. Transfer to a bowl and, using a fork, stir in 3 tbsp chopped dill fronds, 100g crumbled feta and a few torn mint leaves. Season with salt and pepper.

This is perfect for dunking cooked chorizo sausages or king prawns; or spread onto soldiers for soft-boiled eggs, or tossed through a salad of griddled mangetout and served alongside a slow-cooked shoulder of lamb (see page 147).

Kale & Hazelnut (Dairy-Free) Pesto

Wash 2 good handfuls of kale (coarse stalks removed) and dry well in a tea towel. Crush 1 garlic clove and blitz with the kale, 30g blanched hazelnuts, the rind of 1 preserved lemon and 1 tbsp thyme leaves. Drizzle in 100ml extra-virgin olive oil and 1 tsp runny honey, then blitz again until smooth. Season with salt and pepper.

Toss this pesto through boiled potatoes or gnocchi and serve with fishcakes or grilled salmon; dollop large spoonfuls onto cod fillets and bake until the fish is golden and crisp; or serve drizzled over burrata with toasted sourdough.

Sweet Potato Shepherd's Pie

FEEDS SIX—TEN DEPENDING
ON AGE & APPETITE

I came up with this recipe when we were putting on our first Day of the Dead festival at Wahaca. The film *The Book of Life* is popular in our house, and so I cooked this for my daughter's party. Now I make it throughout the winter with any orange root in the mash. It looks sumptuous with its golden topping and the Mexican-inspired raisin and cinnamon-studded meaty filling is sweet and warming when the weather turns colder.

Place the sweet potatoes in a pan of water and bring to the boil. Cook until tender, then drain. Lightly mash with 30g of the butter, using a fork or potato masher, to a smooth purée, season with salt and pepper and leave to cool.

Meanwhile, heat 1 tbsp of oil in a large, deep casserole dish over a high heat and, when hot, add the raisins and cook for a few minutes until just puffing up and changing colour. Remove with a slotted spoon and set aside.

Heat another 1 tbsp of oil in the same pan and add the meat, stirring well to break it up and brown all over, about 5 minutes. Add another splash of oil, reduce the heat to medium and stir in the onion, carrot, celery and spices, seasoning with a little salt and pepper. Fry for 10 minutes to cook out the raw onion flavour before adding the raisins, plum tomatoes, tomato purée and 500ml water. Bring to simmering point and simmer for 15 minutes. Preheat the oven to 190°C/gas 5.

3 large sweet potatoes (about 800g),
    peeled and cut into chunks
40g butter, at room temperature
3 tbsp vegetable oil
65g raisins
750g minced lamb
1 large onion, finely chopped
1 large carrot, grated
2 celery sticks, finely chopped
1 tsp ground cumin
½ tsp ground cinnamon
1 tsp sweet smoked paprika
1 x 400g can plum tomatoes
2 tbsp tomato purée

Spoon the mince into a deep oven dish and spread the mash on top. Melt the remaining butter and use to brush the top, then bake for about 30 minutes until the top is golden and crisp. Remove from the oven, leave to sit for 5 minutes and serve.

Why not try lamb burgers?

Blitz ½ a small onion with a fistful of mint leaves in a mini food processor. Mix with 500g minced lamb, season well and form into 6 small burgers, or 4 larger burgers (depending on the ages of your children). Grill, fry or chargrill for 3–4 minutes each side for medium rare. Serve with oven chips baked with olive oil, a tomato salad and mint sauce and quince jam (for home-made versions of both, see pages 290 and 280). These are also great with 200ml Greek yogurt mixed with 1 small crushed garlic clove, some chopped coriander leaves and one-third of a cucumber, coarsely grated and patted dry.

Fish Tacos

FEEDS FOUR—SIX DEPENDING
ON AGE & APPETITE

My children are obsessed with these tacos, perhaps because they've eaten so many of them with me at Wahaca. They can't believe that they are encouraged to get their hands dirty and make their own, any way they want. At home I use whatever fish looks good in the market: monkfish tails, cod fillets, haddock or gurnard have all worked well (as long as you pick the bones from the latter). You will be amazed at how fast this food can go down; it works a treat when you have a gang of children over for lunch.

First make the guacamole. Check the heat of the chilli by nibbling the tip furthest from the stem. Most generic supermarket chillies are quite mild but, if it is hot, remove the seeds, or leave it out entirely if your children are totally heat-averse.

Put one-quarter of the onion, the garlic, the chilli and salt in a pestle and mortar and mash to a rough paste. Cut open the avocados, remove the stones and scoop the flesh into a large bowl, adding the onion, garlic and chilli paste. Roughly mash the flesh with a fork, adding half the lime juice as you go. When you have a rough guacamole, stir in the remaining lime juice and onion with the coriander and tomato. Season with plenty of black pepper. If it doesn't taste delicious at this stage, think whether it might need seasoning with more salt, lime juice or coriander. When you are happy put it in a bowl on the table.

Season the fish with salt and pepper. Mix the mayonnaise and crème fraîche together and put in a bowl on the table.

Heat the olive oil in a frying pan over a medium heat and fry the fish for a few minutes each side until cooked through. Season with a squeeze of lime juice.

Heat the tortillas in a microwave or a dry frying pan and put them on the table in a basket, wrapped in a tea towel to keep them warm. Place the grated cheese and salsa in separate bowls and add to the table with bowls of Apple Slaw or lettuce. Invite your children to fill their tortillas with whatever they want, roll them up and tuck in.

Kitchen note:

If we are eating en famille we have exactly the same tacos but I just put extra hot sauce on the table for us, home-made or shop-bought. They are also great with chipotle mayo (see page 76).

For the Tacos

600g line-caught cod, monkfish
   or other firm fish
100g mayonnaise
100g crème fraîche
2 tbsp extra-virgin olive oil
2 limes, quartered
8–12 corn or corn and flour tortillas
   (2–3 per child)
150g grated Cheddar
fresh tomato salsa (see page 197)
Apple Slaw (see page 224)
   or shredded lettuce

For the Guacamole

½ red chilli, finely chopped,
   depending on your children's taste
½ red onion, very finely chopped
1 small garlic clove
1 tsp salt, or to taste
3 ripe Hass avocados
juice of 1–2 limes, or to taste
small handful of coriander leaves,
   chopped, or to taste
1 very ripe tomato,
   deseeded and chopped

Chicken Schnitzel with Apple Slaw

I think the girls would eat anything if it came with this sweet, zingy slaw. If you have gluten intolerances in the family you can crumb the chicken with gluten-free cornflakes instead of bread and flour. You can use chicken breast instead of thigh, but the result won't be quite so juicy.

For the Schnitzel

4 slices of stale bread,
    or 150g breadcrumbs
    (for home-made, see page 277)
40g Parmesan, finely grated
small handful of sprigs of thyme,
    leaves picked
40g plain flour, well seasoned
3 eggs, lightly beaten
8 skinless and boneless chicken thighs
30g butter
a little olive oil

For the Slaw

¼ small white cabbage, finely shredded
2 apples, coarsely grated (skin and all)
2 carrots, coarsely grated
½ fennel bulb, finely chopped
½ red onion, finely chopped
2 tbsp sesame seeds, toasted
large bunch of parsley leaves,
    roughly chopped
juice of 1–2 lemons
1 tsp honey
2 tsp tahini
1 tsp Dijon mustard
2 tbsp mayonnaise
1 tbsp natural yogurt

Whizz the stale bread in a food processor to make breadcrumbs, then mix with the Parmesan and thyme. Season with a little salt (the Parmesan is naturally salty) and a grind of black pepper and spread out on a large plate. Spread the flour on another plate and put the eggs in a large bowl.

Toss each chicken piece first in the flour, then in the egg and finally in the breadcrumbs. Put them in the fridge for half an hour to 'set' the crumbs or, if you have made lots, you can freeze them at this stage.

Mix all the shredded, peeled and chopped vegetables together in a salad bowl and toss with the sesame seeds, parsley and the juice of 1 lemon. Shake the honey, tahini and mustard together in a clean jam jar with a tight-fitting lid to get rid of any lumps in the tahini, then whisk into the mayonnaise and yogurt. Season well with salt and pepper. Just before you are ready to eat, dress the slaw; taste a bit and add more lemon juice if the salad needs to be less creamy and a bit sharper.

Heat a heavy-based frying pan over a medium-high heat and add the butter and a drizzle of olive oil. Fry the chicken in batches until golden on the outside and cooked through in the middle, about 3–4 minutes for each side. Serve with the slaw and some golden crispy potatoes (see pages 111 or 129).

Kitchen Note:

Chicken, or even veal, fingers are just as popular as fish fingers in our house and a great source of protein. Cut the thighs into fingers, or bash out some veal and cut into strips. Bread them as above and then either chill in the fridge to firm or freeze for a rainy day. Serve with peas blitzed with salt, pepper and a little crème fraîche and butter to loosen, or just a mild olive oil and some lemon juice.

My Ma's Spaghetti Bolognese

FEEDS EIGHT DEPENDING
ON AGE & APPETITE

I have yet to meet a child who doesn't love this version of the classic and it is a very easy way to introduce some fibre-rich, soft lentils into their diet. We have been known to use this sparingly as a topping for makeshift pizzas, either on puff pastry bases or on Mexican-Style Pizzas (see page 123). There is also something very comforting about feeding your children something you were fed as a child.

Rinse and drain the lentils (if using dried), then simmer in the wine for 25 minutes until tender.

Meanwhile heat the olive oil in a large frying pan and fry the onion, carrot and sugar over a medium heat for a few minutes. Crumble in some of the beef, breaking it up in the pan and frying for a few minutes before adding more and breaking up each time. Continue until you have added all the meat and cook until it is all well browned.

Add the tomatoes and swirl the sherry around in the cans, if using, before adding to the sauce. Season with a little salt and pepper and then add the rest of the ingredients, being careful not to overdo the Tabasco as it is quite fiery.

Add the cooked and drained lentils (or rinsed and drained canned lentils) and cook the sauce over a low heat for at least 20 minutes. Serve with pasta, with some salad leaves or steamed vegetables on the side.

Why not try the quickest, yummiest tomato sauce?
I heat 5 tbsp olive oil in a wide frying pan and fry 3 finely chopped garlic cloves until just turning golden. Add 2 x 400g cans plum tomatoes, rinsed of their juices, breaking them up with a wooden spoon in the pan. At this stage, if you like, add a little chopped rosemary needles or thyme leaves. Season to taste and simmer for 10 minutes. Ta-da! Serve with multi-coloured pasta or fun pasta shapes.

125g dried lentils (or 1 x 400g can)

300ml red wine, stock
    (for home-made, see pages 46–7)
    or water (optional)

3 tbsp olive oil

1 onion, chopped

1 large carrot, diced

1 tsp soft light brown sugar

320g minced beef (not low-fat),
    at room temperature

2 x 400g cans plum tomatoes

2 tbsp fino sherry (optional)

4 tbsp barbecue sauce

1 tbsp tomato purée

2–3 dashes of Worcestershire sauce

few drops of Tabasco

Crispy Chicken Thighs

FEEDS FOUR—EIGHT DEPENDING
ON AGE & APPETITE

So crispy that you would think that they were deep-fried; so simple that you could make them with your eyes shut; so popular with children, hot out of the pan, that this is a recipe that I use repeatedly for feeding my gang and their friends. They can even help cook them. This is mouth-wateringly good served with these smashed courgettes.

Season the chicken thighs generously on both sides and set aside for 15 minutes. Heat a large, heavy-based frying pan over a medium heat and, once hot, add the oil followed by the thighs, skin side down. Fry them for 20–25 minutes without turning, draining the fat into a heatproof dish every 10 minutes or so and checking the colour of the skin. If it looks as if it is colouring too quickly, reduce the heat a little.

Once the skin is crisp and deep golden, turn the thighs over, add the preserved lemon, half the lemon zest and juice, green olives and sherry and cook on the other side for 10–15 minutes, or until the chicken juices run completely clear when pierced with a skewer through their thickest parts.

Meanwhile put the courgettes in a pan large enough to fit them lengthways and cover with boiling water. Simmer for 10–15 minutes until completely tender. Drain, top and tail and put in a sieve or on the draining board. Now cover with a board or plate and weigh down with several cans of beans or a heavy pestle and mortar for 15 minutes to drain. Quarter lengthways, then cut into diagonal chunks. Pop them in a salad bowl and scatter over the remaining lemon zest and juice, herbs, garlic, olive oil and feta and season.

Flip the chicken thighs over to warm the skin side once more, then serve with the smashed courgette salad and lemon wedges.

For the Chicken

8 bone-in, skin-on chicken thighs

1 tbsp olive oil

1 preserved lemon, pulp scraped
    away, rind finely chopped

finely grated zest and juice of 1 lemon

60g green olives, stoned
    and roughly chopped

60ml sherry

lemon wedges, to serve

For the Smashed Courgette Salad

4 medium courgettes

handful each of basil and mint leaves,
    roughly chopped

1 fat clove garlic, finely chopped

6 tbsp extra-virgin olive oil

80g feta, crumbled

Why not try courgette fries?

Fussy eaters may prefer these. Combine 75g ground almonds with 75g finely grated Parmesan and 2 tbsp plain flour and season generously. Cut 3 medium courgettes into 1cm-thick fingers then dip them into an egg beaten with a splash of milk followed by the ground almond mix. Spread out on a lined baking sheet, drizzle with oil and bake in an oven preheated to 220°C/gas 7 oven for 10–12 minutes until golden and crisp. Feeds 4 as a side dish.

Cheesy Polenta Wedges with Veggie Jam

FEEDS SIX OR MORE
IF THEY ARE VERY YOUNG

These are always a hit. Prep the polenta ahead (allow three hours) and keep in the fridge for emergencies. I find that as long as I cover the wedges in a fine carpet of Microplaned Parmesan and a slick of olive oil (which makes them feel very grown-up) my children will eat almost anything on top. Here I serve the wedges with a caponata-inspired veggie stew that has been cooked down until it turns sweet and almost jammy. You could try them with any kind of sauce, from a simple tomato one (see page 225) to leftover bolognese, or serve with melting soft broccoli or wilted spinach. The wedges keep for about a week, well wrapped, in the fridge.

For the Polenta Wedges

100g quick-cook polenta

100g extra-mature Cheddar

20g Parmesan (optional),
  plus extra to serve

30g butter, plus extra for the dish

extra-virgin olive oil, to serve

For the Jam

1 tsp cumin seeds

1 tsp allspice berries
  (or use ground allspice)

butter, to fry

2 tbsp olive oil, plus extra for the polenta

2 red onions, finely chopped

1 red pepper, deseeded and
  cut into bite-sized chunks

1 yellow pepper, deseeded and
  cut into bite-sized chunks

6 garlic cloves, crushed

1 fennel bulb, outer layer
  removed, finely chopped

1 tsp sweet smoked paprika

small handful of thyme or oregano
  leaves, roughly chopped

8 plum tomatoes (or 2 x 400g
  cans plum tomatoes, rinsed of
  their sauce), finely chopped

finely grated zest and juice of 1 orange

1 tbsp red wine vinegar

handful of chopped pitted olives
  (optional)

Pour 400ml boiling water into a pan over a medium heat and gradually whisk in the polenta. Keep whisking until the polenta is thick enough that you need to change from whisk to wooden spoon. Grate in the Cheddar and Parmesan, if using, add the butter and season with a pinch of salt and pepper (I sometimes add 1 tsp Dijon or grainy mustard to the mix, which seems to go down well). Pour into a lightly buttered 32 x 22cm baking dish or oven tray. Cover and chill for a minimum of 3 hours until firm.

To make the veggie jam, toast the whole seeds in a dry frying pan for a minute or so until smelling fragrant, then grind to a powder using a pestle and mortar or spice grinder.

Place the pan back over the heat and add a knob of butter and the olive oil. When sizzling add the onions and cook for 5 minutes until beginning to soften. Now add the peppers, garlic and fennel and cook for another 8–10 minutes before stirring in the paprika, herbs, tomatoes, orange zest and juice, vinegar and olives, if using. Season with salt and pepper and bring up to a high heat. Simmer briskly for a few minutes, then reduce the heat and bubble gently for about 30 minutes until you have a thick paste, stirring every so often to prevent it sticking.

When you are ready to eat, cut the polenta into 12 triangles. Melt a knob of butter and 1 tbsp of olive oil in a non-stick frying pan and fry as many wedges as you need for 2 minutes each side until crisp and golden. Serve with the vegetable jam, lots of grated Parmesan and a slick of extra-virgin olive oil.

Kitchen Note:

Wet polenta, before it sets, is also delicious and very child-friendly. Serve with baked beans, wintery ratatouille, summer aubergine caponata and any kind of ragu. Add a bowl of minty, buttery peas on the side to give them some greens or add some wilted spinach to any of the toppings.

Irresistible Oatcakes

This is a good recipe to have up your sleeve for rainy-day baking. Sometimes we make the flapjacks below, which I find addictive (I hope that the high density of oats and seeds makes up for the sugar and butter). If I am feeling a little more military about our sugar intake, we make these cheesy oatcakes. They are great snacks and very popular for 'picnic' lunches with slices of cheese, cucumber, carrot sticks, cherry tomatoes and pots of hummus and taramasalata for dipping.

Blitz the rolled oats in a food processor with the flour, sugar, baking powder and several pinches of salt.

Cut the butter into cubes and pulse into the mix with the grated cheese. Very briefly pulse in the milk until the mix just comes together. Dust the work surface with a little flour and a handful of oats and roll the dough into a sausage. Wrap in cling film and chill in the fridge for 30 minutes.

Preheat the oven to 190°C/gas 5 and line a couple of baking sheets with baking paper. Cut the chilled dough into 1cm slices and spread out on the baking sheets, spaced about 3cm apart.

Bake in the oven for 15 minutes. Allow to cool for a few minutes before transferring to a wire rack to cool completely.

Why not try golden flapjacks?

Mix 200g jumbo oats with 240g oats that have been briefly whizzed in a food processor. Stir in 200g Demerara sugar, 80g sunflower seeds, 100g raisins and a pinch of salt. Melt 450g butter then stir through the mix. Butter a 50 x 30cm roasting dish or 2 smaller baking tins and spread a thin but tightly packed layer of the mix across the base. Bake in a 190°C/gas 5 oven for 10–15 minutes until a lovely deep golden colour. Score squares through the warm flapjack a few minutes after you have taken it out of the oven, then allow to cool in the tin before cutting into those squares. These are also delicious with 60g peanut butter and 80g grated dark chocolate folded through the mixture.

150g rolled oats, plus extra to dust
120g wholemeal spelt flour, sifted, plus extra to dust
10g soft light brown sugar
1 tsp baking powder
100g chilled butter
150g mature Cheddar, grated
4 tbsp whole milk

Home-Made Baked Beans

FEEDS EIGHT DEPENDING
ON AGE & APPETITE

A great way to make people happy is to rustle up a batch of these and they are blissfully easy to make. The girls eat these with sausages, with eggs, with crispy roast kale chips or simply on toast at the end of the weekend. This recipe is mild but with a lovely smoky depth. Do ramp up the chipotle if you are cooking for friends.

The flavour improves considerably if you can make them a day or two in advance. Soak dried beans overnight and then make them the next day, though canned beans make a good easy shortcut.

If you are cooking your own beans, see method on page 301.

Preheat the oven to 190°C/gas 5.

Heat the oil in a large heavy-based casserole dish over a medium heat. Sauté the onion, garlic, celery and bacon until the onion has softened, about 10 minutes. Add the bay leaves, oregano and Smoky Chipotle Paste and sweat for a further 2–3 minutes before throwing in the remaining ingredients. Season to taste.

If you are using canned beans, add them to the casserole now with 250ml water and bring up to simmering point. If you have cooked your own, throw them in with just a cup of water if the beans look dry (though you will probably won't need to). Cover with a lid and put in the oven for 1 hour or until the beans are juicy but not swimming around in liquid.

Store in a cool part of the kitchen overnight and eat the next day, if you can wait.

Why not try my children's favourite bean salad?

Cover 250g dried borlotti beans with water, add 1 tsp bicarbonate of soda and soak for 1 hour (or longer if you have time). Drain and cover with fresh water in a pan. Cook for 45 minutes or until tender (to make 450g cooked beans). Drain, rinse and allow to cool. Mix the juice of 1 lemon, ½ tsp red wine vinegar, ½ grated garlic clove, 3 tbsp olive oil and 1 heaped tbsp tomato ketchup in a mixing bowl. Stir through the beans, 2 chopped spring onions, ¼ chopped cucumber and 150g chopped cherry tomatoes. Feeds 4.

Ingredients

- 350g dried haricot beans or 3 x 400g cans haricot beans, rinsed and drained
- 3 bay leaves
- 2 tbsp olive oil
- 1 onion, chopped
- 3 garlic cloves, finely chopped
- 2 celery sticks, finely chopped
- 100g streaky bacon, chopped
- 1 tsp dried oregano
- 1–2 tsp Smoky Chipotle Paste (optional, see page 286)
- 1 x 400g can plum tomatoes, chopped
- 2 tsp Worcestershire sauce
- 2 tbsp maple syrup

A Burger Feast

In the summer we like to open our back doors, put some charcoal on our home-made barbecue and invite as many friends as we can fit in the house and garden. These burgers are an easy way to feed a crowd and the children can't help being seduced by these mini versions of the grown-up's food.

Serve any of these burgers with my children's favourite Apple Slaw, Sweet Cucumber Relish or Pomegranate and Tomato Salad (see pages 224, 300 and 215). Ice cream sandwiches (see page 256) make a great pudding.

Straight–Up Burgers

For the Straight-Up Burgers
450g minced beef (not low fat)
½ small white onion, finely chopped
mini burger buns, to serve

Put the mince and onion in a food processor with some salt and pepper and roughly pulse for about 10–15 seconds (if you overwork the meat it will become very stringy). Separate the mixture into 8 equal-sized balls and pat them to make small, flattish burger shapes. Heat up a chargrill until it is smoking hot and cook the burgers for 3–4 minutes each side, depending on whether you like them pink or medium. Serve in buns.

Halloumi Burgers with Avocado & Little Gem

For the Halloumi Burgers
250g halloumi, finely chopped
30g finely grated carrot, squeezed
    of its juices (about 1 carrot)
80g finely grated courgette, squeezed
    of its juices (about 1 courgette)
small handful of mint leaves,
    finely chopped
small handful of thyme leaves
olive oil, to fry
2 Little Gem lettuces,
    separated into 10 leaves
2 avocados, sliced

Mix together the halloumi, carrot, courgette, mint and thyme and season with a little salt and pepper. Scoop small handfuls (about 30g) into the palm of your hand and squeeze into a patty.

Heat a lightly oiled frying pan over a medium-high heat. Cooking them in batches, fry the patties for roughly 4 minutes on each side until golden, pressing them down gently with a spatula as they cook. Remove from the pan and allow to cool down and firm up a bit.

Fill each Little Gem leaf with some sliced avocado and top with a burger.

A Burger Feast
(Continued)

Popeye Burgers

Preheat the oven to 200°C/gas 6.

Blitz the onions in a food processor until they are very finely chopped. Follow with the chicken thighs and bacon and pulse until the chicken is minced. If you are using minced chicken, just stir it through the onion. Season the mixture lightly with salt and pepper and stir.

Pour boiling water over the spinach in a colander until wilted. When the spinach is cool enough to handle, squeeze out as much liquid as possible. Loosely stir the spinach through the chicken until evenly dispersed.

2 onions, roughly chopped
500g boneless and skinless chicken
   thighs (or use minced chicken)
130g smoked streaky bacon,
   rind removed, roughly chopped
200g baby spinach leaves

Using clean hands, shape the mixture into 24 small 5cm patties and place on 1–2 large baking sheets. Slide the patties into the oven and bake for 30 minutes, turning halfway through until all the liquid has evaporated and they are nutty golden brown. Eat hot! (If you are not cooking these immediately keep in the fridge, well covered, for up to 24 hours.) You can also fry these in a little oil in a hot frying pan for 10 minutes each side, but sometimes it's easier to just throw them in the oven!

Cauliflower Cheese with Roasted Cherry Tomatoes

FEEDS FOUR DEPENDING
ON AGE & APPETITE

The secret to a good cauliflower cheese is to steam-dry the vegetable thoroughly after cooking to avoid the sauce becoming flavourless and watery. This version is super-cheesy with lovely bursts of sweetness from the roast cherry tomatoes. It is a firm family favourite.

Preheat the oven to 200°C/gas 6.

Separate the cauliflower into medium-sized florets and cut up the stalk into roughly similar-sized pieces. Cook in lightly salted boiling water for 4–5 minutes until just tender but still with some bite (you want to avoid a mush). Drain thoroughly and leave the cauliflower in the sieve or colander to steam-dry.

Make the sauce: heat the butter in a non-stick pan and, when foaming, stir in the flour and mustard powder and season with salt and pepper. Stir over a medium heat for a few minutes to cook out the 'raw' flavour of the flour. Now add a good glug of milk and whisk or beat with a silicone whisk or wooden spoon. Gradually add the rest of the milk, whisking or beating in between additions to get a smooth, creamy sauce. Stir in the cheese, paprika and nutmeg and remove from heat. Check the seasoning.

Put the now thoroughly dry cauliflower in a shallow gratin dish and scatter with the tomato halves. Pour over the cheese sauce and scatter with the breadcrumbs and Parmesan. Bake in the top of the oven for 20–25 minutes until golden and bubbling. Serve at once with slices of buttered brown bread.

Why not try warming cauliflower mash?
Blitz 900g cauliflower in a food processor to fine crumbs. Transfer to a wide pan and heat with 200g crème fraîche, a knob of butter, 1 tsp Dijon mustard and 50g grated mature Cheddar. Season and steam gently for 5–10 minutes. Feeds a family of 4.

1 large cauliflower

50g butter

3 tbsp plain flour

1 tsp English mustard powder

550ml whole milk

125g extra-mature Cheddar, grated

1 tsp sweet smoked paprika

several good gratings of nutmeg 200g cherry tomatoes, halved

3 tbsp stale breadcrumbs
   (for home-made, see page 277)

30g Parmesan, finely grated

Fish Pie

The Dijon mustard gives the deliciously cheesy topping on this fish pie tang without heat. My husband and I enjoy this comfort food as much as the girls.

Preheat the oven to 200°C/gas 6.

Place the potatoes in a large pan of salted water, bring to the boil and cook for 15 minutes until tender. Drain and mash with 50ml of the milk and 40g of the butter until smooth. Season generously.

Heat a griddle pan over a high heat and grill the spring onions until softened. Finely chop and set aside.

Melt the remaining butter in a pan over a medium heat, add the flour and cook, stirring, for a few minutes. Gradually stir in the remaining milk and the mustard. Season and add the cooked spring onions.

Cut the salmon and smoked haddock into chunks and add to the sauce with the raw prawns. Stir gently to combine and then spoon into a large enough oven dish so that the pie won't bubble over in the oven. Top with the mashed potato and scatter over the Cheddar. Place on a baking sheet and bake for 40 minutes or until the fish is cooked and the mash is crispy.

Why not try crispy pesto fishcakes?

Cook 300g whole floury potatoes (or use leftover mash) for 20–30 minutes until soft. Leave to cool, then peel and mash. Meanwhile boil 500ml water in a pan and poach 250g fish (cod, salmon or haddock) for about 4 minutes until cooked through (or use leftover cooked fish). Drain and flake the fish into the potato with the juice of ½ lemon, 2 tbsp drained, chopped capers and a small handful of dill or 2 tbsp pesto (see pages 218-19 for some of our favourites). Season and mix well. Roll the mix into about 12 little cakes. Put 1 lightly beaten egg and 100g breadcrumbs onto 2 separate plates. Roll the cakes in the egg and then the crumbs. Brush both sides with a little olive oil and fry or bake for 20 minutes at 180°C/gas 6, turning over halfway so that they are golden on both sides. Feeds 3–4 children.

1kg King Edward potatoes, peeled and chopped

475ml whole milk

65g butter

5 spring onions

25g plain flour

1 tsp Dijon mustard

300g skinless salmon, pin-boned

300g skinless smoked haddock, pin-boned

200g raw king prawns, preferably MSC-certified (see page 78), peeled and deveined

50g Cheddar, coarsely grated

Buckwheat Pancakes

Thin crêpes are wrapped around a spinach filling, covered in Gruyère sauce and then baked in the oven until crisp and golden on the outside and soft and cheesy inside. This cunning way to include greens would also work with leeks, pancetta or roasted peppers.

Place the flour and salt in a bowl and stir in the eggs. Mix the milk and water and slowly drizzle into the flour, beating until you have a batter the consistency of single cream. Cover with cling film and place in the fridge for at least 1 hour.

Meanwhile make the filling. Put the spinach in a large pan (you will probably have to do half at a time), cover with a lid and place over a medium-high heat for about 5 minutes until the spinach has collapsed and wilted down, stirring a few times. Drain the spinach in a sieve, pushing with the back of a wooden spoon to squeeze out every last drop of liquid that you can. Put the spinach on a board, roughly chop and then transfer to a bowl.

Whisk the crème fraîche with the eggs, lemon zest, thyme and two-thirds of the cheese. Season with salt, pepper and a generous grating of nutmeg. Mix half of this through the spinach and set aside.

Preheat the oven to 180°C/gas 4. Melt half of the butter and stir it into the batter. Melt 1 tsp of the remaining butter in a heavy-based frying pan over a medium-low heat and, when hot, add one-eighth of the batter. Swirl it around the pan so that it is evenly coated, then allow to cook until bubbles have appeared on the surface, about 2 minutes. Toss the pancake and cook for 1–2 minutes on the other side. Continue with the remaining batter to make a stack of cooked pancakes, laying a piece of baking parchment between each.

Spread a couple of spoonfuls of the crème fraîche mix over the base of a small oven dish. Spread one-eighth of the spinach mix along one edge of each pancake, then roll up and place in the oven dish, seam down. Once you have rolled all the pancakes, spoon over the remaining crème fraîche mix, sprinkle over the rest of the cheese and bake for 15–20 minutes until golden on top. Leave to cool for a moment before serving with a green salad.

Why not try my cheat's 'crêpes'?

These are brilliant for when you are short of time and need to feed children fast.
Dip a flour (or corn) tortilla in an eggy bread mixture (I use 1 large egg beaten with 1 tbsp double cream) and, once thoroughly soaked, fry in butter, topped with any leftover eggy cream. It tastes uncannily like a home-made crêpe. Make it sweet for late breakfasts filled with lemon juice and sugar, or bacon and maple syrup; make it savoury for a super-fast supper filled with sautéed leeks and cheese.

For the Pancakes
300g buckwheat flour
1 tsp salt
2–3 eggs, lightly beaten
400ml whole milk
200ml water
100g butter

For the Filling
800g spinach, washed
400g crème fraîche
3 eggs
finely grated zest of ½ lemon
few sprigs of thyme, leaves picked
200g Gruyère, Beaufort or
    Cheddar, grated
few gratings of nutmeg

Crunchy Cheesy Pitta Pockets

MAKES SIX PITTA HALVES

These are unbelievably moreish, whether you're a kid or an adult. The cheese melts under the grill, mixing with the warm carrot juices, making a ridiculously creamy, stringy filling. The filiing is also delicious just stuffed into hot pittas without going near the grill.

Preheat the grill to high. Briefly toast the pittas so they puff a little, then slice in half and gently open up each half into a pocket. Spread the insides with the softened butter and mayonnaise.

Mix the carrots, cheese and spring onions in a bowl and stuff generously into the pockets. Lay on a baking sheet and grill for 3 minutes until the cheese has melted and the pittas are crisp.

Why not try Gruyère & apple pittas?

Coarsely grate 2 apples, pat dry with kitchen paper, then toss with 100g coarsely grated Gruyère or Emmental. Season with a pinch of ground cumin, a pinch of salt and a smidgen of fresh finely grated horseradish. Butter the pitta pockets as above and spread with mayonnaise. Fill with the cheese and apple mix and grill or eat as they are with slices of cucumber on the side.

3 large wholemeal pittas

softened butter, for the pittas

1–2 tbsp mayonnaise
 (I love Hellmann's for this)

2–3 carrots, coarsely grated

100g mature Cheddar, coarsely grated

1–2 spring onions, finely chopped

Kids' Food (You'll Love Too)

Sicilian-Style Turnovers

Although these sound high maintenance, they are actually incredibly easy to make and the girls love helping to roll them up. They are crispy, versatile, good for packed lunches and children seem to munch happily on them, no matter how healthy the filling. Here I make a sweet-sour chard version dotted with currants.

Preheat the oven to 200°C/gas 6 and lightly oil a baking sheet. Put the baking sheet in the oven to heat up.

Cover the currants with boiling water in a small bowl. Brown the pine nuts in the oven for a minute or so until pale golden.

Run a knife along the chard stalks to remove the leaves. Wash and finely chop the stalks into strips, then wash and cut the leaves into larger strips.

Heat the oil in a pan over a medium heat and soften the onion and garlic, seasoning with salt and pepper. Meanwhile, blanch first the chard stalks and then the leaves in boiling salted water until tender; drain well. Add this to the onion mixture and heat through to evaporate any excess liquid. Drain the currants and add to the chard with the pine nuts. Add the Parmesan, egg, feta and lemon zest and allow it to cool.

Brush a sheet of filo pastry with melted butter and cut into strips about 7cm wide and 30cm long. Cover the remaining filo sheets with a damp tea towel so they don't dry out.

Ingredients

3 tbsp olive oil, plus extra
    for the baking sheet
4–5 large sheets of filo pastry
    (each about 60 x 30cm)
50g currants
4 tbsp pine nuts
300g chard
½ small red onion, finely chopped
1 garlic clove, crushed
50g Parmesan, finely grated
1 egg, lightly beaten
40g feta, crumbled
finely grated zest of ½ lemon
140g melted butter

Place 1 tbsp of the cooled chard mixture at the bottom of each filo strip and fold it to the left to make a little triangle. Keep folding the pastry over the filling – left and right – until all you have is a little strip of pastry and a tidy triangle. Brush a little butter on the strip and fold it over the triangle to seal in the filling. Continue with the remaining filo sheets until you have used up the filling (you should be able to make roughly 22–25 triangles. (If you are not serving immediately you can cover the folded triangles with a damp tea towel and chill until ready to bake.)

Place the triangles on the hot baking sheet and bake for 15 minutes until golden and sizzling. Remove and serve immediately, or leave to cool and reheat later in the oven.

Kitchen Note:
You could try these turnovers with a spinach filling; sweet potato, thyme and feta; or mild curried butternut squash.

Chapter
NINE

SWEET TOOTH

SWEET TOOTH

Puddings weren't a big thing in our house so, once I got to the age where I could cook myself, I had a whole world to discover. I started with crème brûlée, which seemed the height of sophistication in the 1980s; what could be better than the magic of cracking through the golden sugar crust? Next came profiteroles, a real showstopper for a born show-off and a fine way to eat lots of chocolate ganache. From choux pastry I ventured into shortcrust and rough-puff … then into any other pudding I discovered in my parents' cookbook collection.

At university I started hosting large chaotic dinners, where it was all I could do to get my over-ambitious starters and main courses onto the table, much less manage a pudding, so it wasn't until I got back to London that puddings started making a resurgence in my cooking. To begin with, I offered friends the best of the Middle Eastern grocers of Shepherd's Bush: baklavas, figs and tangerines. Piles of quinces would appear in late summer and I would make jars of Jane Grigson's quince paste to serve with cheese, biscuits and bars of chocolate. And I spent a memorably fanatical year, pre-children, perfecting a Mexican-inspired chocolate ganache for chilli-spiked truffles.

Now, with children in the equation, it seems churlish not to have some sort of pudding at the end of a weekend lunch. I was given an ice cream machine for Christmas a few years ago and it turns out that making ice cream is as magical as baking. First, lovingly prepare your base. This might be a simple custard enriched with burnt ombre yolks, whole milk and cream with a whisper of vanilla. Or perhaps it is a lemon-flecked fruit base for a sorbet that lets the pure, sharp flavours of blood oranges or rhubarb sing. This thick cream or purée is then whipped up and churned into a cooling and madly impressive pudding. You can tweak them to create your favourite flavours and I've included some of mine here: berry-rich scarlet-red strawberry sorbet, rich ice cream laced with chocolate sauce and smoky mezcal, and velvety burnt caramel ice cream. It takes time to make but the seductive, melting spoonfuls are worth it, as are the looks on your guests' faces; further proof, if it were needed, that there really is something very nurturing and special about feeding people your own home-made food.

Of course with work, family and friends pulling you in all directions, there isn't masses of time to spare, so I've only included here a rigorously edited list of the puddings that I feel are definitely worth your effort. And there are plenty of shortcuts: you can buy ice cream and just fold in home-made Hazelnut Praline or Raspberry Ripple, or create piles of chocolate-stuffed medjool dates. Pudding doesn't need to be a great undertaking; it just needs to hit the spot when your taste buds are searching for that hit of something a little sweet at the end of a meal.

Chocolate & Banana Bread

I didn't truly discover the joys of banana bread until I went to Mexico. Breakfast there is treated very seriously, and comes in courses. Fruit smoothies, juices and plates of fruit are accompanied by coffee or hot chocolate, followed by waves of freshly baked sweet breads, such as banana bread, cinnamon rolls or cake made with clotted cream in place of butter. Savoury follows next, with endless versions of eggs, roast salsas and sometimes slow-cooked meats. We serve this banana bread on our breakfast menu at Wahaca, toasted and spread with butter.

Preheat the oven to 180°C/gas 4. Butter and line a 900g loaf tin with baking parchment on both base and sides, leaving some overhanging the sides.

Using an electric whisk or stand mixer fitted with the beater attachment, cream the butter and sugar together until pale and fluffy, then beat in the vanilla extract and eggs, each in turn, adding a little flour if the mixture starts to curdle. Briefly mash the bananas and fold into the batter with the chocolate. Sift the flour, baking powder and bicarbonate of soda straight into the batter and fold in using a metal spoon until completely incorporated.

Stir in the yogurt, oil, mixed spice and walnuts, then spoon into the prepared tin. Bake for 1 hour until risen, golden, and slightly split down the middle. Prick the cake with a skewer; if it comes out clean, it is ready; if wet, put the cake back into the oven for an extra 5 minutes before checking again. Cover with foil if the cake is becoming too dark on top.

Leave to cool in the tin for 5 minutes, then lift out, using the baking parchment, onto a wire rack. Allow to cool completely before slicing.

Why not try squidgy home-made chocolate-hazelnut spread?

In a food processor, finely grind 200g roasted hazelnuts and, with the motor running, slowly add 100ml hazelnut, groundnut or vegetable oil, 5 tbsp icing sugar, 2 tbsp cocoa powder, a pinch of salt and 90g melted dark chocolate. Once thick, loosen with 50ml cold water until you have a thick paste. Transfer to sterilised jars and cover with a thin layer of oil. Keeps well for several weeks. Spread over toast and banana bread.

120g butter, at room temperature,
   plus extra for the tin

200g soft light brown sugar

1 tsp vanilla extract

2 eggs

4 very ripe bananas, peeled
   (about 425g peeled weight)

100g dark chocolate (70% cocoa solids),
   chopped into small pieces

250g plain flour

2 tsp baking powder

1 tsp bicarbonate of soda

50g Greek yogurt

2 tbsp rapeseed oil

1 tsp mixed spice

70g roughly chopped walnuts
   (or hazelnuts if you prefer)

Rich Vanilla Ice Cream

Match this with rhubarb, gooseberry or raspberry sauce in the spring and summer; with crushed up gooey meringues, praline, or caramelised sweet breadcrumbs in the winter; and with wickedly dark chocolate sauce anytime, day or night. Use up egg whites in meringues (see page 264), macaroons or whisky sours.

Oil and line a 900g loaf tin with cling film so that the cling film drapes over the sides; if you are planning to scoop rather than slice you won't need to do this bit.

Scrape the seeds from the split vanilla pod with a teaspoon and stir them and the pod into the cream in a large pan. Heat the vanilla cream over a medium heat until just before it boils, then remove from the heat and add the vanilla extract, if using.

While the cream is heating, whisk the egg yolks with the sugar in a bowl until thick and pale. Slowly pour the hot cream onto the yolks, removing the vanilla pod from the pan, and whisk to combine. Return the custard to the pan and heat very gently, stirring, until it coats the back of a wooden spoon; you should be able to run a finger down the wooden spoon and have the custard stay in place without running back over the finger line. Remove from the heat and cover the surface of the custard with cling film (this will prevent a skin forming) and allow to cool.

Place the cooled custard into an ice cream machine and churn until softly frozen. Using a rubber spatula, scrape the custard into the loaf tin and smooth over the top. Cover with the excess cling film (or some cling film, if you didn't line the tin) and freeze for 4–6 hours, or up to a month if well covered, making sure it sits level in your freezer.

Turn out the loaf onto a board, removing the cling film (you might need to dip the loaf tin in just-boiled water to ease it out) and slice, smoothing it with a palette knife, or just scoop with a warmed ice cream scoop.

Why not try machine-less rich vanilla parfait?

Do not be deterred if you have no ice cream machine, this simple old-fashioned ice will serve you beautifully. Crack 4 egg yolks into a bowl and whisk until light and fluffy. Melt 100g caster sugar with 250ml water in a small pan until completely dissolved, then boil the syrup until it reaches the 'thread' stage (at 106–113°C on a sugar thermometer). It will look thick and syrupy and form thin threads when dipped into with a spoon. Pour onto the yolks in a steady stream, whisking all the time and not worrying about some of the syrup flying off in all directions. Add 1 tsp vanilla extract and whisk until you have a thick, creamy white mousse. Whip 750ml double cream and gently fold it into the mousse. Pour into 2 boxes (it is worth making lots), cover and freeze.

flavourless oil, for the tin (optional)

1 vanilla pod, split lengthways

700ml very good double or thick cream

½ tsp vanilla extract (optional if you prefer a more subtle vanilla flavour)

5 egg yolks

100g caster sugar

Ice Cream Sauces

There is something lovely about making your own ice cream when you have time, but as often as not I rely on good-quality shop-bought tubs. Here are some of my favourite ways to 'zhuzh up' vanilla ice cream, whether home-made or shop-bought:

Burnt Caramel Ice Cream

I can never resist this ice cream when I am eating at the River Café. Make a burnt caramel (see page 304) and pour it into the vanilla custard before you churn, or pour it straight onto bought vanilla ice cream. A cup of very strong espresso is also delicious, either churned in when cold, or piping hot and poured on top of a bowl of ice cream.

Insanely Good Chocolate Sauce

Put 200g dark chocolate in a heavy-based pan with 2 heaped tbsp golden syrup, a walnut-sized knob of butter, 150ml whole milk and 150ml double cream. Add a pinch of salt and place over a low heat to melt the chocolate, stirring continuously and being careful not to let it burn. Alternatively heat in short bursts in the microwave, stirring between each burst. Pour over ice cream and eat at once. Drink this with slugs of good mezcal: dark chocolate and smoky mezcal are one of life's great pairings.

Vanilla Sundae with Chocolate Salted Caramel Crispies

Make the chocolate sauce as above and a Salted Caramel Sauce (see page 304). Stir half of the salted caramel through 170g crispy rice puff cereal until thoroughly coated, then sift over 85g cocoa powder so that the rice pieces are entirely coated and no longer sticking together. Serve scoops of vanilla ice cream with either the chocolate or caramel sauces (or preferably both), scattered with chocolate salted caramel crispies.

Vanilla & Raspberry Ripple Parfait

Mash 100g raspberries and 2 tsp caster sugar in a bowl, then pass through a sieve, discarding the seeds. Drop 10–12 raspberries into an oiled and cling film-lined loaf tin, then fill with half the churned vanilla custard. Top with another 10–12 raspberries. Using a skewer, swirl half the raspberry sauce through the ice cream, making sure it goes down into the ice cream and doesn't just sit on top. Smooth over the other half of the churned custard and repeat with the remaining raspberries and raspberry sauce. Cover with cling film and freeze as for Rich Vanilla Ice Cream (see left).

Hazelnut Praline Ice Cream

Toast 120g hazelnuts in a 180°C/gas 4 oven until pale golden, about 5 minutes, then rub with a tea towel to remove the skins. Dissolve 110g caster sugar with 3 tbsp water in a heavy-based pan over a medium heat. Increase the heat and make a dark caramel (see page 304), holding back from over-cooking; you don't want to burn it. Remove from the heat, add the nuts and carefully swirl the pan to cover them with caramel. Pour onto a baking sheet lined with baking parchment and allow to set. Pulse in a food processor, or bash with a rolling pin, to get coarse crumbs. Fold into softened or churning vanilla ice cream, or sprinkle on top. Sensational with any poached fruit.

Strawberry & Balsamic Sorbet with Dark Treacly Ginger Biscuits

MAKES 1.4 LITRES

When it's hot outside and you have had plenty to eat, sometimes you need an injection of refreshing, sharp fruit flavours. This is the time for sorbets and granitas to shine. This sweet, acid lemon-and-berry-rich sorbet conjures up Mediterranean summers like nothing else, with its lick of balsamic. Make it ahead of time so that you can reveal it after a fat lunch or dinner and look like a magician. It goes beautifully with the dark, sticky ginger biscuits below.

Remove the pips from the whole lemon and blitz in a food processor with the sugar until reduced to a paste. Scrape the contents into a bowl, removing any pips that have snuck in.

Purée the strawberries, then mix into the lemon and sugar paste with the lemon juice. Stir in the balsamic vinegar and pour the mix (strained if you prefer to remove the seeds) into an ice cream machine. Churn for about 1 hour, then transfer to a freezer-proof container and freeze for a further 4 hours. If you don't have an ice cream machine, pour the mixture into a lidded freezer-proof container and freeze for 8 hours, stirring it briefly with a fork every 2 hours to break up any ice crystals.

Preheat the oven to 180°C/gas 4 and line 2 baking sheets with baking parchment.

Melt the butter in a pan with the sugar, treacle, syrup and a few pinches of salt, stirring thoroughly. Add the egg and stir it in. Sift the flour, spices and bicarbonate of soda into the butter mixture and stir to combine (it will be a wet and sticky dough).

Drop tbsp of the mixture onto the baking sheets, leaving a tangerine's width between each spoonful to stop them spreading into each other. Bake for about 15 minutes until the biscuits have completely spread out and darkened. They should still be very slightly soft. Let them cool for just a few minutes before prising off the baking parchment and transferring to a wire rack to cool completely. Serve with scoops of the sorbet.

Kitchen Note:

To get a creamy, smooth sorbet every time, use a ratio of 4 cups fruit purée to 1 cup (185g) sugar. For a really creamy texture, replace one-fifth of the sugar with corn syrup. To get 4 cups of fruit purée you need to start off with about 1kg fruit, which you then trim, purée and sieve. Fruits that are high in pectin, such as berries or stone fruit, or high in fibre, such as mangoes and pears, make the creamiest sorbets. It goes without saying that fruit at its best will make the best sorbet. Adding 1–2 tbsp liqueur to the sorbet helps it to stay soft, but any more and it will start turning slushy.

For the Sorbet
3 lemons (1 whole, 2 juiced)
400g caster sugar
900g ripe strawberries, hulled
1 tbsp balsamic vinegar

For the Biscuits
170g butter
175g soft light brown sugar
2 tbsp black treacle
2 tbsp golden syrup
1 egg, lightly beaten
220g white spelt flour
¼ tsp ground cloves
½ tsp ground ginger
½ tsp ground cinnamon
½ tsp bicarbonate of soda

A Light, Silky Panna Cotta

Panna cotta means 'cooked cream'. It is one of my favourite puddings, easier to make than crème brûlée and, with its delicate, creamy texture, goes beautifully with whatever fruit is in season and a trickle of booze. When made well, with less gelatine than any packet suggests, the cream settles into a just-held-together, gently quivering but still perky heap as it comes out of its mould. If this sounds intimidating, set the creams in pretty glasses or deep saucers so that you don't need to turn them out. I lighten mine with yogurt and milk for a touch of acidity. They have to be made in advance, so you can relax over your dinner. You will need six dariole moulds, ramekins or small glasses.

3 x 2g sheets of fine-leaf gelatine

400ml double cream

1 vanilla pod, split lengthways

100g caster sugar

150g Greek yogurt

100ml whole milk

2 blood oranges

6 tbsp tequila

Panna Cotta with Blood Oranges & Tequila

Submerge the gelatine in a bowl of cold water and leave to soften for 5–8 minutes.

Meanwhile, pour the cream into a deep pan with the split vanilla pod and place over a medium-low heat. Allow to warm gently and infuse for 5 minutes, but keep any eye on it and don't allow it to boil. Stir in the sugar and then remove from the heat.

Lift the gelatine sheets out of the water, squeezing to remove any excess water, and add to the hot cream, stirring until it melts away. Scrape the seeds out of the vanilla pod into the cream mixture, then discard the pod. Whisk in the yogurt and milk, then leave to cool completely. Pour into 6 small moulds, glasses or ramekins and leave to set in the fridge for at least 3 hours.

Just before you serve them, peel the oranges, removing all the white pith with a sharp knife, then segment them. If you have used moulds, dip them into gently simmering water, then turn them out onto plates. Pile a few orange segments on top or beside each panna cotta, then sprinkle 1 tbsp of tequila over each before serving.

A Light, Silky
Panna Cotta
(Continued)

Here are some seasonal alternatives to get you through the spring, summer and autumn …

Elderflower Panna Cotta with Gooseberries & Pernod

Infuse the warming cream with 15 fresh elderflower heads or 5 tbsp elderflower cordial. While the panna cotta is setting, place 400g topped and tailed gooseberries in a pan with 65g sugar, 1 tbsp water and 2 tbsp Pernod. Bring to a simmer and cook for 10–15 minutes until soft and sweet. Leave to cool, then serve spooned over the panna cotta.

Buttermilk Panna Cotta with Macerated Strawberries

Follow the main recipe, but make it with 500ml buttermilk and 150ml double cream instead of the cream, milk and yogurt mix. While the panna cotta is setting, hull and halve 1 punnet of strawberries, place in a bowl, and add the finely grated zest of 1 lemon and the juice of ½ lemon. Toss with 1 tbsp sugar and 2 tbsp Muscat. Spoon this over the panna cotta before serving.

Espresso Panna Cotta with Whisky Caramel Sauce

Follow the main recipe, but forgo the yogurt and use 500ml double cream and 100ml whole milk. When stirring in the milk, also add 50ml freshly made and cooled espresso. While the panna cotta is setting, put 225g sugar and 80ml water in a heavy-based pan; stirring until the sugar dissolves and the water comes to the boil. Remove the spoon and do not stir again until the syrup turns a rich golden caramel. Add 240ml very strong good-quality coffee and return to the heat to dissolve. Allow to cool and add 2 tbsp of your favourite whisky. Spoon over the panna cotta before serving (it will also keep in the fridge indefinitely and is delicious poured over ice cream).

Cardamom Custard Tart with Cocoa-Rye Pastry

FEEDS LOTS

This cocoa-rye pastry is adapted from a recipe by Chad Robertson at the amazing San Francisco bakery, Tartine. I fill it with a cardamom-scented custard; its ethereal scent is a lovely contrast to the dark, crisp and earthy pastry case. Using rye flour instead of plain makes the pastry low in gluten, so you need to chill it well once you have made it, then roll it between sheets of baking parchment as it is quite sticky. It is wonderful served with a bowl of fresh raspberries, or try filling the tart case with mascarpone cream beaten with Greek yogurt and decorated with summer berries and icing sugar. Use the leftover pastry to make irresistibly short, crumbly, Oreo-like cookies, perfect for ice cream sandwiches (see overleaf).

For the Cocoa-Rye Pastry
300g butter
125g caster sugar
1 egg, at room temperature
½ tsp vanilla extract
280g rye flour, sifted
125g cocoa powder, sifted,
    plus extra to dust

For the Cardamom Custard
300ml whole milk
300ml double cream
seeds from 6 cardamom pods, crushed
1 vanilla pod, seeds scraped out
9 egg yolks
75g caster sugar

To make the pastry, beat the butter and sugar together for a few minutes in a mixer fitted with the paddle attachment, until it is soft and a pale cream colour. Beat in the egg, then stop the mixer, scrape down the sides and beat in the vanilla, followed by the flour and cocoa powder, until thoroughly combined. Transfer the pastry to a large piece of cling film, pat into a rectangular shape and chill for at least 1 hour or until firm.

Meanwhile make the custard. Put the milk, cream, crushed cardamom seeds, vanilla seeds and pod into a pan and bring to simmering point. Simmer gently for 3 minutes to infuse the milk, then set aside for 10 minutes. Whisk together the egg yolks and sugar in a bowl until light and pale. Whisk the warm milk into the eggs, discard the vanilla pod and pour into a jug. Cover the surface with cling film.

Divide the dough in half, freezing half for another day. Dust both sides of the remaining pastry lightly with cocoa powder and roll out between 2 large sheets of baking parchment or cling film, rotating as you do, so that you have an even thickness of about 4mm. Roll the pastry onto the rolling pin and then carefully transfer to a 26cm loose-bottomed tart tin. Press firmly into all the corners of the tin and then trim the excess dough, leaving an overhang of roughly 5mm. Place in the freezer for 15 minutes to firm up while you preheat the oven to 180°C/gas 4.

Cardamom Custard Tart with Cocoa-Rye Pastry (Continued)

Line the pastry case with baking parchment, fill with baking beans and blind bake for 20 minutes until slightly puffed up. Remove the paper and beans and bake for a further 10–15 minutes until completely cooked, being careful not to let it burn. Reduce the oven temperature to 140°C/gas 1.

Run a sharp knife around the edges of the tart shell to neaten it up. Carefully pour the custard into the tart shell up to the top and bake on the middle shelf of the oven for 35–40 minutes until just set; it should no longer wobble in the middle when you gently move the tin, but you don't want it too firm. Leave to cool completely before serving with a bowl of fresh raspberries.

Why not try Oreo-style ice cream sandwiches?
Roll out the leftover pastry to a 1cm thickness and cut into 4cm rounds. Bake in the oven for 12–15 minutes until crisp. Spread thickly with Rich Vanilla Ice Cream or Raspberry Ripple Parfait (see pages 248–9) and put in the freezer to set for 15 minutes, or overnight. A real showstopper at parties. Makes 8. (See the photo on pages 246-7.)

Rhubarb Upside-Down Cake

There is little so pleasing to bake, or as easy, as an upside-down cake. I have a particular passion for forced rhubarb when in season, it is hard not to be seduced by its beautiful iridescent pink (nor by the bright pink syrup it produces when poached). Do experiment with whatever seasonal fruit you like. I love it with poached plums and star anise, or slices of marinated pineapple in the middle of winter (see page 81), or pears and cardamom in the autumn.

Preheat the oven to 180°C/gas 4 and butter and line a deep 20cm cake tin (preferably not loose-bottomed as the cake can ooze).

For the Cake

200g butter, softened,
     plus extra for the tin
225g caster sugar
3 eggs
75g plain flour
½ tsp vanilla extract
finely grated zest of ½ orange
½ tsp orange blossom water
1 tsp baking powder
½ tsp fine salt
225g ground almonds
75g quick-cook polenta
crème fraîche, to serve

For the Rhubarb

500g pink forced rhubarb, wiped
     clean and sliced into 3–4cm pieces
2 tbsp Pernod
50g caster sugar
finely grated zest and juice of 1 orange
½ tsp vanilla extract

Place the rhubarb ingredients in a pan and poach for 5–10 minutes until the rhubarb is just softened but still retaining its shape. Allow to cool.

Sprinkle 50g of the caster sugar onto the bottom of the cake tin and gently lift the lengths of rhubarb from the syrup onto the base of the tin in prettily arranged circles. You should have some rhubarb left in the syrup for the topping.

In a stand mixer or with an electric whisk, beat the remaining 175g sugar and butter together until pale and fluffy. Beat in each egg in turn, adding a little flour with each. Stir in the vanilla extract, orange zest and orange blossom water. Sift in the remaining flour, baking powder and salt, then add the almonds and polenta. Fold in with a large metal spoon until completely combined but not overworked.

Spoon the batter onto the rhubarb and level out carefully with a palette knife, trying not to move the rhubarb. Bake on the middle shelf of the oven for 35–40 minutes until the cake is firm and a skewer comes out clean when inserted into the centre. Allow to cool in the tin for 5 minutes, then flip the cake onto a wire rack, sitting a plate underneath to catch any syrup. Allow to cool completely before transferring to a serving plate.

Put the remaining rhubarb and juices in a pan and reduce by one-third. Serve slices of the cake with dollops of crème fraîche and the pink rhubarb syrup drizzled over.

Why not try rhubarb pickle?

Using a mandoline or sharp knife, very thinly slice 400g rhubarb into long strips. Fold the strips, along with 1 finely chopped shallot, 1 slice of fresh ginger, 1 sliced red chilli, 2 juniper berries and 1 tsp coriander seeds, into a 1-litre sterilised Kilner jar (or any jar that can be tightly closed). Heat 250ml cider vinegar, 225g caster sugar and 250ml water in a pan until the sugar has dissolved. Pour the warm pickle liquor into the jar over the rhubarb and close the jar. This will be good after a few days and keeps for up to 3 months. Seriously delicious with blue cheese and toast or – if you leave out the shallot – with the cake opposite.

Or why not try a small batch of rhubarb jam?

Layer up 520g rhubarb with 400g preserving sugar (you need this as rhubarb has very little pectin) and the juice of 1 large lemon or 2 oranges. Allow to macerate for at least 2 hours, preferably overnight. Put a small plate in the freezer. Put the rhubarb and sugar in a pan, bring to the boil and boil rapidly for 5 minutes. Remove the plate from the freezer and drop 1 tsp of the jam onto it. If a wrinkly skin forms, it is ready. If not, return to the heat for a minute or so. Allow to cool slightly before pouring into 2 × 400ml sterilised jars.

Honey & Walnut Tart

I am slightly obsessed with honey and find it hard not to buy a locally made jar whenever I see it, no matter how far I am from home or how full my luggage. I find the disappearing bee colonies worrying; imagine a world without honey – worse still all the crops they support – so at home we try to do our bit and plant wild flowers on every scrap of spare earth. Walnuts in the shell are sweeter and less bitter than the shelled variety (and fun for everyone to crack open).

To make the pastry, blitz together the butter, sugar and lemon zest in a food processor. Pulse in the flour and salt until just combined then briefly beat in the egg. Remove the dough from the mixer and knead to bring it together, working it as little as possible. Shape it into a disc and then roll out on a lightly floured surface to 5mm thick and large enough to generously fit a 23cm loose-bottomed, fluted tart tin. Roll the pastry around the rolling pin, then lift and unroll it into the tin. Press the pastry well into the sides and corners of the tin using your knuckles. Cover loosely with cling film and chill in the fridge for 30 minutes.

Preheat the oven to 200°C/gas 6 and place a flat baking sheet in the oven to heat up.

Line the pastry with baking parchment and fill with baking beans. Slide the tart tin onto the heated baking sheet in the oven and blind bake for 20 minutes. Remove the beans, trim the pastry with a sharp knife and bake for a further 7 minutes or until golden. Remove from the oven and reduce the oven temperature to 180°C/gas 4.

Meanwhile gently heat the honey, sugars and butter in a pan until the sugar has dissolved. Remove from the heat and stir in the mixed spice, vanilla, salt, lemon juice and crumbed walnuts. Stir in the beaten eggs until the mix has emulsified and spoon it into the baked tart case. Top with the whole walnuts and slide back into the oven for 20–25 minutes until nut-brown and set. Allow to cool before removing from the tin. Serve in slices with softly whipped cream or ice cream.

Why not try an irresistible treacle tart?

Preheat the oven to 180°C/gas 4. Warm 400g golden syrup and 50g treacle in a pan and stir in 120g stale breadcrumbs and the finely grated zest and juice of 1 large, juicy lemon. Remove from the heat, allow to cool for a few minutes, then stir in 100ml double cream. Spread the mixture over the blind-baked tart base and bake for 15 minutes. Reduce the oven temperature to 160°C/gas 3 and bake for another 15 minutes or until the filling is almost set (it will harden as it cools).

For the Pastry

130g butter, chilled

50g caster sugar

finely grated zest of 1 lemon

225g plain flour, plus extra to dust

¼ tsp fine salt

1 egg, lightly beaten

For the Filling

200g your favourite local honey

60g dark muscovado sugar

40g soft light brown sugar

100g butter

¼ tsp mixed spice

½ tsp vanilla extract

¼ tsp fine salt

½ tsp lemon juice

350g shelled walnuts, two-thirds bashed into rough crumbs, the rest left in halves

2 large eggs, lightly beaten

My Favourite Apple Cake

FEEDS SIX

I grew up eating this cake at my friend Jo's house. Her mother had an Aga, which in London in the 1990s felt both homely and exotic. This is a fluffy pillowy sort of cake, the kind that you want to eat warm with crème fraîche or vanilla ice cream. The apples can be as bashed up as you like, perfect for the autumn when there is a glut of them. Our next door neighbour in Kensal Rise gives us so many from her tree that we normally eat this cake throughout September. Nobody complains. If you can, mix up the varieties of apples for a better flavour and more varied texture. Or make gluten-free by replacing self-raising flour with a mix of ground almonds and gluten-free flour.

Preheat the oven to 160°C/gas 3 and lightly butter a deep 20cm loose-bottomed cake tin.

Place the flour, baking powder, sugar, eggs, almond extract, cinnamon, rum and melted butter into a bowl and mix well until blended, then beat for 1 minute. Pour half of this mixture into the tin and spread out in an even layer.

Thickly slice the apples and lay on top of the mixture in the tin, piling mostly towards the centre. Using 2 spoons, roughly spoon the remaining mixture over the apples. This is an awkward thing to do, but just make sure that the mixture covers the centre well as it will spread out in the oven. Sprinkle with the flaked almonds.

Bake for 1½ hours until golden and shrinking away from the sides of the tin. Leave to cool for 10 minutes in the tin before turning out and cutting into slices.

Why not try baked apples with hazelnut crunch?

Rub together 50g butter and 2 tbsp each of dark muscovado sugar and soft light brown sugar. Sprinkle over 4 large cored cooking apples with 2 tbsp brandy or water. Bake in a 200°C/gas 6 oven for 25 minutes until the apples are soft and the caramel is dark and sticky. Meanwhile rub together 40g each of flour, demerara sugar and butter and mix with 75g chopped hazelnuts. Spread out on a baking sheet and bake on a shelf under the apples for 15 minutes or until golden. Serve the apples with the crunch and custard (I like to scent mine with sea salt and fennel). The crunch makes a terrific crumble topping and is also great on ice cream. Feeds 4.

150g butter, melted,
  plus extra for the tin
225g self-raising flour
1 level tsp baking powder
200g caster sugar
2 eggs, lightly beaten
½ tsp almond extract
½ tsp ground cinnamon
2 tbsp rum
350g apples, different varieties
  if possible, peeled and cored
25g flaked almonds

Pomegranate Meringues with Pistachios

This is a spectacular pudding of bewitching colours, all blushing meringues, vivid green pistachio dust and the sparkle of pomegranate jewels.

Preheat the oven to 100°C/gas ¼ and line 2 baking trays with silicone sheets or baking parchment. In a spotlessly clean bowl, whisk the egg whites with an electric whisk until you have stiff peaks. Now whisk in the sugar, little by little by little, followed by half the pomegranate molasses and a pinch of salt, fully incorporating the sugar with each addition until the whites are stiff again, shiny and voluminous (this takes about 10 minutes).

With 2 teaspoons scoop high heaps of the mix onto the baking sheets, fluffing the tops into peaks. Dust each of the peaks with a sprinkling of the green pistachio nuts, saving half for the final plating. Bake in the oven for 2–3 hours, until the undersides are no longer sticky and peel away easily from the trays. Turn off the oven and leave the meringues to cool inside with the door slightly ajar.

Meanwhile roll the pomegranate firmly along the work surface, pressing down so that you can feel the seeds 'popping' out. Cut the fruit in half over a bowl and tear open to release the seeds into the bowl, discarding the shell and white pith. Blitz half the seeds in a blender and sieve to get a beautiful red juice; keep both seeds and juice for later.

Softly whip the cream until it is thick but still quite floppy and stir in the rest of the pomegranate molasses. Whisk the cream lightly with a wooden spoon until it just holds it shape; you can do this up to 5 hours ahead and store in the fridge.

Put everything together just before you are going to eat so that the meringues don't go soggy. Gather friends to help, it is great fun. Sandwich together the meringues with the cream and lay out on a large platter. Scatter with the pomegranate seeds and pistachios and splash with the brilliant red juice. Bring to the table and bask in glory.

Why not try coconut macaroons?

Mix 5 egg whites with 220g unsweetened coconut flakes, 150g sugar, 2 tsp vanilla extract and ¼ tsp salt. Heat and stir the mix with a spatula in a metal bowl over simmering water until the whites are thick and opaque, about 6 minutes. Let stand for 30 minutes. Meanwhile preheat the oven to 175°C/gas 4 and put heaped dessertspoons of the mix, 5cm apart, on 2–3 lined baking sheets. Bake for 5 minutes, then reduce the oven temperature to 160°C/gas 3 and continue to bake for 10–15 minutes until the macaroons are a creamy gold with nut-brown edges. Rotate the trays throughout cooking for an even colour. Top with a drizzle of melted chocolate and allow to cool completely before peeling away from the baking parchment. Makes about 20.

4 egg whites

210g caster sugar, preferably unrefined for the colour

3 tbsp pomegranate molasses

60g pistachios, finely chopped

1 large pomegranate

400ml double cream

Sticky Coconut Cake with Citrus Syrup

FEEDS EIGHT

This caramelised coconut cake uses spelt, which has less gluten than conventional flour. It is almost impossible to pass by without stealing just one tiny slice. It stays fresh for several days.

Preheat the oven to 180°C/gas 4 and butter and line a 900g loaf tin with baking parchment.

Toast the coconut in a dry frying pan over a medium heat, shaking fairly constantly until you have a lovely combination of golden and white flakes, about 3–5 minutes. Leave to cool, then combine with the ground almonds, spelt flour, baking powder, vanilla seeds, lime zest and salt.

In a separate bowl beat together the butter and honey, then beat in each egg in turn. Fold the flour mixture into the eggs, mix well to combine and pour into the prepared tin. Bake on the middle shelf of the oven for 45–50 minutes until a skewer comes out clean. Check after 30 minutes and cover with foil if the top is getting too dark.

To make the syrup, combine the honey, zests and lime juice in a small pan, stir well and bring to the boil. Reduce the heat to low and simmer for 15 minutes until slightly thickened and sticky. Once the cake is cooked, remove from the oven and pierce with a skewer to make lots of holes for the syrup. Pour over the syrup and leave the cake to cool in the tin before turning out and serving.

Why not try a flourless St Clementine's pudding?

This lemon and orange pudding is gluten free, spectacularly zingy and manages to be both rich and light. Preheat the oven to 160°C/gas 3 and butter a 20cm cake tin or ovenproof dish. Beat 250g softened butter with 180g golden caster sugar and 2 heaped tsp honey until light and fluffy. Add 4 eggs in turn, beating continuously, followed by 1 tsp vanilla extract and the finely grated zest and juices of 1 orange and 2 lemons. Don't worry when the mixture curdles; once cooked it will be beautifully smooth. Fold in 125g polenta and 125g ground almonds and season with a generous pinch of salt. Pour the mixture into the prepared dish and bake for 35–40 minutes until just set. Serve warm with the best cream that you can buy.

For the Cake

150g butter, plus extra for the tin
150g desiccated coconut
75g ground almonds
180g white spelt flour
1½ tsp gluten-free baking powder
seeds from 1 vanilla pod
finely grated zest of 2 limes
½ tsp salt
200g honey
3 eggs

For the Syrup

4 tbsp honey
finely grated zest and juice of 2 limes
finely grated zest of 1 orange
1 tsp orange blossom water (optional)

Carrot & Date Cake with Brown Butter Icing

This is a simple, classic carrot cake given a twist; an irresistible icing made by browning butter until it is richly nutty and ever so slightly salty.

Preheat the oven to 180°C/gas 4 and oil and line 2 × 20cm loose-bottomed cake tins.

Using an electric whisk (or a stand mixer fitted with the whisk attachment) beat the eggs and sugar together for a couple of minutes until they become a little lighter and thicker. Drizzle in the oil and continue whisking for a few more minutes.

Sift the flour, spices, baking powder, bicarbonate of soda and salt into a bowl, then fold into the egg and sugar mix, followed by the carrots, walnuts and dates. Stir until completely combined, then divide between the prepared tins and bake for 35–45 minutes until golden and an inserted skewer comes out clean. Leave to cool in the tins.

Meanwhile make the icing: melt the butter in a light-coloured pan (so you can see the butter change colour), season with a few pinches of salt and place over a medium heat. Cook for 6–10 minutes, swirling the pan frequently, until the large bubbles start popping down into lots of small bubbles. When you see golden-brown speckles on the bottom of the pan, cook for just a little longer until it smells deliciously nutty, watching it like a hawk. Take off the heat as soon as the speckles turn from golden brown to a deep caramel, adding the orange zest and juice to arrest the cooking (it will bubble up a bit). Pour it into a bowl, allow to cool and then chill until just solidified.

Using an electric whisk, beat the solidified butter until fluffy, then add the cream cheese. Keep on beating the mixture, slowly adding the icing sugar until you have a smooth icing. Spread half the icing over a cake, then sit the other on top and spread with the remaining icing. Decorate the top with toasted walnuts and serve.

Why not try a deliciously nutty brown butter biscuit base?
Preheat the oven to 180°C/gas 4 and butter a 23cm loose-bottomed cake tin.
Melt 125g butter in a large pan and cook according to the instructions above. Finely crush 150g each (or 10 biscuits each) of digestives and Hobnobs in a bag with a rolling pin, or in a food processor, then stir into the butter until completely coated. Spoon into the cake tin and lightly press and flatten with the back of a metal spoon. Bake for 10 minutes, then allow to cool. Top with whipped mascarpone or pastry cream and lovely seasonal fruit, or use as a base for cheesecake.

For the Cake

300ml olive or sunflower oil,
   plus extra for the tins
4 eggs
225g soft light brown sugar
250g self-raising flour
1½ tsp ground cinnamon
1 tsp ground ginger
½ tsp ground nutmeg
1 tsp baking powder
½ tsp bicarbonate of soda
½ tsp salt
5–6 carrots (about 275g),
   coarsely grated
150g walnuts, finely chopped
100g medjool dates, chopped

For the Icing

75g salted butter
finely grated zest of 1 orange and
   juice of ½ orange
200g full-fat cream cheese, at
   room temperature
150g icing sugar
handful of toasted walnuts, to decorate

Unbelievably Dark & Delicious Chocolate Cake

MAKES ONE VERY LARGE CAKE

This cake is so popular amongst my friends that it is requested at almost every opportunity. It has a sophisticated edge thanks to the merest hint of cinnamon and a generous scrunch of sea salt.

I stole the recipe from a friend of my parents when I was eight (which gives you an idea of how easy it is to make). Over the years the chocolate base cake has undergone many makeovers, from trays of brownies drizzled with mezcal and salted caramel to being transformed into a myriad of different characters and shapes for children's' parties (edible glitter anyone?). No matter what it looks like when it goes into the oven, it invariably comes out tasting outrageously good.

Preheat the oven to 190°C/gas 5 and butter and line the base of two 20cm non-stick cake tins.

For the Cake
380g butter, plus extra for the tins

380g dark chocolate
(70% cocoa solids), chopped

380g caster sugar

2 small pinches of ground cinnamon

several large pinches of salt

200g plain flour

6 eggs

Melt the butter in a medium pan over a low heat; once melted stir in the chocolate, being careful not to burn it. When the mixture becomes a smooth velvet add the sugar, cinnamon and salt. Stir until the sugar has dissolved, then slowly sift in the flour, stirring to combine. Beat the eggs, then beat into the chocolate mixture a little at a time until fully incorporated.

Pour into the prepared tins and bake in the oven for 30–40 minutes until the outside is dark and delicious looking and a skewer comes out just clean. Leave to cool in the tins for 15 minutes before turning out and cooling on wire racks.

For a Crazy Birthday Topping
4 Mars Bars (157g)

100ml whole milk

3 tbsp golden syrup

90g dark chocolate,
(70% cocoa solids), chopped

500ml double cream

3 Flakes, chopped into 2cm lengths

2 packets of Rolos

1 large packet of peanut M&Ms
(optional)

edible glitter, as many colours
as possible

Meanwhile chop up the Mars bars and melt with the milk, syrup, dark chocolate and 50ml of the double cream. Whip the rest of the cream until it just holds its shape.

Sandwich the cooled cakes together with the whipped cream and pour over the Mars Bar sauce. Scatter the various chocolates and the glitter over the surface of the cake in a higgledy-piggledy fashion, getting as many over-excited little helpers as you dare.

Kitchen Note:
If you want a chocolate pudding fix fast, try stuffing half squares of dark chocolate inside medjool dates and bake in a 180°C/gas 4 oven for 3 minutes for an easy, after-dinner treat. Or grill sourdough toast covered with slabs of dark chocolate sprinkled with sea salt, a pinch of chilli flakes and plenty of extra-virgin olive oil for 5 minutes until melted, then serve with vanilla ice cream.

An Easy-Peasy Not Quite Christmas Cake

This is a simple and delicious alternative to a traditional Christmas cake, made in half the time but with all the same rich, boozy molasses flavours.

Preheat the oven to 160°C/gas 3 and butter and line a 25cm loose-bottomed cake tin with baking parchment.

Put the almonds on a baking sheet and warm through in the oven until a pale golden, 5–10 minutes. Allow to cool and then roughly chop and set aside.

Meanwhile roughly chop the figs with the apricots. Put them in a pan with the raisins, wine, brandy, orange zest and juice and spices. Bring to boiling point and then simmer very gently for 5 minutes. Turn off the heat and let the mixture stand for 10 minutes.

Stir the butter and sugar into the fruit mixture and let stand for a further 5 minutes while you sift the flour, baking powder and bicarbonate of soda into a large bowl. Stir the eggs briskly into the warm fruit mixture, followed by the almonds.

Now make a well in the middle of the flour and pour in the cake mixture. Fold briefly to combine, pour into the prepared tin and bake for 45–50 minutes until an inserted skewer comes out clean. Leave to cool in the tin for 10 minutes before turning out onto a wire rack. Serve wedges of the cake with warmed honey and large dollops of crème fraîche, but be warned: if you make this too soon before Christmas it is liable to vanish.

Kitchen Note:

You can do a great cheat with mince pies at Christmas too. Make a batch of mincemeat (easy-peasy) following a traditional recipe but with extra rum, brandy and slithered almonds stirred in. This keeps almost indefinitely and is best made at least a month or so ahead. Then buy the best mince pies you can and, before heating, gently prise off the lids with a teaspoon and add a small heap of extra mincemeat. Pop the lids back on and heat in the oven as usual until hot and golden. Pop onto plates, open up again and fill with rum butter. Replace the lids and top with lashings of double cream, ice cream or both (in my father's case). Pools of the boozy, buttery, creamy juices will leak out onto the plate for mopping up with the sweet pastry. For optimum results pour over an extra slug of Calvados, Cognac, dark rum or tequila (it is Christmas).

125g butter, softened or at room
temperature, plus extra for the tin

90g blanched almonds

250g dried figs, stems cut away

70g dried apricots

120g raisins

350ml red wine

3–4 tbsp Cognac or brandy

finely grated zest and juice of 1 orange

1½ tsp ground cinnamon

pinch of ground cloves

200g muscovado sugar

230g plain flour

1½ tsp baking powder

1 tsp bicarbonate of soda

2 eggs, lightly beaten

Coconut & Jasmine Rice Pudding

FEEDS FOUR—SIX

Talk about comfort food. If you can't get hold of wholegrain jasmine rice, which has a lovely nuttiness, stick to white. Coconut sugar is now available in delis, health food shops and online and has a wonderful butterscotch flavour, but soft brown sugar will also be delicious. When mangoes are out of season, this pudding is delicious just with a spoonful of strawberry or raspberry jam in the middle.

Preheat the oven to 150°C/gas 2.

Mix together the rice, sugars, coconut milk (and the can of water), vanilla extract, orange blossom water, if using, and lime zest in a 500ml ovenproof dish. Stir in 1 tbsp of lime juice and bake slowly in the oven for about 1½ hours until the rice has absorbed most of the liquid but is still moist, giving it a stir every half hour or so. Check the grains after the cooking time; they should be plump and tender, so return to the oven for another 15 minutes if not.

Meanwhile toast the flaked coconut in the same oven on a baking tray until pale golden all over.

Once cooked, remove the rice from the oven and allow to cool, then cover with cling film and chill in the fridge for at least 2 hours.

When ready to eat, peel and dice the mangoes then toss with the rest of the lime juice; it doesn't matter if not all the pieces are the perfect size.

Stir the yogurt or cream through the pudding; you want a lovely loose consistency that can drop easily from the spoon, like a loose risotto. Serve topped with the mangoes and toasted coconut.

Kitchen Note:

This makes an insanely good breakfast. Take down the sugar a little and substitute 50g of the rice for chia seeds, stirring them into the pudding in the final half hour of baking. You might need to loosen the rice with a little more yogurt than usual. Try topping with raisins cooked in a spiced rum syrup, caramelised apples or prunes steeped in Earl Grey (see page 28).

150g Thai jasmine wholegrain rice

25g coconut sugar

30g caster sugar

1 x 400ml can coconut milk (plus the empty can full of water)

½ tsp vanilla extract

1 tsp orange blossom water (optional)

finely grated zest and juice of 2 limes

couple of handfuls of unsweetened flaked coconut

2 Alphonso mangoes

100–150ml coconut yogurt, Greek yogurt or double cream

STORE CUPBOARD

STORE CUPBOARD

For me, 'store cupboard' describes any space in my kitchen that houses ingredients. In its most literal sense it could include my freezer, in which nestles loaves of sourdough to whip out for last-minute dinners (see page 276), or stocks, Thai curry pastes or chopped herbs to defrost and turn into fast soups, stews or even interesting omelettes (see pages 164 and 206). It could also include my fridge, where I keep opened jars of home-made jams, chutneys, mayonnaises and other sauces alongside bottles of bought mayonnaise, mustards and so on.

The latest scientific evidence indicates that relatively new conveniences such as bought sauces and other ready-prepared foods – most of which contain emulsifiers and other additives – suppress good gut health. Home-made sauces and pickles, on the other hand, usually contain ingredients such as vinegars and raw olive oil that are good for the gut. I balance our lives with as much home-made food as I have time to cook, using bought-in ingredients that I know will add last-minute flavour and spice when time is short. I do not browbeat myself if I have to fall back on buying prepared ingredients occasionally: who can manage to cook from scratch every night? I know that when I have time I'll make and store recipes that will sit perfectly happily for weeks, sometimes months, ready to pull out and add real oomph to my food at a moment's notice.

This is the essence of home cooking: storing food and ingredients in your kitchen that will come in handy when you are tired and hungry after a long day, or when you are time-poor and frenzied because you have ten people arriving for dinner that night. It is about knowing what is in your kitchen, so that you are able to cheat time and prepare food as if by magic. At its most boring it is household management; at its most exciting the ability to stun your friends by producing mouth-watering food with ease and speed.

So this chapter contains a few recipes that I find indispensable to our ever-changing menus at home. Whether a simple home-made mayonnaise, a chilli-tomato jam (we seem to eat it with everything), or spice mixes that transform simple, thrown-together dinners, this is a toolbox of recipes that I turn to again and again. I hope that you will try them and fall in love with them as we have. They make our everyday food more fun and more delicious.

Kitchen Note:

Quite a few of the recipes in this chapter involve storing the finished product in sterilised jars or bottles. To sterilise containers, put them through the dishwasher, or wash in hot, soapy water, then rinse well and place in a preheated oven (220°C/gas 7) for 10 minutes, or fill with boiling water for 10 minutes, then dry thoroughly.

Freezer Essentials

We spend lots of money on state-of-the-art freezers for good reason; freezing food keeps it fresh, arresting the growth of microorganisms and enzymes that cause food spoilage. Sweetcorn, peas and broad beans are classic examples of ingredients that are often frozen as soon as they are picked, prohibiting the conversion of their sugars into starch, thus keeping them more tender, delicious and sweet. I use my freezer to stock up on good ingredients when I have access to them (such as after a visit to our local Sunday market) which allows us to have great food at our fingertips for the week that follows. I also squirrel away leftover pastes, stews, soups and stocks for a rainy day. We're planning to move house soon and I am already planning space for an even bigger freezer than I bought last time … I always, always want more room in the freezer.

For best flavour and texture, home-frozen foods should be used within six months. Freezer bags and a good marker pen are essential. I never remember what went into the bags and when, even though I am convinced that I will; somehow freezing makes food lose all identifiable features. My mother keeps a freezer book, adding and crossing off food as it goes in and out of her freezer, but that is one step too organised for me!

What I Freeze On A Weekly Basis

— *Sourdough bread*
— *Grass-fed milk from the market*
— *Puff pastry (and sometimes shortcrust)*
— *Home-made ice creams and sorbets*
— *Butter (imagine running out?)*
— *Smoked mackerel fillets*
— *Meat or fish from the market*
— *Stock, in cleaned-out plastic milk bottles*
— *Peas, sweetcorn, broad beans, berries*

Other Things That Freeze Well

— *Fruit purées*
— *Curry pastes*
— *Chopped lemon grass*
— *Good-quality chorizo and black pudding*
— *Most soups and stews*
— *Chopped leftover herbs*

A Few Thoughts on Bread

Bread gets a bad rap these days, as does gluten. It has become associated with a number of health complaints in recent years, even though only one per cent of the population is unlucky enough to have coeliac disease.

There are some reasons to be wary of certain types of bread. After the Second World War, wheat was aggressively hybridised to yield more and to facilitate industrial baking. These modern strains of wheat (and flour) contain significantly fewer micronutrients than older varieties and more intolerance-triggering compounds. Some millers leave so little vitality in basic white flour that, by law, they must add synthetic nutrients in an attempt to make good the deficit. And some bakers reduce fermentation time by using additives and enzymes (which in the UK are not declared on labels). These are some of the reasons why so many people find they are intolerant to mass-produced loaves, that leave them feeling bloated and uncomfortable.

There has also been a rise in lifestyle and diet trends that see gluten as the number one enemy, but ignore bread made from less-processed strains of wheat, or bread that has been allowed its traditional slow rise (such as sourdough bread with all of its associated health benefits from the fermentation process). I'd suggest finding a local bakery and chatting to them. Many use ancient varieties of wheat, organic flours and whole grains in their baking, together with slower production methods. Bread from a proper bakery not only tastes much better than a mass-produced loaf, but is more nutritious and gentler on your digestive system.

I used to make my own bread at home but now, time-poor, I buy sourdough or other good-quality loaves and freeze them for the week ahead. We get through a lot as a loaf comes good for any occasion: toasted for breakfast, or topped with purple sprouting broccoli sautéed in olive oil for dinner (see page 210). When it starts looking tired and stale, I whizz it up to make breadcrumbs, which I leave to dry overnight. These become constituent parts of fast pasta dishes during the week (see pages 167 and 215), or, when fried in butter, a favourite fast pudding (see the prune and Armagnac pudding on page 28). With a single loaf I can feed my family well in a myriad of tasty and economical ways that leave us feeling satisfied but sprightly. For me this is the very definition of a superfood. If I still haven't convinced you, here are some of the extra things we do with fresh bread … and that which is getting past its best.

Pan con Tomate

Rub 4 slices of bread from a fresh crusty loaf with a large peeled garlic clove. Slice 1–2 juicy, ripe beef tomatoes in half and rub onto the bread. Drizzle with your best extra-virgin olive oil, season well and serve. Slices of cured ham and/or cheese work well with this.

Bruschetta

Toast or grill slices of bread and rub with a large peeled garlic clove. Drizzle with your best extra-virgin olive oil and slice in half. For a simple tomato bruschetta, chop 100g ripe baby plum tomatoes and mix in a bowl with a pinch of sugar, salt and pepper and some good olive oil. Marinate for up to 1 hour and spoon onto the toasts.

Crostini

Thinly slice a small ciabatta or baguette into roughly 10–15 slices. Rub with 2 peeled garlic cloves, drizzle with olive oil then place on a wire rack over a baking tray. Grill until golden and crisp, about 1–2 minutes. Turn over and grill for another 1–2 minutes.

Serve With:
— *Cooked cannellini beans (see page 301) blitzed with garlic, lemon juice and olive oil and scattered with black olives and parsley*
— *Blackened aubergine purée (see page 68) with sliced radishes*
— *Mexican crab mayonnaise (see page 76)*
— *Pickled beetroot and goat's curd*
— *Cauliflower salad (see page 95)*
— *Smashed courgette salad (see page 227)*
— *Grilled asparagus with romesco (see page 73)*
— *Blue cheese, watercress and rhubarb pickle (see page 259)*

Breadcrumbs

Chop leftover stale bread into large chunks, then blitz to crumbs in a food processor. Place on a plate or baking tray and leave to dry overnight in a warm, dry environment covered with a tea towel (or use a warming oven or drawer if you have one).

Fried Breadcrumbs

Melt 50g butter in a wide frying pan. Toss through 75g breadcrumbs until coated in butter. For sweet crumbs, add 1 tsp demerara sugar and a pinch of salt; for savoury, fry 1 crushed garlic clove in the butter before adding the crumbs, then add a pinch of salt. Makes 1 small jar.

Quince Jam

I can't do without this jam. We have it on everything from lamb chops to slow-cooked meaty braises and bring it out after dinner whenever we are serving cheese. Its blushed pink colour and floral taste are total heaven. It is not quite as beautiful as a clear quince jelly but it is far easier to make, which makes it a winner in my book.

Wash and roughly chop the quinces, then pop into a large pan and cover them with 400ml water. Bring to the boil and simmer until the fruit is completely tender.

Push the fruit through a sieve or, if you have one, it's easier to work it through a mouli (aka a food mill). Discard the seeds and skin. Weigh the purée you are left with and then place in a pan with an equal weight of sugar. Stir over a low heat until the sugar has dissolved, then increase the heat and cook, stirring frequently, until the purée thickens and starts leaving the sides of the pan. It will turn a deep dark rose-red colour. Transfer to sterilised jars (see page 274 for method). This will keep for up to 1 year.

Plum, Vanilla & Star Anise Jam

This jam is amazing with a fresh, crusty baguette and lots of butter as well as on croissants and scones. Place a plate in the freezer. Halve and stone 1.2kg large red plums, put in a large pan with 300ml water and bring to a boil. Simmer for 5 minutes until the plums are soft, then reduce the heat and add 800g granulated sugar, 1 star anise and 1 scraped vanilla pod and its seeds. Stir until the sugar has dissolved, then return to the boil and cook for 5 minutes. Take the jam off the heat, remove the plate from the freezer and drop 1 tsp of the jam onto it: if a wrinkly skin forms after a minute, it's ready; if not, return to the heat for a minute or so, and put a clean plate in the freezer. Continue to test, taking the jam off the heat each time, until the jam on the plate wrinkles. Allow to cool slightly then pour into four 250ml sterilised jars and top with tight-fitting lids. Store in a cool dark place for up to a year.

2kg quinces

preserving sugar

Ma's Five-Sugar Marmalade

MAKES ABOUT TWENTY JARS

My grandmother used to make a good marmalade and after she died my mother started making it too, partly in an effort to stay close to her. My mother's ten-year quest to make the best marmalade has been closely aided by my father, who had his own interests to look after. Seville orange time has become a quasi-religious affair in our family, such is our collective love of my mother's famous jam. As the season draws near my siblings and I vie with each other to book bedrooms at home so that we can claim to have helped in the marmalade-making process and go home with the larger share of these precious jars. The dark, sticky, treacly jam that she has perfected over the years is the simply the best that you will ever taste.

Four different sugars are used in this recipe on top of the traditional preserving sugar, each adding depth and nuance of flavour. The resulting pectin content is low, so it needs twice the length of cooking as conventional recipes. Right at the end we add whisky; its flavour can't be deciphered in the finished article but it adds an unmistakably intriguing note. Even if you do not have time to make the marmalade when the season comes round, you can buy a stash of the oranges for the freezer and make it at a later date. Once you have tried this stuff, running out is not an option.

Cut the oranges and lemons in half and boil them in 3 litres water in a very large pan for 30 minutes. Remove the fruit and scrape out the insides into a muslin. Cut the skins into very thin strips (the thinner the better since they thicken and expand during cooking) and cut the long strips in half. Tie up the muslin bag, return it to the water with the peel and simmer for 2 hours. Remove the bag and strain the contents back into the water, discarding the pith and pips.

3kg Seville oranges

1 large sweet orange

3 lemons

1.5kg preserving sugar

2kg Demerara sugar

500g dark molasses sugar

500g dark muscovado sugar

3 large tbsp black treacle

180ml whisky

Add the sugars and treacle to the pan. Bring to the boil then reduce the heat and simmer gently for about 2 hours, being careful not to let it boil over. Meanwhile, sterilise the jam jars (see page 274 for method) and put a saucer in the freezer.

After 2 hours of simmering test the marmalade by putting ½ tsp onto the saucer in the freezer for a few minutes. If it is still runny when you push it with your finger, simmer the marmalade for a further 15 minutes and test again. Once you have achieved the desired consistency stir in the whisky and decant into the jars, making sure to put the lids on tightly while the jars are still hot.

Squash Ketchup

I first came across pumpkin ketchup in LA about a decade ago when I was checking out the Mexican food scene. I got hooked on its rounded, sweet taste and beautiful colour. I make it in the autumn and winter. If you are in full-on summer replace the butternut with the same quantity of ripe tomatoes to make a more traditional ketchup.

650g peeled and diced
    butternut squash

3 tbsp olive oil

6 cloves, or to taste

1½ tsp ground coriander seeds,
    or to taste

1 tsp black peppercorns, or to taste

2 onions, roughly chopped

2 celery sticks, roughly chopped

2 fat garlic cloves, roughly chopped

1kg very ripe fresh plum tomatoes
    (or use drained and rinsed
    canned tomatoes)

160ml cider vinegar, or to taste

2 tsp celery salt

1½ tsp salt

1 tsp mustard powder, or to taste

2 bay leaves

165g brown sugar, or to taste

1 cinnamon stick

1 chipotle chilli, stem removed

Preheat the oven to 200°C/gas 6.

Toss the squash in 1 tbsp of the oil, season, then roast in the oven for 20–25 minutes until soft. Meanwhile grind the cloves, coriander seeds and peppercorns to a powder using a pestle and mortar.

Heat the remaining oil in a pan over a medium heat and fry the onions, celery and garlic for 10 minutes until beginning to soften.

Roughly chop the tomatoes and add to the pan along with the roasted squash. Add the remaining ingredients, including the ground spices, and bring to the boil, then reduce the heat and leave to simmer for 1 hour.

Discard the bay leaves, cinnamon (and chilli if you don't want it too spicy), then transfer the mixture to a food processor or blender and purée until smooth. Return to the pan and continue to cook over a low heat for 20–30 minutes, stirring frequently until nice and thick. Adjust the sugar, vinegar or spice to your liking.

Transfer to a sterilised jar or bottle (see page 274 for method), leave to cool, then seal with a tight-fitting lid. Leave in a cool place for 2 weeks before using for the flavours to meld. Once opened, this will keep in the fridge for up to 1 month.

Tomato & Chilli Jam

Tomato & Chilli Jam

Addictive Tomato-Bonnet Jam

MAKES TWO JAM JARS

1.5kg very ripe tomatoes,
   washed and roughly chopped

2 large onions, roughly chopped

8 garlic cloves, roughly chopped

3 heaped tbsp peeled and finely
   chopped ginger

2 large Scotch Bonnets,
   deseeded and finely chopped

juice and finely grated zest of 4 limes

300g Demerara sugar

300g preserving sugar

200ml red wine vinegar

4 star anise

2 tbsp coriander seeds

1–2 tsp salt

I slather this sweet, mildly fiery jam on cheese, sausages, ham or eggs. It is worth making bigger batches so that you can give some to friends. Add another Scotch Bonnet if you like your jam with more of a kick.

Pulse the tomatoes, onion, garlic and ginger in a food processor for about 5 seconds to get a rough salsa. Add to a pan with the rest of the ingredients and bring the mixture to simmering point. Simmer, stirring regularly, for 40–50 minutes, then stir frequently for a further 15 minutes until most of the water has evaporated, leaving behind a sticky, thick jam.

You can test if the jam is ready by putting ½ tsp onto a saucer and placing in the freezer for a minute. If the jam thickens to your liking when you put your finger to it, it's ready. If not, you can continue simmering for a while until it thickens some more. This jam does not do a classic 'set', it is a little like a thick, sticky salsa (that tastes amazing)!

Spoon the jam into clean, sterilised jars (see page 274 for method), leaving a 1cm gap at the top of the jar. Leave to cool and seal tightly. Store in a cool place as you would jam, and once opened store in the fridge.

Kitchen Note:
Wash your hands thoroughly after chopping the Scotch Bonnet, or a trip to the loo can become pretty painful!

Smoky Chipotle Paste

MAKES ABOUT ONE LITRE

In Mexico, this smoky, fiery, slightly sweet paste is known as 'chipotles en adobo' meaning chipotles 'in a marinade' (or sauce). It is probably the biggest-selling chilli product in the country, made with dried, smoked jalapeño chillies (the chipotles). Once you start using it you will find yourself wondering how you ever did without it. The paste improves any stew, pasta sauce, dressing or mayonnaise.

Wash the chipotles in cold water and drain. Snip off the stalk end of each chilli with scissors, which will allow the water to penetrate their tough skins. Put in a pan, cover with water and simmer for about 40 minutes until completely soft. When the chillies are soft, remove from the pan and rinse off any seeds.

200g chipotle chillies (about 65)
1 large Spanish onion, roughly chopped
1 whole head of garlic,
   cloves roughly chopped
3 tbsp fresh oregano leaves or a few
   good pinches of dried oregano
1–2 tbsp thyme leaves
2 fresh bay leaves
1 tsp cumin seeds, crushed
4 tbsp olive oil
175ml good-quality cider vinegar
175ml good-quality balsamic vinegar
3 tbsp tomato purée
7 tbsp Demerara or palm sugar
2 tbsp salt

Put the onion, garlic, herbs and cumin seeds into a blender (or use a stick blender) with 200ml water and 6 of the chillies. Purée to a smooth paste.

Heat the olive oil in a large, heavy-based pan until it is smoking hot. Add the spicy onion and chilli paste and fry for about 3 minutes, stirring continuously with a spatula to prevent it catching and burning.

Add the vinegars, tomato purée, sugar, salt and another 100ml water and cook for 5 more minutes before adding the rest of the chillies. Cook for 5 minutes, then purée the mixture and continue to cook for 10 more minutes over a low heat, stirring every so often to stop the sauce from burning. Taste to check the seasoning, adding more salt, sugar or vinegar if the flavours need balancing.

Store in clean, sterilised jam or Kilner jars (see page 274 for method). It lasts for months, like ketchup. These jars make great presents at Christmas.

My Mother's Classic BBQ Sauce

MAKES TWO MEDIUM BOTTLES

olive oil and butter, to fry

1 large Spanish onion, finely chopped

2 garlic cloves, crushed

700g tomato ketchup

1–2 tsp chilli powder
   or 2–3 tsp Smoky Chipotle Paste
   (see left), or to taste

2 tsp celery seeds

110g soft light brown sugar

150ml cider vinegar

150ml Worcestershire sauce

Tabasco, to taste

You can vary this sauce by using various hot pepper sauces instead of the chilli powder or chipotle paste, or you may prefer to use less sugar. This sauce will keep in a jar (or an old ketchup bottle) almost indefinitely in the fridge and is very useful for giving an extra kick to pasta sauces or stews ... almost anything that uses tomatoes in fact. It makes a wickedly smoky, sticky marinade for chicken pieces or spare ribs to throw on the barbie.

Heat a glug of olive oil and a knob of butter in a pan and add the chopped onion. Fry over a low heat until soft, but not coloured, about 10 minutes. Add the garlic and fry for a minute more.

Add the remaining ingredients, season generously with salt and pepper and bring to the boil. Simmer gently for about 20 minutes before whizzing with a stick blender. Adjust the seasoning to add further heat as you like. You can also add a slug of sherry for taste. Allow to cool before transferring to a sterilised bottle or jar (see page 274 for method). Once opened, store in the fridge for as long as you would normal ketchup.

Home-Made Mayonnaise & Variations

MAKES ONE & A HALF CUPS

A BLT is not the same without Hellmann's but there's a time and place for home-made mayonnaise. It really comes into its own if you are splashing out on giant prawns or making summer crudités or home-made fritters. Here is my fail-safe recipe, with a few alternatives below (and see page 76 for chipotle mayo).

Whisk the egg yolks, a pinch of salt, the mustard and vinegar in a china or glass bowl. Slowly drizzle in the oil, drop by drop, whisking furiously. Keep whisking, slowly adding the oil until it has all been amalgamated into the mayonnaise. If necessary thin down with 1 tbsp of water.

If you are using a food processor follow the recipe, slowly adding the oil as the blades are turning. I sometimes like to add a small pinch of sugar to my mayonnaise to balance the bitterness from the olive oil. If the mayonnaise splits, put an egg yolk into a clean bowl and whisk it as you add the split mayonnaise, drop by drop. The mayonnaise will come together again.

Aioli

This is really just a mayonnaise mixed with crushed garlic. Follow the basic mayonnaise recipe, adding 1 crushed garlic clove, to the yolk base. Increase to 2–3 garlic cloves for an extra garlic hit. Amazing with chips, wonderful with burgers.

Lemon Aioli

Follow the recipe for aioli, adding 1 tbsp freshly squeezed lemon juice to the yolk base instead of the vinegar. Heaven with steamed asparagus or raw crudités.

Anchovy Mayonnaise

Mash 4 anchovy fillets to a paste with 1 fat garlic clove. Mix with the yolk base, reducing the mustard to ¼ tsp and cutting the vinegar back to 1 tbsp. Incredible with lamb or fritto misto, particularly deep-fried cauliflower and calamari.

Wasabi Mayonnaise

Add 2–3 tbsp of wasabi paste to the mayonnaise recipe instead of the mustard. Nice and fiery with any kind of tempura.

Saffron Mayonnaise

Boil a kettle; add a large pinch of saffron to 2 tbsp boiling water and set aside to infuse for 10 minutes. Add 1 crushed garlic clove, to the yolk base, substituting the white wine vinegar for sherry vinegar. Add the saffron water to the finished mayonnaise. Excellent with fish stews, bouillabaisse and globe artichokes.

2 egg yolks, at room temperature
½ tsp Dijon mustard
2 tsp white wine vinegar
175ml extra-virgin olive oil
175ml sunflower or groundnut oil
pinch of sugar (optional)

Hollandaise Sauce

Hollandaise has a bad reputation. In spite of the horror stories about curdled sauces, it is not difficult to make. The secret lies in how you are going to eat it. At brunch you can whizz it up in front of friends and keep them busy with large Bloody Marys as you cook. It won't take long and you can serve the sauce straight away. It gets trickier if you are making it for a dinner. The sauce doesn't sit well, so if you are not going to use it immediately keep it in a bowl suspended over a pan of simmering water, to maintain an even, warm temperature. If the sauce does split, just whisk in a trickle of cold water and it should come together again.

To make the white wine reduction put all the ingredients in a small pan and simmer until reduced by two-thirds. Keep any leftover in a jam jar in the fridge. It can be used for other emulsions such as Béarnaise (see below) or salad dressings.

Melt the butter in a pan. Put the yolks in a heatproof bowl suspended over a pan of simmering water, making sure the water does not touch the bottom of the bowl. Whisk the yolks by hand, or using an electric whisk, until light and fluffy. Add 1 tbsp of cold water and keep whisking. Turn the heat off and start adding the butter in a slow dribble, whisking all the time, just as you would emulsify a mayonnaise (see left). If you add this too quickly it will split, at which stage you just whisk in 1 tsp of cold water. Once all the butter is incorporated, whisk in the white wine reduction and lemon juice and season with salt and pepper (white if you have it). Keep over the warm pan until you are ready for your sauce.

Béarnaise Sauce

Substitute tarragon vinegar for the white wine vinegar in the reduction above and add 1 tbsp chopped tarragon leaves to the finished sauce. This is a classic accompaniment to steak.

Mousseline Sauce

Whip 100ml double cream and whisk into the hollandaise sauce for a delicious, frothy sauce for spooning over asparagus or artichokes in the summer.

For the Sauce
175g butter
2 egg yolks
1½ tsp White Wine Reduction (see below)
squeeze of lemon juice

For the White Wine Reduction
250ml white wine vinegar
1 bay leaf
5 black peppercorns
½ shallot, chopped
1 allspice berry or a good grating of nutmeg

Vinaigrette & Herb Sauces

My Classic Vinaigrette

A tangy, silky French dressing transforms salad leaves, steamed vegetables, avocado or leftover pasta. The components are also good for you: oils rich in Omega-3 and acidic vinegars full of good gut bacteria. The ratio of ingredients below really works for me. Making this large a quantity (I even make double) may feel a bit extravagant, but store it in a Kilner jar and you'll be able to make a knockout salad in moments. Experiment with different vinegars (sherry, raspberry, red and white wine, cider, balsamic), oils, mustards and sugars.

1½ heaped tsp Dijon mustard
3 heaped tsp soft light brown sugar
150ml red wine vinegar
500ml extra-virgin olive oil

Mix the mustard, sugar and salt and pepper in a jar large enough to hold all the dressing. Add the vinegar and whisk lightly to dissolve the salt and sugar. Pour in the oil and store in a cool, dark cupboard. Shake well before using. *Makes about 600ml.*

Salsa Verde

This is an Italian herb sauce and not to be confused with the Mexican green tomatillo sauce by the same name. It is a beautiful accompaniment to fish, meat and vegetables. I use a touch of basil and mint in my version, but you could also try it with tarragon if eating with fish.

2 garlic cloves
5 anchovy fillets
1–2 tbsp salted capers, soaked in water
    for 1 hour, then rinsed well
large bunch of parsley leaves, chopped
small handful of basil leaves, chopped
small handful of mint leaves, chopped
1–2 tbsp red wine vinegar
1 tsp Dijon mustard
75ml extra-virgin olive oil

Smash the garlic, anchovy and capers to a paste and then add the herbs. You could use a food processor but I prefer to mash it in a pestle and mortar to retain the rough texture of the herbs within the paste. Season with the vinegar, mustard and plenty of freshly ground black pepper. Stir in enough olive oil to make a spoonable sauce and serve as fresh as possible. It will keep for a week in the fridge but it does lose its lovely fresh flavour. *Makes a bowlful.*

Mint Sauce

This is an ingenious little recipe, perfect for preserving the armfuls of fresh mint that grow uncontrollably in our small garden every year. This sauce revs up any lamb dish, from chops to slow-cooked shoulder, burgers or a classic roast.

40g soft light brown sugar
½ tsp salt
250ml boiling water
165ml cider vinegar
120g mint leaves, washed and
    finely chopped

Put the sugar and salt in a bowl and pour over the boiling water; stir to dissolve. Pour in the vinegar and stir in the chopped mint. Store in sterilised jam jars (see page 274 for method). This keeps well in a cool, dark cupboard for 6 months. *Makes a large jar.*

Stunning Spice Mixes

Throughout history fortunes were made in the pursuit of spices. Spices were considered so precious that they were traded in place of money ... and sometimes even their weight in gold. Desired for their healing properties as well as their aphrodisiac qualities, spices also added enormous flavour to food that was, in a world without refrigeration, often past its best.

I buy mine in bulk when I am abroad, or from Asian grocers where they are a fraction of the cost of the small glass jars you find in supermarkets. I store them in large sealed tubs. There are lots of good spice mixes available to buy, but you can't beat the taste and smell of spices that you have freshly ground yourself. The most time-consuming part is getting the spices out of the cupboard and measuring them. After that, you just warm and grind. All the recipes below last well for several weeks and make enough for multiple uses, but their intense flavours will gradually fade over time.

Chinese Five-Spice

This powder is spectacular: its blend of citrusy Sichuan pepper, aniseed-flavoured fennel seed, star anise and sweet cinnamon is perfectly designed for the fatty, rich taste of duck and pork. Slow meat braises or fast noodle dishes become exquisitely aromatic.

1 tbsp Szechuan peppercorns
1 tbsp cloves
1 tbsp fennel seeds
7 star anise
1 long cinnamon stick

Warm a dry frying pan over a medium heat. Add the Sichuan peppercorns first and gently toast for 1 minute to release the aroma. Grind in a pestle and mortar and sieve, keeping the fine powder and chucking away the woody husks left in the sieve. Now toast the rest of the spices for a few minutes, shaking or stirring the pan from time to time. Once they smell fragrant, grind them into a pestle and mortar or spice grinder and mix them into the Sichuan pepper. Store in a small jam jar and use within a week or so.

Garam Masala

This blend comes from northern India. Traditionally it contains black and green cardamom, black and brown cumin, cinnamon and cloves. No two spice blends are ever the same, so experiment with the spices you have and make it your own. This makes enough for a few meals. I use it in the base of vegetable and meat curries, lentil dishes, rubbed onto meat before grilling and even sprinkled onto scrambled eggs or curried picnic eggs.

2 small cinnamon sticks
15 cloves
1 tbsp cumin seeds
2 tbsp coriander seeds
seeds from 15 cardamom pods
    (half green and half black,
    if you can find them)
1 tbsp black peppercorns
2 dried red chillies
1 tsp ground nutmeg

Heat a dry frying pan over a medium heat and once hot add everything except for the nutmeg and cook, stirring continuously, for 1 minute until it all begins to smell toasted. Remove and leave to cool. Grind to a fine powder in a pestle and mortar or spice grinder, sifting out any woody husks. Stir in the ground nutmeg at the end.

Stunning Spice
Mixes (Continued)

1 tbsp black peppercorns

2 tsp cloves

1 tbsp allspice berries

1 small cinnamon stick

2 tbsp coriander seeds

2 tsp cumin seeds

½ nutmeg, freshly grated

1 tsp ground ginger

Middle Eastern Seven-Spice

Slightly spicy and warm, this combination is delicious when rubbed over lamb shoulder or combined with lamb or beef in koftes, as well as sprinkled into sautéing onions to make a pilaf.

Follow the method for the garam masala (see page 293), stirring in the grated nutmeg and ground ginger at the end.

Dukkah

This irresistibly nutty, spiced mix is served throughout the Middle East with small bowls of olive oil as a dip for bread and crudités at the beginning of a meal. I love it sprinkled on egg dishes, salads and olive oil.

30g pistachios

30g hazelnuts

10g sesame seeds
   (black and white if you have both)

1 tsp coriander seeds

1 tsp cumin seeds

1 tsp caraway seeds

2 tsp ground turmeric

1 tsp salt

Put all the ingredients in a food processor and blitz quickly to break everything up into small pieces. Store in an airtight jar for up to 1 month.

Kitchen Note:

The Olive Oil Granola with Oodles of Nuts & Seeds (see page 27) is exquisite when turned into a more savoury, spiced creation. Halve the amount of sugar in it and toss in 1 tbsp coriander seeds, 2 tsp fennel seeds, ½ tsp cumin seeds, 1 tsp cayenne pepper, 2 tbsp soy sauce and the leaves from 3 rosemary sprigs before you bake it. Perks up salads, breakfast yogurt or egg dishes.

Hot & Fiery
Chilli Oil

MAKES A LARGE BOTTLE

This is an indispensable part of my store cupboard arsenal. It adds zing to even the simplest plate of food, keeps for ages and makes a terrific present. Keep a bottle of it on the table for ladling over anything from tacos and tostadas to salads and stir-fries.

Smash the garlic cloves with a heavy object to remove the skins easily. Heat a deep, wide-bottomed pan over a medium heat and toast the sesame seeds for 4–5 minutes until pale golden all over. Remove from the pan and set aside.

Heat 200ml of the oil in the same pan over a medium-low heat. Add the garlic and chillies and gently cook until the garlic has turned soft and golden, about 5 minutes. Add the salt, sugar and sesame seeds and pour in the remaining oil to stop the chillies cooking any further.

With a slotted spoon, transfer the chillies and half the seeds to an upright food blender and blitz to a coarse crumb. Now add the rest of the oil and seeds and leave to cool. Store in a clean, sterilised bottle or jar (see page 274 for method).

Punchy peanut oil
Follow the recipe above, adding 90g peanuts to the oil with the garlic and chillies and cook until they turn golden. Half blitz as above for a wonderfully nutty addition to the oil. I add it into the base of stir-fries or drizzle over Asian or Mexican dishes.

6 fat garlic cloves

30g sesame seeds

400ml sunflower oil

25g chiles de árbol (or other hot,
   dried red chillies), stems removed

2 tsp salt

2 good pinches of caster sugar

Mouth-watering hot sauce
Pound 4 garlic cloves with 2 tbsp fish sauce, the juice of 3 limes and 1–2 tsp of the chilli oil above. Use to dress stir-fried rice, noodles, deep-fried tofu or banh-mi sandwiches (see page 146).

Rose Harissa

This Middle Eastern spicy paste lasts for weeks in the fridge and peps up anything from lamb chops, sausages and grilled chicken bits to Middle Eastern salads and party food. I scent it with a touch of rose water, which gives it a beautifully exotic taste.

1 red pepper, halved, core
   and seeds removed
2 tomatoes, halved
1 red onion, peeled and quartered
4–5 fresh red chillies
6–8 garlic cloves (unpeeled)
150ml olive oil
1 tbsp cumin seeds
1 tbsp coriander seeds
1 tsp fennel seeds
large handful each of coriander
   and mint leaves
3 tbsp red wine vinegar
1½ tsp salt
1 tbsp brown sugar
2 tsp chilli flakes
1 tsp rose water (optional)

Put the red pepper in a bowl with the tomatoes, red onion, chillies and garlic. Toss in a few good splashes of the olive oil, season well with salt and pepper and transfer to a baking tray, with the tomatoes cut side down. Roast in the oven for 40–50 minutes until they are looking charred and softened, then set aside to cool.

Meanwhile, warm a dry frying pan over a medium heat. When the pan is hot (but not searing hot) add the spices and gently toast them for a few minutes, just long enough to unlock their fragrance. Grind to a powder using a pestle and mortar or spice grinder.

When the vegetables are cooked and cool, slip the skins off the garlic cloves and tip everything into a food processor. Add the fresh herbs and ground spices and pulse to a rough purée. Stir in the remaining oil, vinegar, salt, sugar, chilli flakes and rose water, if using. Store in clean glass jars in the fridge.

Kitchen Note:
A much simpler option (reflected in the taste) is to whizz the chillies, garlic and spices together without roasting and store under oil in the fridge.

Two Sweetly-Sour Sauces

Pomegranate Molasses

The distinct concentrated juices of pomegranates add a delightfully sweet and slightly sour flavour to meats and puddings alike. Try drizzling over a whole cauliflower before roasting, or carrots and parsnips with a sprinkling of ras el hanout, or over a whole shoulder of lamb before slow-cooking. It's equally good in ice cream, cakes and meringues (see page 264) or exotic fruit salads.

Roll 3 pomegranates across the work surface, pressing down firmly to 'pop' out the seeds from the bitter, white membrane. Cut the fruits in half and empty the juice and seeds into a blender, picking out any membrane. Whizz the seeds and pour through a sieve. You should get about 350ml of juice depending on the size of the fruit. For every 250ml of juice add 1 tbsp lemon juice and 2 tbsp caster sugar. Bring to the boil in a pan and simmer briskly until the mixture has reduced to a wonderful, syrupy consistency. Cool and store in the fridge. If you have leftover juice consider it a cook's perk and drink with relish!

Tamarind Paste

As with pomegranate molasses, tamarind paste is one of those essential cook's ingredients that is used to balance other flavours in dishes. It provides a deliciously sour background note in South-East Asian curries, soups and sauces, and it is often paired with chipotle chillies in Mexican cooking (see Flash-Baked Salmon with a Smoky Tamarind Glaze, page 193), to even out sweetness and heat in sweet-sour glazes and sauces for seafood.

Dried blocks of the pulp or boxes of fresh pods can be found online or in Asian grocers. Peel the fresh pods of their outer husks and then cover these (or dried blocks) with boiling water. Leave to sit for 10 minutes and then push the contents through a sieve to produce the tamarind paste. Lasts a week in a fridge, or you can freeze it in ice cube trays. Makes a great marinade for seafood or salmon with the Smoky Chipotle Paste (see page 286) or add it to a classic margarita. I also add it to Thai curries for a lovely sour note.

Two Speedy Veggie Pickles

A Quick Carrot & Radish Pickle

120ml red wine vinegar

120ml rice wine vinegar

4–5 tbsp caster sugar

2 tsp salt

2 carrots, cut into thin matchsticks

6 radishes, washed and finely sliced

½ red onion, halved and finely sliced

1–2 fresh red chillies,
   finely sliced (optional)

½ tsp allspice berries

1 tsp black peppercorns

3 fresh bay leaves

I find vinegars are an indispensable ingredient in my store cupboard, giving a beautifully fresh zip and zing to food. As with cucumber relish below, which also relies on vinegar for its sparkle, this pickle provides a great contrast to rich food, lightening it and heightening its flavours.

Combine the vinegars, sugar, salt and 240ml water in a pan, bring to the boil and simmer until the sugar has dissolved. Pour into a heatproof bowl.

Add the vegetables, spices and bay leaves, stir again and allow to sit for at least 30 minutes. I love this in the banh-mi sandwiches (see page 146), or served alongside the chicken liver pâté (see page 74), or just with lunch at weekends when we are eating salad and cheese.

Sweet Cucumber Relish

75ml white wine vinegar

4 tbsp caster sugar

2–3 small round shallots or 1 large
   banana shallot, finely sliced

2cm piece of ginger, peeled and
   finely grated

1 large cucumber, halved lengthways
   and finely sliced

This is a refreshing relish that you can heap onto grilled or poached fish or barbecued chicken, or pack into little tubs for a picnic lunch of bread, cheese and ham. I love the slight kick from the chilli, but if you leave it out you will still have a wonderfully sweet-sour summer salad.

Put the vinegar and sugar in a small pan with 75ml water and a large pinch of salt. Bring to the boil and simmer for a few minutes until the sugar has dissolved. Remove from the heat and leave to cool.

Meanwhile, combine the rest of the ingredients in a pretty bowl and pour on the syrup when it is cool. Leave in the fridge for at least 1 hour to chill thoroughly and allow the flavours to mingle.

Home-Cooked Beans or Chickpeas

MAKES ABOUT 750 GRAMS

The soft, creamy texture of home-cooked beans is a totally different thing to some of the hard, pellet-like pulses you find in cans. If you can get into the habit of grabbing a packet of dried beans from the cupboard and covering them in water whenever you think of it, you will find that it is really easy to cook your own beans from scratch. Soaking reduces cooking time by 30–60 minutes. Your reward will be the creamiest, most delicious beans that cost little and provide a mass of nutrition; a real superfood.

Tip the beans into a large bowl and cover with plenty of cold water. Add the bicarbonate of soda and leave to soak overnight. The beans can be left like this for up to 2 days, so you can cook them whenever you find a suitable moment.

When ready, drain and rinse the beans and put them in a large pan with plenty of water, the garlic, bay leaves and peppercorns, if using. Bring to the boil and simmer gently for 30–60 minutes (cooking times vary enormously), topping up with boiling water as needed and skimming the surface of the water a few times to discard any scum that rises to the surface. Cook until completely soft. Drain, keeping the cooking water, which is full of flavour and goodness for soups and stocks.

Kitchen Note:

If you are buying canned chickpeas, I find the Napolina brand is the best and that the cartons of beans are softer than the cans.

300g dried cannellini or
   borlotti beans, or chickpeas
2 tsp bicarbonate of soda
3 garlic cloves, bashed once
   with the flat of a knife
2 bay leaves (optional)
½ tsp peppercorns (optional)

My Definitive Shortcrust Pastry

I have been making this pastry for years. It essentially relies on a ratio of 2:1 flour to butter, which makes a very crumbly, buttery and deliciously crisp pastry. Handle it as little and as lightly as possible, ensure all the ingredients are chilled, and rest the pastry after making: those are the three golden rules to ensure a perfect pastry every time. Once you have made on a few occasions, you will find that it takes 10 minutes to pull together, plus resting time. A fast, gratifying recipe with the most delicious results.

Put the flour, salt and butter – or butter and lard – into a food processor and blitz for 20–30 seconds. Add the egg yolk and blitz again until it is incorporated. Now add just enough of the egg white to make the mixture bind together (reserve the remaining egg white). Roll into a ball, flatten slightly and wrap in cling film. Chill in the fridge for at least half an hour to rest, preferably 1 hour.

Lightly butter a 24cm loose-bottomed tart tin and then coarsely grate the chilled pastry evenly into the tin, allowing extra pastry for a small overhang around the edges. Press into shape evenly across the base and up the sides with your fingers. Sprinkle the pastry with a little flour and roll flat with a small glass. Prick the base all over and put in the freezer for 20 minutes (this will stop the pastry from shrinking too much in the oven). Preheat the oven to 220°C/gas 7.

To blind-bake, cover the pastry base with baking parchment and baking beans. Bake for about 10 minutes, then remove the beans and paper, brush the base with the remaining egg white to seal it and keep it crisp and return to the oven for further 5–10 minutes or so until golden brown.

Kitchen Note:

To make a sweet pastry, reduce the amount of flour by 10g and replace with 30g sifted icing sugar. To make a bigger tart, use the amounts of flour given below, remembering to stick to the ratio of 2 parts flour to 1 part fat.

For a 26cm tin: 210g flour / For a 28cm tin: 260g flour / For a 32cm tin: 340g flour

170g white flour, spelt or sifted
    wholemeal, plus extra to dust
pinch of salt
85g chilled butter (or, for even better
    results, 60g butter and 25g lard),
    chopped, plus extra for the tin
1 egg, separated, white lightly
    beaten with a fork

Store Cupboard

Salted Caramel Sauce

This is adapted from the *Violet Bakery Cookbook*, which is one of my favourite baking books. Once you have got the hang of the method you will find yourself coming back to it time and time again. I use it to make the chocolate salted caramel crispies in the most wicked ice cream sundae imaginable (see page 249).

Put the cream and vanilla pod into a small pan and bring to simmering point. Turn off the heat, scrape the vanilla seeds into the cream and allow to infuse while you make the caramel (or if you want to skip this step just measure out the cream with ½ tsp vanilla extract and set aside).

Put the water, sugar and syrup into a heavy-based pan and measure out the rest of the ingredients so they are all ready to go. Put the pan over a medium heat and stir with a wooden spoon to dissolve the sugar. The moment the sugar has dissolved, put the spoon down, increase the heat and simmer the sugar briskly, without stirring, until patches start to darken in places. Swirl the pan to disperse these patches through the syrup and keep heating until the whole lot has turned a deep caramel colour. At this stage hold your nerve and keep heating so that the colour darkens a little more. This is now a burnt caramel, which you can use to turn into caramel ice cream or praline (see page 249).

To finish making the sauce keep heating until you see a wisp of smoke. Immediately remove from the heat, pour in the cream, lemon juice, butter and ¼ salt, stirring furiously to arrest the cooking. It will bubble up angrily at first but keep stirring until it is smooth. Pour into a plastic container to cool and then keep chilled and covered in the fridge for up to 2 weeks, or 3 months in the freezer.

Kitchen Note:
This makes the most amazing base for salted caramel buttercream icing on cupcakes and cakes. Just beat 75g of it with 125g softened butter until smooth and then beat in 1 tsp vanilla extract, 1 tbsp milk, a few pinches of fine sea salt and 500g sifted icing sugar. It makes a great coffee buttercream too; beat in 50ml really strong espresso coffee instead of the milk and use to sandwich a coffee and walnut sponge cake.

130ml double cream
½ vanilla pod, split lengthways
4 tbsp water
250g caster sugar
2 tbsp golden syrup
1 tsp lemon juice plus 1 tsp water
65g butter, cut into small cubes
¼ tsp salt

Soft Curd Cheese

It is becoming easier and easier to find good farmhouse soft curd cheeses but it is fun to make your own when you have time. It's also incredibly easy. Here's how. You need a muslin or a very clean sock for this recipe.

Put the milk and salt in a pan and bring to just below boiling point. Take off the heat and slowly stir in the lemon juice until the milk starts to split. Set aside for 20 minutes to allow to separate.

Line a colander with a layer of muslin and sit it over a bowl or pan. Carefully pour the curds into the lined colander, leaving behind the watery whey, and leave to drain, squeezing occasionally. Alternatively spoon into the sock and tie up around your tap. Chill if you have time.

You can make the cheese up to 2 days before you want it, but if making on the day you need it just make sure you leave yourself 2 hours to make it from scratch. You can make ricotta with the leftover whey, too, if you feel inclined!

1.5 litres whole milk
   (cow, sheep or goat's)
½ tsp salt
juice of 1½ lemons

INDEX

Page references in *italics* indicate photographs.
(V) indicates vegetarian recipes; (VO) refers to
a recipe that has a vegetarian option.

C

D

E

F

G

O

P

ACKNOWLEDGEMENTS

Thank you to everyone who has helped make the impossible possible:

The book instrumentals

Bob Granleese and Melissa Denes at the *Guardian* (I love my column). Antony Topping and Claudia Young at Greene & Heaton (for making things happen). Laura Hassan at Faber & Faber (wow). The Dream Team: Tara Fisher, Rosie Ramsden, Luke Bird and Charlotte Heal. Lindsay Davies, Daisy Radevsky, Clara Grace Paul, Emma Miller, Georgia Levy, the Kitchen Co-operative, Rivets & Rags, Wei Tang, Lucy Bannell, Clare Sayer, Ben Murphy.

For food inspiration

Stevie Parle, Claire Ptak, Joe Trivelli and Blanche Vaughan. Skye Gyngell, Margot and Fergus Henderson, Darina and Timmy Allen, Jacob Kennedy, Yotam Ottolenghi, Claudia Roden, Alice Waters, Anna Jones, April Bloomfield, David Tanis, Food 52, Nigel Slater, Dan Saladino, Sheila Dillon, the Aldeburgh Food Festival, Caroline Cranbrook, Angela Hartnett, Ewan Venters, Saritha Pilbrow, Lexi Hill-Norton, Fuchsia Dunlop, David Thompson and all the other chefs and food-writers who constantly give me wonderful ideas and whet my appetite.

To the whole Wahaca team

In particular Mark Selby, Courtney Smart, Carolyn Lum, Gavin Healy, Jo Fleet, Hugo Selby and my kitchen team – Chris Buckley, Edson Cintra, Leo De Cruz, Amardeep Singh, Bledi Jahjaga and Erik Vajda – you all make going to work amazingly good fun.

To my support network

Laura Harper Hinton and the Fork to Fork team. Sophie Hoult, Lynda Stachowiak, Laura Real. Sam Baker, Lauren Laverne and Sara Cox. Lucy Cleland, Chloe Billington, Jo MacPherson, Marika Lemos, Elly James, Charlotte Lascelles, Ed Lascelles, Dorothea Avery, Lizzie King, Loubie Vaughan, Emily FitzRoy, Stacey Duguid, Caroline Irby, Cecilia Selby, Simon Bullivant, Claude Botha. To all my friends and family for being endless guinea pigs and for putting up with me. Toots, DD and Finn Miers – steadfastly solid. Niki and Probyn Miers, the constant editors, babysitters, architects, recipe testers. To my girls Tatiana, Ottilie and Isadora, who give me endless pleasure, and last but definitely not least to my husband Mark, just for being him.

About the Author

Thomasina Miers was the winner of BBC *MasterChef* in 2005. She is a cook and food writer whose work has ranged from cheese-making and running market stalls in Ireland, cheffing with Skye Gyngell at Petersham Nurseries, to co-founding the restaurant group Wahaca, winner of numerous awards, including *Observer Food Monthly*'s Best Cheap Eats, several design awards and three-time winner at the Sustainable Restaurant Association Awards. Her previous books include *Cook*, *The Wild Gourmets*, *Mexican Food Made Simple*, *Wahaca – Mexican Food at Home* and *Chilli Notes*. She has presented various cookery TV programmes and writes a regular column, 'Weekend Cook', in *The Guardian Weekend* magazine. She is the mother of three children and lives in London.